GOING DEEP

CRIS CARTER

with JEFFRI CHADIHA

GOING DEEP

HOW WIDE RECEIVERS
BECAME THE MOST COMPELLING
FIGURES IN PRO SPORTS

HYPERION

NEW YORK

Copyright © 2013 by CC80 Enterprises, Inc.

Library of Congress Cataloging-in-Publication Data has been applied for.

ISBN: 978-1-4013-2485-8

Design by Renato Stanisic

FIRST EDITION

10   9   8   7   6   5   4   3   2   1

THIS LABEL APPLIES TO TEXT STOCK

We try to produce the most beautiful books possible, and we are also extremely concerned about the impact of our manufacturing process on the forests of the world and the environment as a whole. Accordingly, we've made sure that all of the paper we use has been certified as coming from forests that are managed, to ensure the protection of the people and wildlife dependent upon them.

Contents

Prologue

I n early January 2012, just one day after another thrilling Sunday of
NFL action captivated the country, I appeared on ESPN's *Mike and
Mike in the Morning* radio show to talk about the previous weekend's
action. Host Mike Greenberg started the conversation by focusing on
the drama unfolding within the New York Jets at the time, namely star
wide receiver Santonio Holmes being benched for pouting about his
offense and quarterback Mark Sanchez in a loss. But I saw the discussion a different way. I wanted to talk about the personalities of wide receivers and why teams need to understand exactly what they are dealing
with at the position.

Wide receivers are a unique breed. There is a certain swagger that
comes with playing the position, an unshakable confidence that can
swerve in the wrong direction if the player is unchecked or, worse, underestimated. Coaches need to be mindful of such potential problems
yet also fully aware of how much can be gained when these fierce personalities are unleashed in the right manner. As former New Orleans
Saints wide receiver Joe Horn once said, you can't become a great NFL
receiver if you don't have a little pit bull in you.

Once I finished that interview, two things were apparent: (1) wide
receiver had become a complex, fascinating position, and (2) I was in a
unique position to discuss how a job I held for sixteen seasons had

evolved to such fascinating levels. From the time I started my career as a supplemental draft pick for the Philadelphia Eagles in 1987 to my retirement in 2002, the position of wide receiver exploded in the NFL. Receivers went from being obscure and unassuming to being known for their electric play and—in some cases—their over-the-top personalities. In the process, they became some of the most heavily discussed athletes in America's most popular sports league.

The NFL has been enamored with quarterbacks since the day it went into business. Receivers, on the other hand, have gone from being just one part of the offense to the unrivaled celebrities of many teams. In some cases, it's just their sheer athleticism that blows people's minds, especially when it comes to oversized targets like Detroit's Calvin Johnson, sure-handed legends such as Jerry Rice, and jaw-dropping speedsters like Randy Moss. They've altered the way the position both looks and produces with their rise in the game.

At their best, wide receivers can transform offenses and fascinate fans. When the Arizona Cardinals reached their only Super Bowl, during the 2008 season, it was Larry Fitzgerald who drove their success by consistently mystifying defenses with his potent mix of grace and grit. Terrell Owens wasn't around for most of the Philadelphia Eagles' post-season success in 2004, thanks to a late-season broken leg, but he made the most of his opportunity in Super Bowl XXXIX. He went from having major surgery to catching 9 passes for 122 yards in that loss to New England.

It's also not even worth debating that three of the most magical plays in Super Bowl history belong to wide receivers: Pittsburgh's Lynn Swann's leaping catch—juggling and eventually grabbing a Terry Bradshaw pass for a 53-yard gain—while falling over Dallas cornerback Mark Washington in Super Bowl X; David Tyree clutching a football to his helmet with his right hand as he's wrestled to the ground by New England safety Rodney Harrison in the New York Giants' upset of the undefeated Patriots in Super Bowl XLII; and Mario Manningham, another Giants receiver, managing to keep his feet inbounds as he snares a perfectly thrown pass from Eli Manning in New York's win over the Patriots in Super Bowl XLVI.

Fans never tire of watching such plays, but they're just as easily drawn to the combination of talent and flashy temperament that has become a trademark of the wide receiver position in recent years. The same people who can't stand Terrell Owens and Randy Moss couldn't stop talking about them when they were in their primes. Keyshawn Johnson wrote a book entitled *Just Give Me the Damn Ball!* and openly feuded with his head coach in Tampa, Jon Gruden. Some receivers have won championships (Michael Irvin, Plaxico Burress), others have flopped (former first-round picks like Philadelphia's Freddie Mitchell and Detroit's Charles Rogers), and a few have come out of nowhere to blow us away with their skills (Steve Smith, Victor Cruz).

What all these players have in common is the hunger and supreme confidence to believe they can do anything in a position that has become so vital. The more the NFL has grown into a predominantly passing league, the more it has enabled receivers to blossom into marquee performers. But there are certainly more factors that play into what's happened to this position. That's why I started thinking it was time to finally make some sense of this phenomenon.

I wanted to reveal to readers the stories they've never heard, theories about the position that only get discussed in front offices, and explanations on what these players mean to the league today . . . as well as why the NFL can't go forward without them. Ultimately, this book is meant to be both fun and insightful. It's not about preaching or putting down some of the more controversial receivers in the game. Hell, I was one of those players! Instead, it's about taking the audience on a football-observing journey, one meant to help comprehend a position that mesmerizes in so many ways.

Many key people and events led to wide receivers reaching their current place in the game. I learned that much while playing during the most important years of that evolution and I've seen even more while working as an NFL analyst for ESPN. There's no question that the league is as wide open as ever, that the passing game has dominated offensive strategy. But what *Going Deep* will do is give readers the same perspective that I was trying to explain during my radio interview: a complete understanding of why wide receivers are the most compelling athletes in the world today.

CHAPTER 1

Head Games

had just settled into a nice vacation in the Bahamas in mid-February 2012—one that I sorely needed after another long season of analyzing the NFL for ESPN—when my cell phone rang. I hadn't expected anybody to be calling me from the United States—least of all Randy Moss, my old teammate with the Minnesota Vikings. Randy and I hadn't talked in well over a year, and our most recent interaction, one that had occurred indirectly, didn't exactly generate love for each other.

That incident was one that I take blame for starting. While appearing on an ESPN radio show, I was asked about Randy's chances of returning to the NFL after his "retirement" in 2011, and I did what I normally do: I gave my honest opinion. I explained to the hosts that Randy was easily the most talented receiver I had ever played with and that his disappearance from the league had little to do with his ability. Instead, it had everything to do with his attitude.

You're talking about a player who had 954 receptions, 14,858 yards, and 153 touchdowns at the time—numbers that made him one of the best ever to play the position. But Randy also had one glaring flaw that turned people off over the course of his career. As I told the host that day, Randy has a quit mechanism in him. It was hard to understand because he wasn't a bad person and he also loved playing football. It's just that when times turned bad, he was usually the first person to pack it in.

And me being me, I wasn't about to tone down that stance for the masses. What I said was this:

> The one thing you have to address with Randy Moss is not a conditioning thing. It's not an age thing. It needs to be addressed. I believe it's the elephant in the room. It's the thing called quit. And Randy, not like any other superstar I've ever met, he has more quit in him than any of those other players. So I need to address that. I think that's what [New England Patriots head coach Bill] Belichick did when he brought him over from Oakland. He told him he wasn't going to have it.

By the time those statements hit the airwaves, I expected that people would be talking about them. I also assumed it would reach Randy, who eventually fired his own shot back at me. Via Twitter, he said:

> **@criscarter80 its sad how u stroked ur own ego when u were suppose to b my mentor!then u wonder why karma bites u in the ass!#goodlukwithhof**

I'll be the first to say that my relationship with Randy should've never reached that low point. I also felt the jab about the Hall-of-Fame process was a cheap shot. I hoped that I had earned the right for my day to eventually come, but I also never felt that karma had anything to do with it.

Randy must have felt the same way when he called. Though our friendship has been filled with ups and downs that I'll get into later in this book, I still sensed that I was one of the few people he really trusted in the game. When I heard his voice, I was even more convinced of that. The first thing Randy said was "We need to talk." He followed that up by saying that there was no reason for people to suspect there was "a beef" between us because that was far from the truth. Randy even added that the last thing he wanted was "for our children to grow up thinking that we don't get along."

The most surprising part of that conversation wasn't that Randy had initiated it. It was that it happened at all, especially since I had criticized an aspect of his game. If there's one thing I've come to know it's that people who spend most of their lives playing the wide receiver position tend to have a hard time seeing the world around them. It's something that we all have inside of us, an inherent selfishness that makes us believe our interests are as important as, if not more than, anybody else's on our team.

That selfishness isn't necessarily a bad thing when it's channeled in the right way. However, it can be a huge problem if it gets out of control. I knew Randy had that selfishness in him. I did, too. It's what helped us dominate what has become the most compelling position in professional sports. Every weekend during football season, fans expect amazing performances from their team's star wide receivers. The by-product of that expectation is that many of the game's best players in recent years have soaked up the attention that comes with that spotlight . . . and pined for ways to keep it squarely on themselves.

But I'll be honest: Wanting the limelight was never Randy's major problem. As much as he fascinated people with his freakish combination of size (he is 6'4" and 210 pounds) and breathtaking speed, he never cared for the spotlight in the way stars such as Chad Johnson and Terrell Owens did at the height of their careers. Randy's issue was that he was so damn unreliable when faced with adversity. He'd worn out his welcome in Minnesota in 2004 and Oakland in 2006 for exactly that reason. When the New England Patriots traded for him in 2007, Randy enjoyed the best years of his career. Three years later, Belichick traded him back to the Vikings, likely because the head coach sensed Randy was about to get sideways with that franchise as well.

As it turned out, Randy wound up with two other teams that year. Minnesota placed him on waivers after four games because he was dogging it. Tennessee picked him up and rarely threw him the ball. But that wasn't where it ended for Randy. Once the lockout that killed most of the 2011 off-season concluded, there wasn't a single team that wanted to pay for the services of a player who'd been the game's most dangerous receiver for most of his career.

When I spoke to Randy, I told him that all was forgiven as far as we were concerned. I also reminded him that I'd always vowed to be honest with him and I was about to do so right then. "That guy I saw in 2010?" I said, referring to Randy's 28-reception season. "I don't know who that was."

When Randy explained that he wasn't happy about his performance that year, I was happy to know that, even at age thirty-five, there was still a chance for him to turn things around. He felt that Belichick had misled him, which ultimately fed the same distrust that has always been a huge part of Randy's personality. The moment Randy thought the Patriots had shit on him, he decided to take a bigger shit on everybody else. What he didn't understand was that, in the end, he was doing more harm to himself.

Randy likely thought there was no way the league would ever have a team that didn't want him. He couldn't see how all the headaches he had caused throughout his career could affect him to that point. Wide receivers can be like pretty girls that way. The more they hear how beautiful and desirable they are in their youth, the harder it is for them to ever think the day might arrive when they don't look so good anymore.

I'll never make the mistake of thinking that I understand why all receivers act the way they do all the time. I don't have special powers and I'm not interested in being football's version of Dr. Phil. What I do understand is the position. Randy Moss didn't become one of the most majestic and mystifying athletes in the game by sheer coincidence. He became that because he played a position that so easily demands attention.

Quarterbacks, by nature, are less dynamic. They typically say and do the right things because their words and actions carry so much weight, both inside and outside of the locker room. One mistake in judgment becomes a weeklong debate on *SportsCenter*. Even the smallest glimpse into their personal lives can lead to a feature story in *People* magazine. Quarterbacks don't need to seek attention. It's part of their job description.

As for other positions, it's hard to find any that compare to receivers as far as interest levels. Running backs handle the ball plenty, but the days of the feature back have almost disappeared. Most of today's teams believe in a running-back-by-committee approach, using several ball carriers who, in turn, face more questions about their long-term job security. Offensive linemen have never been trained to seek the spotlight and most defenders rarely have the opportunity to showcase their personalities in the same manner receivers can.

As I said earlier, wide receivers are naturally selfish people. We almost have to be that way. Remember, we didn't select the position to block. We need the ball in our hands to be effective. We don't get to handle it on every play like a quarterback does and we certainly don't have the luxury of having it handed to us in the way a running back does. We need a lot of things to go right for us to succeed—a smart play call, a good snap, effective blocking, and an accurate pass, among others—but we're cool with it. Once the ball is in the air, that's our time to shine.

I spent sixteen seasons playing wide receiver in the NFL and I can honestly say that you can get addicted to the spotlight you attract. We've seen it happen with Terrell Owens, Chad Johnson, and plenty of others. They get so wrapped up in the attention that comes with the job that it becomes their identity. The problem with that is that it doesn't last very long in the league.

The players who tend to enjoy the steadiest careers attract the spotlight solely for their on-field accomplishments. If you watch three of the best at the wide receiver position in recent years—Arizona's Larry Fitzgerald, Detroit's Calvin Johnson, and Houston's Andre Johnson—you see a number of similarities. They're all big, sure-handed, and quiet. They let their production do the talking and that's enough for them to sleep well at night. They play the game for admirable reasons: sheer love of the sport, an appreciation for the art of the craft, the desire to excel. Landing a reality show or gaining millions of Twitter followers isn't something that drives them to greatness.

But don't make the mistake of thinking that they want the ball any less than a more controversial player like Terrell Owens. Former Indianapolis Colts wide receiver Marvin Harrison is a future Hall-of-Famer who never liked the limelight when he played. The man caught 1,102 passes in his career and he talked about as often as a mafia kingpin facing federal indictment. But Marvin would let former Colts quarterback Peyton Manning know when the ball wasn't coming his way enough. He would simply do it in a sly manner—maybe coming off the field after a failed possession or while standing with Manning on the sideline—to let him know it was time for his touches to increase.

Jerry Rice had a similar style in San Francisco. He once threw a tantrum in a 35-point win over the Washington Redskins in 1998. His chief complaint? He had caught only 4 passes in that contest, a crisis that led to him screaming at then head coach Steve Mariucci on the sidelines late in that contest. Rice yelled that he was basically "a decoy" and that he didn't even know why he'd traveled to that game. Mariucci just stood there quietly, knowing full well that the national television audience was catching every bit of the future Hall-of-Famer's tirade.

Mariucci was so concerned about the issue that he called a sure-fire touchdown opportunity for Rice when the 49ers forced a turnover a few minutes later. It would've been a great way to appease the star receiver if Mariucci actually could've found him. Instead of running out to the huddle for that play, Rice was sitting on the bench with his helmet off, pouting. So that sure-fire touchdown went to some other lucky receiver.

Rice might have looked bad in that moment, but he made up for it afterward. When the game ended, he ran up to Mariucci, put an arm around the coach's shoulder, and apologized.

"I went crazy, didn't I?" Rice said.

"Yeah, you are a psycho," Mariucci responded.

"I know. I can go off every now and then."

Still, the tantrum worked. Rice apologized publicly the next day and the ball started coming his way more often. The next week Mariucci called six of San Francisco's first ten plays for Rice in the 49ers' win over Atlanta. When the game's greatest receiver (and player, as far as I'm concerned) finished with 8 receptions for 162 yards and 2 touch-downs, everybody in that franchise likely breathed a lot easier going forward.

Every great receiver can relate to that feeling of being underuti-lized. Many of us have had moments we regret as well. One of my most memorable came toward the end of the 1995 season with Minnesota. We were 8-7 going into a potentially season-ending game against the Cincinnati Bengals, and our playoff chances basically ended by half-time of that contest. By that point, I was thinking about my chances of resetting the league record for receptions in a season. I had established the mark with 122 receptions in 1994, but Detroit's Herman Moore had surpassed that with 123 catches prior to our game with Cincinnati. I wanted that record back. I needed it back.

Keep in mind that the mid-1990s were a time when receivers were playing out of their minds and you truly earned the right to be consid-ered among the very best. We all understood that Rice was in his own class, given how long he'd been playing and the numbers he'd put up in San Francisco. After him, there was a serious competition for the runner-up spot on the list of the day's top wideouts. You had Moore, Michael Irvin, Sterling Sharpe, Isaac Bruce, Tim Brown, and a bunch of others. In 1995 alone, *twenty-three* different players had more than 1,000 yards receiving.

It used to be that a 1,500-yard season was a big deal. Suddenly, you had players on the same team hitting that mark. The same was true for the 100-catch season. Reaching that point before those years was like dropping 60 points in an NBA game. It was rarefied air. Plus, I'd bet that most of the game's best receivers knew what everybody else was doing in those days. I know that I was keeping track. There were too many resources to study up on what other players were doing, too many times when you'd hear Chris Berman celebrating their feats on ESPN instead of yours.

I wasn't the only person thinking about that receptions record, ei-ther. Our offensive coordinator, Brian Billick, approached me in warm-up drills and said he was going to give me plenty of opportunities to reset the mark. The only problem was that his promise never materialized. I needed 9 receptions to surpass Moore and the second half of that contest was disastrous. We couldn't execute consistently. We played lethargically. We basically watched Cincinnati, one of the league's worst teams, outperform us in a game that meant even less to them when it started.

When I ended up with just 7 receptions (giving me 122 catches on the year), I fumed in the locker room afterward. Making matters worse, the media found me at exactly the moment when I was most heated. By the time that question-and-answer session had ended, I had blasted Billick for his play-calling, ripped into my teammates for quitting in the second half, and lamented both the defeat and our extinguished playoff hopes. The one comment I remember saying publicly that probably looked the worst was fueled by my notorious pride. As I told the reporters that day, the only thing that mattered to me at the end of that game was that record.

I don't think it's hard to understand why some receivers can reach that point. We've always wanted the ball but we've never been rewarded for our success in the ways we've seen recently. When I was a kid, pro football wasn't nearly as available as it is today. You watched two or three games on Sunday—generally featuring the local team or one within the region—and then you had *Monday Night Football.* There was no ESPN and no fantasy football, so no stat-crazed fan base. Aside from the quarterbacks and a few players here and there, there wasn't much individuality in the game.

That was before constant highlights, more focus on the game, and more opportunity for receivers to prove their value. The NFL we see today is a far cry from the one I grew up with in the 1980s. Back then it was a game of speed and power, one fueled by dominant running attacks and fierce defenses. Now it's a game of speed and finesse, a league that old-school types refer to as "basketball and grass." In that kind of world, where offensive coaches are always looking for freakish athletes to create mismatches against undermanned defenses, receivers had the opportunity to become bona fide superstars.

The popularity of the position also had plenty to do with the fundamental nature of it. People can relate to receivers because catching a football is one of the most basic things you can do on a field. Anybody can do it. You see people throwing the ball around when you drive through NFL stadium parking lots on game days and they're doing the same thing when the contest has ended. Sure, anybody can throw a football, but it takes arm strength, accuracy, and certain fundamentals to do it correctly. Being a receiver just means running forward and catching the ball when it comes your way. And when you think about it, nobody gets together with his buddies to re-create blocking schemes.

I even believe that some receivers brought their own unique personalities to the game before we ever recognized them. As an ESPN analyst, I spend a lot of time talking to fellow ex-players about today's game and their own experiences. Tom Jackson, another ESPN broadcaster and a linebacker who played with the Denver Broncos from 1973–86, once agreed that he remembers some interesting characters from his own playing days. He wouldn't identify one memorable person, but the story he provided about this player was enlightening:

The Broncos were preparing to leave for a road trip, and Tom was one of the first to recognize a problem with the bus that would take them to the airport: One of the receivers wasn't on it. This wouldn't have been such a big deal if the player had been ten minutes late for the team's departure. Even twenty minutes could've been explained away. But after an hour, Tom, his teammates, and his coaches were all wondering what the hell had happened. This was during the 1970s. It wasn't like there were cell phones in those days. You were off the grid the minute you got stuck in traffic.

It wasn't until the team had been waiting for more than ninety minutes that the receiver finally pulled his car into the parking lot and boarded the bus. When he came down the aisle, Tom wondered why nobody was asking why the guy was so late. That concern changed as soon as Tom saw his teammate's right hand. It wasn't a car accident that had held him up, nor was it some sort of family emergency. Instead, the receiver's explanation had everything to do with a more basic need: He was carrying a plastic bag filled with three boxes of Church's fried chicken.

That story tells me this position was destined to be a little different from the start. It just took a few decades and a certain set of circumstances to bring us to where we are today. We needed the television networks to take the popularity of the game to an entirely new level. We needed innovative minds to revolutionize football and open up the passing game. We also needed a run of quarterbacks the likes of whom we'd never seen before in the 1980s and 1990s—legends like John Elway, Dan Marino, Warren Moon, Jim Kelly, and Brett Favre, who started throwing the football in ways we'd never imagined.

Those signal-callers received ample credit for what they did for offensive fireworks in their day. What we didn't know was how much they were creating a platform for receivers to become bigger stars in their own right. I remember the best pass-catchers of the 1980s—most notably Jerry Rice, Steve Largent, James Lofton, and Art Monk—as gifted performers in dynamic offensive schemes. Over the last two decades, we've become more accustomed to the idea of teams building their offenses around featured receivers . . . along with those receivers ranking among the loudest voices in the locker room.

When the New York Giants upset the heavily favored and undefeated New England Patriots in Super Bowl XLII, it wasn't Giants quarterback Eli Manning who predicted a victory in the same way Joe Namath did for the New York Jets in Super Bowl III. It was wide receiver Plaxico Burress, who also caught the game-winning touchdown pass. The Patriots also had the league's most prolific offense ever that season and not only because they had Tom Brady playing quarterback. The arrival of Randy—who caught a league-record 23 touchdown passes in 2007—ultimately transformed a very good offense into a legendary one.

In addition to those players, we've seen far more receivers in recent history serving as the faces of their teams than ever before. Before

Drew Brees arrived in New Orleans and helped the Saints win Super Bowl XLIV, Joe Horn was the most prominent player in that franchise. Rich Gannon may have won the league MVP with the Oakland Raiders in 2002, but for many years Tim Brown was the only star on that team. Even Michael Irvin—despite all his off-the-field issues—was a driving force in the Dallas Cowboys dynasty in the 1990s. Troy Aikman was the quarterback and Emmitt Smith the star runner, but Irvin was unquestionably the heart and soul of those teams. Ask anybody who'd spent time around them during those glory years.

The only problem with this trend is that sometimes teams make the mistake of putting too much responsibility on wide receivers. I've long believed that players at that position shouldn't be team captains because there are too many reasons the job is beyond their capabilities. The New York Jets discovered as much during the 2011 season. They started the year with great ambition, eager to challenge for the AFC East title and hopeful that wide receiver Santonio Holmes, a team captain, could help lead them there. By January, they were sifting through the wreckage of their season and trying to decide if Holmes should even remain on the roster.

Those issues revolved around one area: Holmes wasn't happy with the quarterback. The more erratic Jets starter Mark Sanchez became, the more Holmes sulked. There were reports that Holmes wouldn't attend the quarterback-receiver meetings that Sanchez arranged each week and that teammates privately disliked the receiver's attitude. Holmes's situation became so toxic that former offensive coordinator Brian Schottenheimer actually benched him during a game late in the season.

Now, does any of this surprise me? No. The minute the Jets elected Holmes as a captain, they were making a huge gamble. This was the same guy who had won the Most Valuable Player award in Pittsburgh's win over Arizona in Super Bowl XLIII and then became such a headache for the Steelers that they traded him for a fifth-round pick two years later. That's a pretty hard feat to achieve. But the Jets probably felt like they had a steal at the time, and they did for a bit. Holmes played very well in his first season, making clutch catch after clutch catch and helping New York reach the AFC championship game in 2010.

That success was enough to make them forget the type of receiver they had acquired. They probably figured that Holmes was more mature than Sanchez and that he'd help the young quarterback blossom. Instead, Holmes became the same player he'd been for the Steelers. Only this time, it wasn't off-the-field issues that hurt his standing with the team. It was the same trait that had been growing in him since the first time he ever lined up as a receiver. He had a natural inability to deal with a world where the football wasn't constantly coming his way.

Holmes's 2011 season with the Jets was also an example of another characteristic common in receivers: We want more than what we have. If we catch five balls, we want seven. If we catch seven, we want ten. If we go to the Pro Bowl, we want to start. If we lead the league in receptions for one season, we want to do it every year after that.

In the case of Holmes, I guarantee you that he loved the idea of being in New York because it was a step up. When he was in Pittsburgh, he was part of a franchise that already had plenty of star power on both sides of the ball. Ben Roethlisberger was the two-time Super Bowl–winning quarterback while fellow receiver Hines Ward was the heart of the offense. Outside linebacker James Harrison was the Defensive Player of the Year in 2008 and strong safety Troy Polamalu was widely considered one of the best defenders in the game. Even head coach Mike Tomlin, the man who produced a Super Bowl win just two seasons after replacing Bill Cowher, had a higher profile.

The minute Holmes arrived in New York, he was hailed as a savior for an offense that needed a big-play threat. He likely ate that up, all the while believing this was his opportunity to show the world what he could really do. Does that make him any different from most receivers? Not at all. Holmes probably thought he'd take his game to the next level in his new franchise, which can be a common mistake for some wideouts.

We saw Deion Branch leave the New England Patriots—just one season after helping them win their third Super Bowl in four seasons—for a forgettable five-year tenure with Seattle. Peerless Price signed a huge deal with the Atlanta Falcons in 2003 after making a name for himself during four seasons in Buffalo. He never enjoyed a 1,000-yard season after that point and lasted only two years with that franchise. Dallas fans also have to remember the free-agent flop of Alvin Harper. He left the Cowboys as a number two receiver in 1994, eager to make big money as a number one target after helping that team win two Super Bowls. He wound up in Tampa Bay, then Washington, New Orleans, and finally Dallas again. In all, he caught 67 passes over the final five seasons of his career.

These receivers all wanted the same things I wanted when I came into the league. They wanted the world to see how truly exceptional they were, how much they could do for a team with the ball in their hands. That they lost sight of their own limitations isn't surprising. The more we succeed at the position—regardless of how much help we get from fellow players and coaches—the more we believe it's all the result of our own extraordinary skills.

It's that level of confidence (or cockiness) that makes the best players at the position great. It's also why teams will put up with plenty of headaches if a receiver can put them over the top. When Randy Moss was at his best in Minnesota, I know for a fact that head coach Denny Green was willing to give him a long leash. Randy was so dangerous that all you had to do was keep him motivated on game days. His talent would take care of the rest as long as he had his head on straight.

I'll give you an example. When Minnesota reached the NFC championship game in 2000, I knew it might be one of my last opportunities to reach the Super Bowl. I had come close back in the 1998 season and that year still ranks as the most heartbreaking moment in my career. We had lost one game all season and yet the Atlanta Falcons upset us at home in the NFC title game. To this day, people still consider that Minnesota team one of the best to never win a championship.

Since Randy had been a rookie on that 1998 team, he understood full well how hard it was to reach another NFC title game. We talked about it plenty as we advanced through the 2000 playoffs and especially during the week prior to that contest with the Giants. I still remember thinking about the significance of that moment as I was driving to get a haircut on the Friday before we left for New York. It was a ritual that Randy and I always had before games. We'd go to our favorite barber in Minneapolis on Friday mornings and be ready for the cameras come Sunday.

Only this time, Denny decided he wanted to change the team schedule on that Friday morning and hold a mandatory meeting prior to our departure. He called me as I was driving toward the barbershop, asking that I give the message to Randy. When I got ahold of Randy, I could sense him getting upset before I got all the words out. He was already so close to the shop that he didn't see the need in turning around.

I tried explaining to Randy that we had to be at the meeting. I also reminded him that it would be fairly easy to find a barber in New York who could come to our hotel and provide the same service. We'd done it before.

But Randy wouldn't hear it. "I've got to get my hair tight," he said. "We're going to New York!"

There are probably still teammates and coaches who never learned why Denny changed that mandatory midmorning team meeting to a set of individual position meetings that everybody managed to make before we left that Friday afternoon. I didn't discuss the adjustment with anybody and I doubt Randy even thought twice about it once he tightened up his hair. I do know there weren't any other players on that team that could've made a head coach as accomplished as Denny Green reconsider how he handled his team just two days away from playing for a Super Bowl bid. I also can't think of another position where it was plausible for a player to pull that kind of stunt (and, by the way, we lost 41–0, which was the worst defeat ever in NFC championship game history).

Randy's decision that weekend confirmed for me that receivers had reached a point that the NFL ultimately had to accept. The game had evolved so much that we'd become major power brokers. Instead of being satisfied with mainly blocking for running backs (as was the case for many prior to the 1970s) or being part of a system (such as in the 1980s), offenses were starting to utilize us in ways we never quite imagined. That dynamic has created its share of amazing talents and it's also produced plenty of unique characters.

The 1990s started with plenty of coaches being hyped for their genius and ability to create potent, high-scoring offenses. A couple of decades later, it was apparent that wide receivers played a huge role in all that praise being thrown around to the men on the sidelines. Coaches like Denny Green understood what was happening and embraced it. Others fought against it and discovered that it wasn't so easy to win without such talents.

What can't be denied is the impact receivers have had on the NFL over that time. Some have left their marks with their exhilarating play. Others have done it with a combination of personality and production. A few have even made the term "diva" the most common way to describe those who become too controversial for the job, once again proving that it's taken all types to help the role of receivers evolve.

Yet all have made the position more interesting than any other job in the world of pro sports. And the issue most worth exploring isn't just what they're doing with all that status today. Instead, it's how wide receivers actually reached this formerly unimaginable point in the first place.

CHAPTER 2

Same Name, Different Game

I didn't start off wanting to be a wide receiver. In 1973, when I started playing organized football at eight years old, it wasn't a glamorous position. I could probably name about five wide receivers in the entire NFL at that time, and it wasn't because I felt like they didn't have a valuable place in football. It's just that there weren't many who really stood out. Catching passes just didn't seem that cool of a job.

Growing up in Middletown, Ohio, I watched football as much as any kid in my neighborhood, but the game was different back then. The team mattered more than the individual in those days. You followed perennial powers like the Dolphins, Cowboys, Raiders, and Steelers because they exemplified unity and cohesiveness. Even the nicknames of that time gave you a good feel for how fans looked at the NFL: "the No-Name Defense," "the Steel Curtain," "the Doomsday Defense." If you're wondering why all the cool monikers went to the defenses back then, just consider what was happening on offense.

As kids, we knew the quarterbacks got all the glory. We also understood that running back was an attractive position. It always seemed like the best athletes wanted to handle the ball as much as possible, which meant working out of the backfield. You wanted to be like O. J. Simpson, Franco Harris, or Walter Payton. If you dreamed about being an NFL receiver one day, you were heading for a career where very few fans were likely to remember your name.

I was a quarterback when I started playing football and I loved the role. On my first play in peewee football, I raced 67 yards for a touchdown and fell in love with the game. It fed my ultracompetitive spirit and felt like a natural fit for my athletic skill set.

But I also had to learn to tone down my desire to win at that young age. In that same first game, I got so angry at a teammate for making a weak attempt at tackling an opponent that I threw a tantrum. I threatened to fight anybody who wasn't willing to lay it on the line that day, to compete as hard as me. Looking back, it wasn't the best way to start my career. My oldest brother, Butch, reminded me of that when he dragged me off the field and lectured me about how team sports were played.

I couldn't help myself, though. I always wanted to win and believed that everybody else around me should want to win just as badly. You learn as much growing up in a four-room apartment with five siblings and a single mother. You don't escape that kind of poverty without ample willpower. The minute you let up on your ambition just a little bit, your wildest dreams are a lot less likely to ever be realized.

I remember my mother, Joyce, always telling us that she couldn't afford college for us kids. If we were going to go, we had to work hard in school and earn a scholarship somehow. My mom truly believed in using sports as a way of creating educational opportunities. She had gotten pregnant with her first child as a high school senior, so she wanted her kids to grow up with more opportunities than she ever had. She raised us to be leaders.

I guess that's why quarterback suited me. I loved playing basketball, and the quarterback position offered me the same options: I always had the ball in my hands and I dictated the action. Having the chance to make things happen was the most enjoyable part of playing football. I figured I'd be playing that position for years, but that was before I became a ninth grader at Middletown High School, before I realized that my destiny in football meant having to move to a position I had never played.

Friends of my older brothers would see me doing my thing on the freshman team—you couldn't play on varsity until you were a sophomore—and they'd always tell me, "You're not going to be playing quarterback on varsity, Li'l Carter. It's not going to happen." That was their way of saying that my high school wasn't ready for a black quarterback. It also was a good reason for me to start thinking about the next best place for me to play once I moved up a grade.

Since I was lanky and athletic, I thought receiver would be the most sensible choice. I liked the position mainly because it offered me the easiest chance to start as a tenth grader. I always felt comfortable catching the ball and I knew how to position my body to go after it. It was almost like I was going up for a rebound in basketball. I could work the angles, read my defender, and then separate just as the pass was falling into my hands. I felt like a natural.

If I was going to be a receiver, there were at least two players at the time whom I wanted to emulate. The first was Paul Warfield, a man I watched racing by defensive backs when he was with the Miami Dolphins in the early 1970s. Warfield had grown up in Warren, Ohio, played at Ohio State, and later starred for the Cleveland Browns, so that made him cool enough in my eyes. He also made his own position switch before becoming a Hall-of-Fame receiver—Warfield had been a college running back—so I identified with him even more.

The other player who opened my eyes to the position was Pittsburgh's Lynn Swann. The Steelers played their home games only five hours from Middletown. They were always on television because they were in the same division with the Cleveland Browns and Cincinnati Bengals. I could see Swann at least four times a year on my family's television set and even more once the Steelers became a championship dynasty. I would bet you there are plenty of receivers who migrated to the position solely because they watched him excel for the best team of the 1970s.

The impressive thing about Swann was that he played during a time when numbers really didn't matter. He caught only 336 passes in his nine-year career and he never gained more than 900 yards in any season. What he gave the game was flair and a knack for making the big play on the biggest of stages. Of all the great catches made in Super Bowl history, I'd guarantee you most fans would put the one he made in Super Bowl X on their top five.

In that contest, Swann raced up the sideline as Steelers quarterback Terry Bradshaw unleashed a deep pass. It wasn't just that Swann caught the ball while Dallas Cowboys cornerback Mark Washington grappled with him on that 53-yard play. It was the way Swann made the catch—timing his leap perfectly, maintaining his balance as Washington stumbled to the ground, and clutching the ball as he tumbled to the turf. That play changed the entire look of football. Instead of merely being a brutish sport dominated by men imposing their will on one another, a wide receiver could intimidate in a different way: He could beat you with grace.

I won't say Swann was the only player to transform the position, but he definitely had the greatest platform. The man won four Super Bowls during his career and he made a lot of big plays. His style and athleticism set him apart from a team known for its bruising, blue-collar image. Without even trying, Swann was proving how cool it could be to do things that sent fans' hearts racing.

What's also interesting about Swann, as I later discovered, is that he never felt limited by his position when he entered the NFL. When he was a sophomore at USC, he once had an old friend, B. Wayne Hughes, tell him that he needed to make more game-changing plays if he wanted to help his team win. Swann thought the guy was nuts. He ran his routes properly, caught the passes thrown his way, and blocked enthusiastically for star runners like Anthony Davis and Sam Cunningham. In Swann's mind, he was doing everything right.

Still, that wasn't enough evidence to keep Hughes, a USC alum and local businessman, from asking Swann a simple question over dinner one night: Why did a receiver so gifted look so ordinary in the biggest games? It was a radical thought in those days because a player as blessed as Swann didn't realize how much he could impact a game as a receiver. After watching game film and scrutinizing his play, Swann saw what his friend meant.

"What I saw was that Wayne was right," Swann told ESPN.com. "I wasn't the guy making the big catch in the big games. I wasn't the guy breaking the tackles and making a long gain after I got my hands on the ball. I was a team player. I played well. But I didn't do anything that was defining. And I decided to change that."

The Lynn Swann I watched play for the Steelers—the one who would be the Most Valuable Player of Super Bowl X—was a man who had that very mind-set, and it was stunning. Since I grew up in the Midwest, I watched the NFL because I wanted to see teams throw the football. I could watch plenty of running teams in college on Saturdays, with everybody from Michigan and Ohio State to Oklahoma and Nebraska sticking with the three-yards-and-a-cloud-of-dust strategy. The NFL was willing to be more open because it wanted to entertain fans. You couldn't just do that with handoffs and field goals.

The league needed more players like Swann and Warfield. It needed more ways to involve them in the game. It wasn't like there wasn't crazy talent at the position, because, as Hall-of-Fame receiver James Lofton said, "You could watch players like [Baltimore's] Lenny Moore or [San Diego's] Lance Alworth back in the 1960s and see that they had skills. The first Super Bowl touchdown was [Green Bay's] Max McGee and he was a six-three, 205-pound man. Even [Packers Hall-of-Famer] Don Hutson ran a 9.7 hundred-yard dash. So there were always guys who could do the job."

"In [the 1970s], receivers were ingrained in the entire offensive picture," said former Dallas Cowboys wide receiver Drew Pearson. "They weren't just there for big plays. I can't tell you how many times I had to line up tight and block a defensive end on a running play. You threw on third downs so you had to be more physical."

I didn't grow up watching those great old-timers featured in the wide-open American Football League. But I did see the steady progress the NFL was making with the pass. The more I saw where the game was going by the end of the 1970s, the less I cared about having to give up my job as a quarterback.

I was a starting wide receiver by the time my sophomore year at Middletown High began. As it turned out, that was one of the smartest moves I ever made in my life.

By the time I started playing wide receiver in high school the NFL game had changed dramatically enough for me to see the possibilities of staying at that position. In 1978, just two years before I started catching passes for Middletown, the league had made two of the most significant rule changes ever to improve offensive productivity. The first allowed offensive linemen to use their hands when pass blocking, so long as the players positioned their mitts inside defenders' shoulders (linemen previously had to keep their hands pressed together while warding off pass rushers with their forearms and elbows). The second prevented defensive backs from having any contact with receivers more than 5 yards beyond the line of scrimmage.

As a teenager trying to make a name on his high school team, such alterations to the game didn't catch my attention immediately. What I did eventually notice was how the NFL opened up in the late 1970s as a result. The AFC always threw more than the NFC, but suddenly all quarterbacks had more time to throw because the pass protection was better. Receivers also had more room to operate because defensive backs—even the ones who still tried to find ways to put their hands on opponents—couldn't mug them whenever they wanted. The game became smoother, faster paced, and more reliant on speed and quickness.

If you look back at 1973, the first year I started playing organized football, there were only three receivers in the entire NFL who caught more than 50 passes. Only one, Philadelphia's Harold Carmichael, gained more than 1,000 receiving yards. Aside from the random big play, receivers didn't really catch your eye. Most players, if I had to guess, didn't really try. They had to make the most of whatever came their way because teams were only throwing about twenty times a game.

Those players likely had the same mind-set that Swann had when he was an underclassman at USC: Do your job, be a good teammate, and make something happen when the ball comes your way. As Carmichael said, "You didn't know anything else so you did what you were told to do." James Lofton added: "If you go back thirty or forty years ago, catching a pass was a real valuable commodity. The ball didn't come your way very often so you had to make the most of it. Why else would [former Oakland Raider and Hall-of-Fame receiver] Fred Biletnikoff cover himself in so much stickum? He had to catch what came his way."

Thank God the owners at that time knew how vital it was to increase scoring and keep defenses from running wild. That's something people tend to forget in today's NFL, where the best offensive teams average around 300 or more passing yards a game. In the 1970s, catching passes meant facing the possibility of somebody knocking your head off. Former Steeler and Hall-of-Fame cornerback Mel Blount, who was 6'3" and 205 pounds, could do it easily. He'd walk up to the line of scrimmage, crouch down at an angle that positioned his backside to the middle of the field, and dare you to beat him to the inside. Most receivers in that era couldn't do it.

"Mel Blount was having a field day against people," Drew Pearson said. "The only time I ever caught passes against Mel was on first down, when he was playing off [the line of scrimmage]. Once you got to third down—and he knew your team was throwing—he'd get so close that you could feel him breathing on you. In situations like that, [former Cowboys receiver] Tony Hill and I knew we were going to be decoys. Because we weren't getting by him."

Carmichael said the Washington Redskins used to have a coverage for him called the Sequoia Axe. Since he was 6'8", the Washington defenders wanted to intimidate him by taking out his legs. Whether it was a cornerback or a linebacker, Carmichael knew somebody was going to be aiming at his lower body every time he ran a route. "That was an era where people thought anything goes," Carmichael said. "They'd clothesline you. They'd throw forearms at your head. They'd go helmet to helmet. The St. Louis Cardinals were one team that loved to hammer you back then. I always felt good playing a team that had just played them because you knew guys would be beat up."

Younger receivers coming out of college had an even harder time adjusting to that environment. When the Houston Oilers spent a fourth-round pick on Steve Largent in 1976, they were expecting big things from a wideout who had enjoyed an All-American career at the University of Tulsa. Instead, Largent looked lost when facing the more aggressive cornerbacks in the NFL. He'd grown accustomed to beating defenders who mainly played zone coverage in college. Getting assaulted on every route had been something he never expected at the professional level.

"The guys were huge and they had no problems grabbing you by the shoulder pads or hitting you in the head," said Largent, who would eventually become a Hall-of-Famer, leading the NFL in career receptions, yards, and touchdowns when he retired in 1989. "That's how the game was played. It got to a point that the Oilers traded me to Seattle during my first training camp. I was so slow to adjust that they thought I'd never learn to get off the line of scrimmage. I had to come to the realization that I had to do it. If I couldn't, I wasn't going to be around very long."

The Oakland Raiders' defensive backs—vicious hitters like Jack Tatum and George Atkinson—had a scarier idea of how best to attack receivers. They made their names by going high to blow up opposing wideouts. Tatum was so nasty that New England Patriots wide receiver Darryl Stingley was paralyzed from Tatum's brutal hit in a 1978 preseason game . . . and he never apologized for it. Atkinson was just as vicious; during a 1976 game, he gave Swann a concussion by clubbing the unsuspecting receiver in the back of the head.

That hit by Atkinson led to former Steelers head coach Chuck Noll claiming that "a criminal element" had emerged in the NFL and that defenders like Atkinson should be "kicked out of the league." Atkinson responded by filing a $2 million lawsuit against Noll and the Steelers for slander. The entire affair culminated in a ten-day trial in a San Francisco federal courthouse in 1977, with Noll, Swann, Atkinson, and even league commissioner Pete Rozelle taking the stand. It was a messy case, one thoroughly embarrassing for the NFL and ultimately unsuccessful for Atkinson. It also was a critical moment for wide receivers all over the league.

That lawsuit must have been the impetus for the league to rethink what was happening to offensive football. The decision-makers may have wanted to open the game up for quarterbacks, but they also had to consider what was happening to wide receivers. It was bad enough that the most graceful athletes on the field were barely seeing the football. But they were also likely to be assaulted every time they raced off the line of scrimmage. "Keep in mind, it wasn't like receivers were coming into the league with personal trainers and nutritionists," Pearson said. "Nobody was physical back then. I didn't even lift weights before I got to Dallas."

There surely was plenty of complaining on the defensive side of the football when the rules changed in 1978. But there also had to be a heightened anticipation of what could happen with a few more advantages being handed to the offense. For one thing, the likelihood of notable coaches and players winding up in court again over such nonsense seemed laughable. More plausible was the notion that the game would become even more entertaining as the years went on. "The league started getting smart," Pearson said. "It realized that defense may win championships but offense puts fans in the stands. And exciting offense keeps them coming back."

It was only a coincidence that the next player to really elevate the position entered the NFL in the same year those rules changed. But if you watched San Diego's John Jefferson just a few times, you would think it was fate. Jefferson had extraordinary timing. He mesmerized when the ball was in the air, because he had the same exceptional gifts as Swann. He could contort his body, leap as if propelled off a trampoline, and snatch anything that came within inches of his soft hands. Jefferson made even the most difficult of receptions look routine.

Jefferson became the first player in league history to surpass the 1,000-yard mark in each of his first three seasons, and he literally was at the forefront of a receiving revolution. While quarterbacks predictably received plenty of credit for the passing game opening up in the late 1970s, receivers also were doing things they'd never done before. In 1977, just one year before those rules changes, Pearson *led the league* with 870 receiving yards. In 1981, fifteen different receivers hit the

1,000-yard mark with three tight ends joining them (Kellen Winslow, Joe Senser, and Ozzie Newsome). The NFL didn't just look different anymore. It was different.

As a high school kid in Middletown at that time, I could feel my own competitive juices burning as I saw the pro game opening up. I caught 27 passes as a senior and 10 of those went for touchdowns. That was probably around the time when I started to learn how receivers could whine so much for the football. If I had managed to catch twice as many passes during my final high school season, I might have scored twice as many times (at least that's how I figured the math in my head). And trust me, I let my quarterback and coaches know I was open every time I had the chance.

I had become so good by that point that I was moving closer to a major decision. I had long dreamed of following Butch into the NBA, where he was in the midst of a six-year career, and I was receiving plenty of major college attention. Schools like Purdue and Kentucky were all high on my list of suitors. Georgetown was a dream school as well, but head coach John Thompson didn't recruit me. Louisville was another favorite institution, especially because of the team's up-tempo playing style, and I was a big fan of assistant coach Wade Houston (whose son, Allan, later played in the NBA).

The only problem with pursuing basketball in college was my height. I was about 6'2½" and I never felt comfortable with the idea of going far in the NBA with those dimensions (Butch was a 6'5" shooting guard who had made his name playing for Bobby Knight at Indiana from 1976–80). I also understood the value of looking at simple math. The NFL had twenty-eight teams when I graduated high school in 1984, while the NBA had twenty-three franchises. The United States Football League (USFL) also had started in 1983, and it had eighteen teams of its own a year later. Overall, there were roughly two thousand more jobs to be found in pro football if I wanted to go that route.

I also didn't lack for suitors as a college recruit. Michigan, Notre Dame, Pitt, USC, and Ohio State were all on my list of favorite schools. Michigan had just lost one of the most exciting receivers in college football history in Anthony Carter. Notre Dame had history and a head coach, Gerry Faust, who had made his name as a legendary high school coach in Ohio. Pitt also had a dominant program, even with All-American quarterback Dan Marino heading to the NFL the year before I would've arrived.

Still, the place I longed to go most was USC. It had tradition and talent, and Los Angeles looked pretty good to a kid from Ohio. The only problem was its recruiting process. One of USC's assistants was supposed to come watch me at basketball practice during my senior year but he never actually showed up. Talk about being pissed. I had been excited all week for that visit. When my basketball coach told me the USC assistant wasn't coming, I dropped the Trojans from my list without even wondering why they couldn't keep their commitment.

Ultimately, Ohio State was the school that won out. I decided that while I was sitting with my mother in our kitchen one day during my senior year. I had reached the point where I was tired of all the questions from strangers about where I was going to college. Every school that offered me a scholarship seemed attractive at some point, but I needed to move forward with my life. Finally, I asked my mom where she wanted me to go. Up to that point, she had never offered an opinion.

"I always had a dream that one of my boys would go to Ohio State," she said.

That really was all I needed to hear. I was her youngest son. And I figured that God was talking to me through my mother. So later that night, I called up head coach Earle Bruce and told him I was accepting his full ride to Ohio State. That was the end of my recruiting process.

Along with my mother's desire, I liked the idea of being a Buckeye because the school would let me play basketball if I kept my grades above a 2.5 GPA. However, Butch didn't think sentimentality should figure into my decision. He had watched the Buckeyes for years and he knew how much they loved to run the football during the Woody Hayes era. Even though Woody had retired in 1978, Butch didn't see the point. In his eyes, I was throwing my career away before I ever stepped foot onto a college field.

"Why would you want to go there?" he asked me one day. "They don't throw the football."

"Well, they've never had a receiver like me," I responded.

"Really," Butch retorted. "Have you ever heard of a guy named Paul Warfield? He went there and they never threw him the ball."

"That's exactly my point," I said.

What Butch couldn't understand was that Coach Bruce had convinced me that he knew what to do with a talented receiver. He never promised any freshmen that they would play in their first season, but he did make it clear that he'd be disappointed if I didn't earn a first-string spot once I joined the team. That's how much the NFL was affecting college football by that point. It was making traditionally conservative coaches think long and hard about the best ways to utilize their assets in the passing game.

Now I definitely wasn't focusing on the NFL when I first arrived at Ohio State. I had too many things to consider when it came to adjusting to life at the college level. I struggled so much in my first practice with the varsity squad that even my coaches were a little concerned. I kept slipping on the turf, stumbling into my routes, and dropping easily thrown passes. My problems eventually reached such a low point that Coach Bruce walked by one of his assistants and said, "Does anybody know what happened to Cris Carter? That's not the guy we recruited out of Middletown."

I eventually regained my confidence and my stride a few days later and earned a starting job as a freshman. I also gained valuable inspiration from watching the pro game. The more you looked around the league, the more you saw stars emerging every season. You had newcomers like Mike Quick in Philadelphia, Cris Collinsworth in Cincinnati, and the two Marks (Clayton and Duper) in Miami, fresh faces who were making an immediate impact on the sport. You also had crafty veterans like Lofton, Largent, and Pittsburgh's John Stallworth—experienced targets who knew exactly how to make the most of their newfound freedom.

All these players had the requisite skills to excel at the professional level—reliable hands, crisp route-running, and the ability to exploit rules designed to increase their effectiveness. A few even had something that was much less common for the position at the time: personality.

I laughed the first time I saw the Washington Redskins "Fun Bunch" in 1982. The group consisted of three wide receivers (Art Monk, Charlie Brown, and Virgil Seay) and two tight ends (Rick Walker and Don Warren), and they revolutionized pass-catching for one reason—they literally made it fun. Starting with a first-round playoff win over the Detroit Lions that season, they began a habit of meeting in the end zone following a touchdown, forming a circle, and rising in unison for a group high-five. It was a routine they likely created during some down time in practice, but it definitely caught on quickly. In those days, you rarely saw anybody doing something that demonstrative in the middle of a pro football game.

Flair wasn't something the NFL embraced or marketed. The league was corporate and conservative by nature, and you could feel it in every aspect of the game you watched on television every Sunday. If you were a receiver with a little bit of swagger to you, you rarely had a chance to showcase it. Instead, you tried your best to fit in with the team and did little to draw attention to yourself.

The irony of this trend was that every time a new celebration ritual started in pro football, a wide receiver was at the forefront of it. In 1965, the New York Giants' Homer Jones decided to create his own form of punctuating a score after noticing that teammate Frank Gifford tossed the ball into the stands once he reached the end zone. So whenever Jones scored that season, he'd stop, brace himself, and slam the ball into the turf as hard as possible. Jones called the move a "spike" and, without even intending to, launched a trend that has been part of football ever since.

A few years later, an explosive junior receiver at the University of Houston named Elmo Wright decided to do his own thing when it came to scoring touchdowns. He had started out by throwing the ball into the stands—like Gifford—after scores during his sophomore year, but the NCAA eventually outlawed that celebration. A year later, in Houston's first game of the season, Wright caught a short pass against Florida, high-stepped away from a defensive back diving at his feet, and kept high-stepping all the way to the end zone. He didn't know that it looked like he was actually dancing his way to a touchdown, not even when people started booing him. But when his teammates found him on the sidelines later and praised his spontaneity, he decided to make it his trademark.

The NFL first learned about Wright's "moves" in 1973, when he was a member of the Kansas City Chiefs. He caught a touchdown pass against the Houston Oilers, immediately started high-stepping, and then spiked the football exuberantly. Nobody had seen anything like that from a pro football player, not even in the wild and crazy days of the American Football League in the 1960s. But it's also fitting that a receiver was responsible for it. It gave people a little indication of what was going on in their minds.

In an interview with the *New York Times* years later, Wright said he felt like he'd "created a monster" by introducing the world to touchdown dances. He also explained that "a player who only has to run patterns and score touchdowns isn't thinking long term. He's thinking, I have to get into the end zone and score a touchdown. Wanting to do a dance is an inducement and a motivation to train harder and focus. Players use that in order to play well." I understand exactly what Wright was saying. As much as wide receivers want to be team players, there's something inside us that naturally wants to stand out.

As classy as Swann was in his day, I can remember him and Stallworth waving their Terrible Towels on the sidelines when the Steelers were closing in on a big win. Pearson said he used to have his own variation on the spike, where he'd windmill the ball or take it between his legs before spiking it. Former Cowboys head coach Tom Landry used to encourage his players to celebrate after a score so long as they kept things under control. Pearson actually crossed the line one game when he scored and tried to throw the ball into the end zone seats. He stumbled after releasing the ball, hyperextended a knee, and never found Landry supportive of touchdown celebrations after that. "He wasn't very happy with me," Pearson said.

A star like John Jefferson had swag before people even started using that term to define somebody who was cool. You saw it in his space-age-style goggles and the sheer energy he brought to the position. If future Hall-of-Famer Charlie Joiner was the old-school, consummate professional of the Chargers receivers back in the early 1980s, then Jefferson was the image of young rebellion. He didn't have to act like a revolutionary. His game embodied the very idea of it.

Still, when I think of flair in the late 1970s and early 1980s, I think more about receivers who earned their reputations on special teams. Billy "White Shoes" Johnson was never a dominant pass-catcher in the league—he averaged about 24 receptions during a fourteen-year career spent mostly with Houston and Atlanta—but he thrived as a return man who thrilled fans with his "Funky Chicken" dance after touchdowns.

Butch Johnson was no different when he played for Dallas from 1976–83. He had only two seasons when he caught more than 25 passes, but you can bet longtime Cowboys fans can recall his "California Quake." Every time Butch reached the end zone, he'd hold his arms above his head, shake his entire body as if he were succumbing to a full-scale spasm, and then drop to his knees as he used his hands to simulate six-shooters firing away at imaginary villains. "Butch Johnson was one of my favorite players because he brought excitement to the game," said Joe Horn, who made four Pro Bowls as a wide receiver with the New Orleans Saints from 2000–06. "He made me want to dance."

It's easy to say these were just special teams' stars who were making the most of their opportunities for individual recognition. I'd argue that they were receivers frustrated by not having more opportunities to do something with the ball in their hands. Yes, they did their jobs and they did them well. But like every receiver, they had to be pining for the chance to take advantage of all the possibilities that were coming from a league that was embracing the pass more than ever.

It's especially hard to wait for those opportunities in football because the game isn't set up for flair to be easily showcased. It's not like basketball, where a flashy player can reveal his individuality in various ways, whether it's through exceptional ball handling, acrobatic drives to the basket, or jaw-dropping dunks. You don't have time to think about how creative you can be in the middle of a football play. You start by trying to execute your assignment, and then your instincts take over once the ball is in your hands. That's why flair in the NFL only happens after a play ends.

Even when my career started taking off in college, I didn't have a signature celebration after a big play. If I scored a touchdown or made a difficult catch, I usually just raised the ball above my head in the way a grade-school student might lift his hand to answer a question from his teacher. If I was really excited, I'd extend both arms upright in a way that would mimic an official signifying a touchdown. Yes, it was boring and predictable, and trust me, I would've rather been far more outlandish in those moments.

When I was in practice I developed a reputation for being quite the showman. I'd spin the ball on the turf when I got into the end zone. I'd toss it in a defender's face after an acrobatic catch or talk trash whenever I had the opportunity. There were plenty of days when fans watching practice would stand up and cheer if I did something spectacular. And every time that happened I ate it up.

I also was thrilled by the first time I ever saw a player celebrate a touchdown in a wild manner. That was back in 1974, when USC running back Anthony Davis scored a touchdown in a 55–24 win over Notre Dame and performed a little shimmy while on his knees in the end zone. I don't think Davis had planned it that way; he had tripped on his way over the goal line. But once he was shaking on the turf while holding the ball over his head, I thought it was the wildest thing I'd ever seen. I knew I had to add that kind of flavor to my game someday.

My college coaches, however, weren't so keen on that idea. They'd get on me about it in practices, and I was smart enough to not be so demonstrative in games. If I even thought about doing something crazy after a touchdown in public, I probably wouldn't see the ball or the field for the rest of the game. That's how they treated you at Ohio State. They knew they could make any player expendable each Saturday.

It seemed like the NFL had its own issues with creative license, because things changed in that sport after a few years of funky moves. The NFL earned its nickname as the "No Fun League" precisely because it felt it necessary to banish celebrations considered "excessive." By 1984, "the Fun Bunch" was just a bunch of receivers who had to find another way to stylize their touchdowns. The individual touchdown dances still existed, but even the players who performed them paid a subtle price for them. As Elmo Wright told the *New York Times*, people forget most of the six years he spent in the NFL as well as the records he set at the University of Houston (he still holds the NCAA mark for averaging 27.7 yards per catch in 1968). His mark on the game still revolves around one thing: He's the first man to ever perform an end zone dance on a football field.

Carmichael also said there was an unspoken danger that came with being too outgoing a personality: It could cost you your career. "We didn't have free agency back then, so we didn't have the confidence that came with knowing you could always find another job," Carmichael said. "In those days the team had a lock on you and you'd hear stories about players getting blackballed. If a team didn't like a guy, you'd hear that he'd been traded and then the next team to get him would cut him. After that, he'd be gone."

John Jefferson easily paid the biggest price at that time. Even though he didn't celebrate touchdowns the way Wright and Billy "White Shoes" Johnson did, he developed a huge following in San Diego. He was the man who hyped up fans in pregame drills and then excited them even more after kickoff. But when it came time to get paid for what he brought to the Chargers, Jefferson couldn't get any traction with then owner Gene Klein. Despite making three Pro Bowls in his first three seasons, Klein refused to renegotiate Jefferson's contract and increase his salary. That contract dispute ended with the Chargers trading Jefferson to Green Bay after the 1980 season, and he never surpassed the 1,000-yard mark again.

The statement Klein seemed to be making back then wasn't hard to miss: No receiver is bigger than the team. Though Jefferson was a star to everybody who watched the game—and cost the Packers two first-round picks, two second-round picks, and wide receiver Aundra Thompson to acquire him—Klein saw him only as a commodity, a replaceable one at that. But even as Jefferson was vanishing into the land of frozen tundra, it would've been hard to ignore what was happening to wide receivers around the NFL.

As much as some people weren't ready for wide receivers showcasing themselves, those players were reshaping the game. They were revealing that receivers weren't afraid to push the boundaries of social convention, that it was okay to bring a little personal style to a game that could be so punishing. Such panache reminded everybody involved that the game was meant to be both physical and fun. The players worked too hard during the week to stifle their emotions when Sundays finally arrived.

The closer I got to the NFL, the more I sensed the league was moving in a direction that would be beneficial for men who caught passes for a living. By the time I had become an All-American at Ohio State in 1986—and as I told my brother, Coach Bruce found a way to get the most out of my talents—the league was as exciting as it had ever been. Dan Marino was setting all kinds of records in Miami for Don Shula, a head coach who had never been confused for a man with a gunslinger's abandon. The 1983 draft class (featuring Marino, John Elway, and Jim Kelly) was being hailed as the greatest collection of quarterback talent ever, while the 1984 draft started with New England making Nebraska's Irving Fryar the first receiver ever to be selected with the number one overall pick. The USFL also had generated opportunities for even more creative ideas about how to move the ball through the air.

When I look back on those years, I realize that more receivers could've become dominant in the 1970s. It wasn't like there was a shortage of them. The only things holding them back were mediocre quarterback play, a lack of creativity, and a league filled with frightening defenses. Once the NFL started throwing the football more consistently, there never seemed to be a problem when it came to finding people to catch it.

Still, I couldn't know how much the game was about to change for wide receivers in places like San Francisco, San Diego, and Houston. The quarterbacks may have been gaining plenty of attention by then, but there were other forces at work as well. The notion of what a wide receiver could do for an offense was just beginning to take hold in some of the most imaginative minds the game has ever seen. And for somebody like me—a lanky, talented college kid brimming with ambition—it was exhilarating to think about the possibilities that could come with being in the right place at the right time.

CHAPTER 3

A Whole New World

My dreams of becoming an NFL wide receiver became a nightmare in the summer of 1987. By that point I had become the first receiver in Ohio State history to be named first-team All-American and I was part of a strong group of wideouts who'd be eligible for the 1988 draft. There was also Notre Dame's Tim Brown (who would win the 1987 Heisman Trophy), South Carolina's Sterling Sharpe, Miami's Michael Irvin, and Tennessee's Anthony Miller, among others. Six receivers would eventually be selected in the first round of that draft, a record that stood until 2004. I surely would've been the seventh if I hadn't screwed up my senior season at Ohio State.

The NFL passing game had blossomed so much by the mid-1980s that I knew I was becoming a hot commodity. By the end of my freshman season, I was already attracting attention from a lot of people. Before Ohio State played USC in the 1985 Rose Bowl, our equipment manager grabbed my arm and told me he wanted to introduce me to somebody he knew on the sidelines. He said the guy's name was Bobby Moore and that it would be a meeting I'd never forget. I didn't know Bobby Moore was the name given to former Minnesota Vikings star wide receiver Ahmad Rashad until I was face-to-face with the man. But the equipment manager was right: I didn't take the moment lightly.

My friend told Rashad that I was a great player and that "you'll be watching this guy in the NFL for a long time." Rashad graciously listened and shook my hand. A few hours later we were talking again. By that point, I had caught 9 passes for 172 yards, both Rose Bowl records. Even though we lost 20–17, Rashad did a postgame interview with me. I also ran into another person who surprised me with his introduction.

His name was Norv Turner and he was USC's offensive coordinator and a man who would later become an NFL head coach in Washington, Oakland, and San Diego. Turner lauded me for my impressive college career start and my performance that day. He then apologized for never showing up on that recruiting visit when I was a high school senior. He told me that a snowstorm had hit Kansas City as he traveled through the Midwest. When faced with the decision of coming to see me or going back to Los Angeles, he chose to return home.

I appreciated Turner's honesty and graciousness. I also hadn't held anything against USC for what happened in the recruiting process. I knew I'd made the right decision in going to Ohio State, and my Rose Bowl performance validated that choice. In fact, my football career was going so well that I gave up the idea of playing basketball for the Buckeyes that winter. Football was going to be my ticket into professional sports.

Wide receivers were becoming bigger weapons in most teams' offenses by that point. There were still only a handful of receivers getting paid big money but the upside of the job was limitless. The NFL had changed so much that New England had made Irving Fryar the top pick in the 1984 draft. No receiver had ever been selected that high, and we're not talking about a man who played in some pass-happy college offense. Fryar had been a star wingback at Nebraska, a player who had caught 40 passes as a senior. His potential value to an NFL team made plenty of people take notice of how receivers were rising up in the world.

In those days, it was especially hard to find bigger receivers, so I felt confident that there would be a nice market for my services once my eligibility expired. So did a man named Norby Walters, an ultra-hip entertainment agent who was trying to branch out into pro sports. Walters and his partner, Lloyd Bloom, had been talking to potential NBA players, but what they really wanted most were guys with futures in the NFL. They started pursuing me as soon as my freshman year ended.

I met Walters for the first time that summer after flying to Miami to do a photo shoot for *Playboy*'s All-American football team. As soon as I met him, I knew immediately that this dude was different from other agents out there. He was fifty-four years old and about as cool as an aging white guy could be. He managed a lot of black entertainers at the time, and he even acted black. Norby Walters didn't stroll through a room; he strutted. He didn't just talk the King's English; he threw out so much slang that he was like a geriatric Eminem.

I don't know if Walters spent a lot of his youth around black people, but he definitely understood how to reach them. By the time I sat down to talk with him, I sensed I was missing out on something. Walters had already signed between six and ten likely first-round picks to contracts by then. And I'm not talking about guys who never did anything in the NFL. I'm talking about future pro stars like Jerry Ball and Rod Woodson. Those players were heading into their senior years and they already had deals with Walters and Bloom. Even though I knew it was wrong, I thought it was worth working out a similar arrangement with those two.

It wasn't like I was sitting on a pile of cash back in Middletown. My brother Butch had played in the NBA, but my family was still poor as hell. If my mother came to Columbus to watch me play, we could barely afford to go eat at a local restaurant after the game. That's what made Walters's pitch such an easy sell. The more he realized that I was as broke as many college kids, the more convinced I was to take the things I wanted.

One of the first questions that Walters asked me was about competition. He asked if I had a booster who took care of me at Ohio State. When I said no, he then asked if I had a car. He knew I was preparing to move into my own apartment after spending my freshman year in a college dorm. It wouldn't hurt to have some nice transportation to help me get around campus.

Walters also had the trump card for any teenager—he could give me immediate access to the world of celebrity and entertainment. If I wanted to fly across the country to see Janet Jackson, it wouldn't be a problem. If Kool and the Gang was coming through Columbus, I never had to worry about tickets for my friends or myself. I was already a big man on campus. As he put it back then, Walters had the ability to help me live even larger.

I ultimately agreed on a deal that was similar to what Walters was giving most of his clients at the time. He gave me $10,000 to sign my name to a contract and promised to pay $500 per month. The deal was simple: As soon as I finished my senior year at Ohio State, Walters would have a post-dated contract with my name on it and I wouldn't have to worry about representation. All I had to do was keep quiet and keep catching passes.

I guess that is both the beauty and the curse of youth. You're brash enough to think you can do anything yet ignorant enough to not understand how much trouble you can create for yourself with a colossal mistake. At nineteen years old, it seemed as if everything I'd wanted was coming together neatly. I was a college star. I had money in my pocket. And I could see the NFL opening up to wide receivers in ways that it never had before.

If 1984 was a critical year in my own evolution as a player, it was also memorable for another reason: It was the first time I ever heard of a wide receiver named Jerry Rice. That fall, I was reading *USA Today* when I came across an amazing story on this guy at a small college named Mississippi Valley State. They called him "World" (because there wasn't a pass in the world he couldn't catch), his quarterback "the Satellite" (his real name was Willie Totten), and his coach "the Gunslinger" (Archie Cooley). The story talked about how nobody could cover Jerry or keep him from catching an average of about 15 balls a game or track him down in the open field. When I saw highlights of him on television, I was even more blown away.

The lasting memory of watching Jerry on that grainy film was this:

a skinny receiver gracefully snatching passes out of the air, then racing off as if a street gang were trying to beat him down. He didn't just look fast on those tapes. He looked like he was playing at an entirely different speed from everyone else on the field. When I later discovered that he had run something like a 4.71 40-yard dash at the NFL combine, I couldn't believe it. You never saw people with speed that ordinary blowing past defenders.

The first thing I wondered about Jerry was whether it was the competition he faced that made him look so good. Even though there were still plenty of NFL players coming out of historically black colleges in those days, there was far more overall talent at the bigger schools. Jerry could've looked great against players who were likely to be working normal jobs when their eligibility expired. The results might have been totally different if he were taking on cornerbacks in the Southeastern Conference or the Big Ten on a weekly basis.

What I didn't know then was that San Francisco 49ers head coach Bill Walsh had been watching Jerry that same year. The 49ers had been on a road trip when Walsh saw a similar video of Jerry's highlights while sitting in his hotel room. It's one thing to impress a nineteen-year-old college kid who's just starting to make a name for himself in college football. But when you catch the attention of a prominent NFL coach—that year Walsh was on his way to winning the second of his three Super Bowls in seven years—there's definitely something special about your game.

Walsh saw an extraordinary weapon in Jerry, a player who could make the 49ers' potent offense even deadlier. And believe me, the 49ers were already as dangerous as any team in the league when it came to throwing the football. They had a star quarterback in Joe Montana and an assortment of reliable playmakers. The main idea behind the 49ers' system—which eventually became known as the "West Coast offense" after former New York Giants head coach Bill Parcells mockingly called it that—was to get five players into pass patterns on every play. You needed a mobile quarterback like Montana because your offense was vulnerable to blitzing, but the 49ers worked that system to perfection.

More than anything, Bill Walsh helped get quarterbacks more comfortable throwing the football.

In many ways, Walsh was a visionary long before he became an NFL head coach in 1979. When Walsh became head coach at Stanford in 1977, he found a gangly, speedy receiver named James Lofton on his roster. It didn't matter that Lofton had caught just 12 passes during his first three years in college. It didn't even matter to Coach Walsh that Lofton didn't have a reception in the first game of his senior year.

Walsh showed Lofton footage of Cincinnati Bengals wide receiver Isaac Curtis—whom Walsh had coached as an assistant with that franchise—and he promised Lofton that he had everything it took to be a similar game-changer. "After that first game of my senior year, he told me that I'd have a game where I'd catch twelve passes," Lofton said. "I might not have been rolling my eyes to his face but I was doing it in my mind. But sure enough, we played Washington five or six weeks later and I had twelve receptions for 192 yards and three touchdowns."

In those days, Walsh was doing the very thing that excited me most about football. He was redefining the times, breathing new life into the game, changing the way coaches conducted business. If his offense was having a bad practice, he wouldn't growl and threaten players. He'd simply say he had to do a better job of calling the plays during the rest of the session. When he was at Stanford, he once let his team's inability to execute a trap play frustrate him. He responded by telling the players that such a routine running play could do one of two things: (1) it could lead to a 2-yard gain that would result in the home crowd groaning, or (2) it could lead to a 30-yard gain and result in the star running back dating a pretty girl after the contest.

What I liked most about Walsh was that he saw wide receivers as crucial weapons on offense. They weren't just there for a reception when running plays didn't work. They weren't just meant to make a big play here or there when major yardage was needed. They could catch a pass on first, second, or third down. Instead of using the run to set up the pass, as had been conventional wisdom, Walsh went the opposite route: He used the pass to set up the run.

It was a philosophy he had learned during his days as an assistant with Cincinnati. "Bill Walsh would always be the first to say that his offense came about mainly because he coached with a team that was trying to simply survive in the seventies," said Brian Billick, whose NFL career included stints as offensive coordinator of the Minnesota Vikings and head coach of the Baltimore Ravens. "The Bengals couldn't afford the high-priced players and their running game suffered because of it. So they came up with the idea of supplanting the running game with [short] passes. When the game changed, Bill was on the cutting edge of all that, but I would also say it was a coincidence that things played out that way."

The West Coast offense was critical to the evolution of receivers because it required everybody to know what everybody else was doing. You didn't just run your route and look for the ball. There was a specific timing to everything. Receivers had to understand spacing and the importance of taking certain splits on certain plays. In a lot of ways, the West Coast offense was like the first Apple computer. It used to be crazy to think of a day when everybody would have a personal computer. Well, the same was true of wide receivers thirty years ago—it was hard to imagine a time when a receiver would have such an impact on the NFL.

It wasn't that the idea of the short passing game was new to pro football (Paul Brown had introduced it to the game decades earlier). Walsh simply took it to another level. "Defenses had gotten so good at stacking the line of scrimmage and playing man-to-man that offenses had to adjust," said Steve Largent. "They would commit eight guys to the run and not give you much time to pass. The Chicago Bears' Forty-Six Defense in the eighties was like that. And the adjustment was to get the ball out quick. When I first started playing in 1976, quarterbacks would take seven-step drops and throw downfield. Then teams started figuring out that shorter passes were better. The guy who came up with that was Bill Walsh."

"The West Coast offense had been around for a while before Bill Walsh started winning Super Bowls with it," said Steve Mariucci, an

NFL Network analyst who served as head coach for both the San Francisco 49ers and the Detroit Lions. "And those high-percentage throws helped the passing game open up. But at that time, it was still a predominantly traditional set. You used two backs, two receivers, and a tight end. And having two wide receivers on the field meant that one person was going to be the featured guy. You always have a number one and a number two receiver in the West Coast. Whether it was Dwight Clark at first or Jerry later, the number one receiver got a lot of balls."

Jerry was the perfect fit for the 49ers in that regard. He had 1,682 receiving yards and 27 touchdowns in his senior season at Mississippi Valley State. He also had more than 100 receptions in each of his final two years of college football. As great as Walsh's Niners offense was at that time, it didn't have a weapon like that. Veterans like Dwight Clark and Freddie Solomon were reliable, but Jerry was transcendent. He was also eager to prove that he belonged in the NFL, even though he played at such a small school.

Jerry proved himself at the 1985 Blue-Gray Football Classic, when he earned MVP honors while embarrassing defenders from more prominent programs, and he never lost his drive once the 49ers made him the sixteenth overall pick in that year's draft. "I was just hungry," Jerry said. "I wanted to prove myself every chance I got. If I had a great game, I always came back hungrier for the next one. I never wanted to be complacent. I didn't even take a vacation for the first ten years of my career."

Jerry quickly set the bar for up-and-coming receivers like myself. He did it partly because he expanded the idea of what receivers could do on the field. When Jerry was setting all those records in college, he only had to worry about his own job. With the 49ers, he had to understand how the defense was trying to attack him and everybody else on offense. "Bill always emphasized the importance of being a complete receiver," Jerry said. "My job was easier because I was always on the same page as our quarterback."

Now I won't say Walsh was the only person responsible for wide receivers gaining greater prominence in the 1980s. From 1982 to 1991,

Washington Redskins head coach Joe Gibbs won three Super Bowls, two of them with sophisticated schemes and gifted receivers like Gary Clark and future Hall-of-Famer Art Monk. The San Diego Chargers were still running "Air Coryell" (so named for head coach Don Coryell) long after they dealt star wide receiver John Jefferson to Green Bay in 1980. They also acquired Wes Chandler, a playmaker cut from the same cloth as Jefferson, and added him to a mix that already included quarterback Dan Fouts, wide receiver Charlie Joiner, and tight end Kellen Winslow, all future Hall-of-Famers in their own right.

The USFL also had a huge influence on the passing game at that time. One head coach, the Houston Gamblers' Mouse Davis, had brought his wide-open style from the Canadian Football League to the States in 1984 and ran wild with it in his first year. That run-and-shoot offense spread the field with four wide receivers and gave quarterback Jim Kelly so many options that Houston became the first pro football team to ever have two receivers (Richard Johnson and Ricky Sanders) with more than 100 receptions in a single season. That same year the NFL's Houston Oilers signed another former Canadian Football League product—quarterback Warren Moon. Within four years, the Oilers were spreading the field with four wide receivers and seeing what could happen with that many weapons set in motion.

For Warren, the NFL played at an even slower pace than what he was used to during his career with the CFL's Edmonton Eskimos from 1978–83. "When I first got into the league, it was really heavy on the West Coast offense," Warren said. "The 49ers were having so much success with it that everybody was using it. But it was also a straight two-back, two-receiver, one-tight-end system. Coming from Canada, I was used to an offense where you took advantage of all the space [CFL fields are ten yards longer and thirteen yards wider than those in the NFL] and the seams. Once we started using four receivers at the same time in my third year, things really took off. That's when the NFL really started to open up because then you had teams like Atlanta, Detroit, and New Orleans doing the same things."

As those offenses evolved, so did the need for different personnel.

After a while, the ball wasn't going to the running back or even the tight end as often. Most teams were finding ways to get three or four wide receivers on the field, and that meant the game was becoming more situational. Suddenly, you could exploit a team's third cornerback or a slow-footed safety who was caught in coverage. As the 1980s went on, the more the NFL became about mismatches.

The Oilers were so explosive at the position that they sent three different receivers (Haywood Jeffires, Curtis Duncan, and Ernest Givins) to the Pro Bowl in 1992. "That success gave them more exposure, more credibility, and better paychecks," Warren said. "We had pretty good success with the offense, but more teams would've jumped on board if we had won a championship. Because we never got to the Super Bowl, some people didn't believe fully in it. But they did see the schemes and things did evolve from there. It became okay to have four wide receivers on the field—we didn't even have a tight end on the roster—or to find somebody who could work in the slot."

I actually didn't personally embrace the run-and-shoot offense for one reason: I believed in offensive balance. The more you ran the football, the more it opened things up for receivers downfield. Plus, it never seemed like the players who came into the NFL out of those gimmicky offenses did much. They'd catch a bunch of passes at the college level and then get exposed by better defenders in the pros.

There were plenty of traditional receivers I liked at that point in my own career. I was a huge fan of Philadelphia's Mike Quick because he was an explosive receiver with a build (6'2", 190 pounds) similar to my own. New England's Stanley Morgan, a dude who could really fly, was also high on my list of favorites, as was Lofton, a man who had serious track skills and transitioned them into NFL success in Green Bay. And if I had to pick somebody to emulate when it came to route-running, that would've been Henry Ellard of the Los Angeles Rams. He had everything you'd want in a receiver: quick feet, fluid hips, soft hands, and the ability to get in and out of his breaks without wasting any motion.

When I dreamed about being an NFL receiver, these were the players who had everything I wanted. Their success on the highest level was also having a ripple effect on everything that was happening in college. Even at a school so committed to the run as Ohio State, you had coaches looking for ways to innovate their own offense. You'd see our coaches talking with assistants from other programs in order to find ways to throw the football more consistently and effectively. We were still a team that revolved around the running of All-American back Keith Byars in the 1980s, but I was also seeing my share of touches for the Buckeyes.

My first receivers coach was Jim Tressel, who also coached the quarterbacks and later served as the team's head coach from 2001–10, and he'd always say, "We're coming to you, C.C. Be ready." After my sophomore season, I had another talented coach arrive at Ohio State, a graduate assistant named Urban Meyer. He'd often tell me that I was going to be an All-American but I had to push myself. He told me my success would come down to my intensity, my mind-set, and my ability to push myself harder than I had in past years. I wasn't surprised years later when Urban won two national championships as Florida's head coach and eventually took the same position at Ohio State in 2011. He looked like a star from the moment he stepped into the profession.

With coaches like that, it wasn't hard for me to succeed in college. By the end of my junior season, I had set school records for career receptions (168), single-season receptions (69), and single-season receiving yards (1,127). But all those good vibes evaporated the minute I got a phone call from my coaches at Ohio State in June 1987. The next thing I knew, I was sitting down at a table in a Columbus-area Bob Evans Restaurant. Across from me sat a couple of men who scared the shit out of me: FBI agents.

They started the conversation by telling me the only positive thing I could hear: "Cris, we're not after you." I took as much comfort in that comment as I could, because everything I learned after that point was unsettling. A few years earlier, when I signed with Norby Walters, he had seemed like a cool dude—the kind of guy who easily bonded with black athletes because of his swagger and smooth-talking nature—but the stories the agents told me about him painted a different picture. Most notably, federal investigators had linked him to an organized crime figure named Michael Franzese, claiming the mobster had given Walters and Bloom $50,000 to start their sports agency.

What I also found out was that a rival agent in Chicago supposedly tried to steal some of the players who had signed with Walters and Bloom. Once that happened, Walters and Bloom allegedly sent some people over to the agent's office to rough him up. In the process, a secretary sustained some injuries, and some prosecutors issued subpoenas to see what Walters and Bloom were up to. Once those investigators started searching through the files that Walters and Bloom kept, it wasn't long before they stumbled across a lot of post-dated contracts. And one of them had my name on it.

The agents told me they had that document but they wanted to know more, especially whether Walters had ever threatened me. Though nothing like that had ever happened to me during my relationship with Walters, I did know that Brad Sellers, a star on Ohio State's basketball team, also had signed with Walters and, like a lot of players who had joined Walters, Sellers later decided to go with another agent. That didn't go over well. Walters had once told me in passing that he would break Sellers's legs for backing out of the deal.

I had dismissed that threat when Walters first said it, figuring it was just an angry old man frustrated by losing some money. When the FBI agents brought it up, I wasn't so dismissive. I sensed there was going to be serious trouble coming out of this. As I later learned, these investigators were only starting to unravel all the dirt that Walters and Bloom had done during their days as sports agents.

The FBI ultimately conducted a seventeen-month investigation that ended with a federal grand jury indicting Walters and Bloom on charges that included racketeering, mail fraud, and conspiracy to commit extortion. The agents had signed fifty-eight college athletes overall—in football and basketball—and gave them all the same deal I got. What made those arrangements even messier was the fact that several athletes had deserted Walters and Bloom. Before the FBI ever clamped down on the agents, they were suing players all over the country for breach of contract (Walters and Bloom ultimately had their racketeering convictions overturned on the grounds that they didn't receive a fair trial, but their breach-of-contract suits proved unsuccessful. Walters did later plead guilty to mail fraud.)

I hadn't fallen into that kind of controversy, but there was plenty for me to face that summer. Instead of preparing for my final year at Ohio State and a chance to enhance my stock for the NFL draft, I got a phone call from Buckeyes head coach Earle Bruce. I was sitting in my apartment when he told me I was ineligible for my senior season. Within hours I was talking with lawyers, hoping to find a solution to my sudden problem.

I also had to break the news to my girlfriend, Melanie, whom I had started dating in February of that year. She didn't know much about sports and her parents hadn't been crazy about her seeing me. When they first learned that we were together, they wanted her to end it because I'd been suspended for smoking marijuana. When I found out about my ineligibility, I knew that would create even more concerns with her family.

So I tried to explain it to Melanie as smoothly as possible after picking her up on campus. "Mel," I said, "I did something wrong and it's going to be in the papers."

"What did you do?" she asked.

"I took some money from an agent."

"Is that bad?"

"It will be okay."

When we pulled into my apartment complex later that day, the scene in the parking lot shocked Melanie. Camera crews, photographers, and reporters were everywhere, waiting for me.

"Oh my God!" Mel said. "My parents will kill me if they ever see me around this. You have to get me out of here."

I drove away as fast as I could, but it didn't take long to see that my troubles would only worsen. Ohio State had the option of appealing the suspension and the NCAA later ruled that I might sit for two to four games before my eligibility was restored. Ohio State athletic director Rick Bay wasn't hearing that, though. He said I could finish school and keep my scholarship. As for playing football, he vowed that I would never wear an Ohio State uniform again.

I left Columbus a couple of days later. I never went back to the locker room. I never met with Coach Bruce. I did get some phone calls from some disappointed teammates and Coach Tressel, but that was it. I knew the climate around campus wouldn't be in my favor. I had lost my amateur status, and I at least had to start thinking about life away from college.

I soon learned the NFL wasn't crazy about that idea. The NFL draft had already come and gone in April—underclassmen weren't allowed to enter the draft at that time anyway—and the NFL didn't want me to come into the league as a supplemental pick, given my issues with agents. I responded by threatening to sue on the grounds that the league was preventing me from earning a living. The league eventually allowed me to enter the supplemental draft that summer, along with Charles Gladman, a running back from Pittsburgh who lost his eligibility because he wouldn't cooperate with an investigation into illegal agent payments to college players.

It all happened so fast that it felt like a whirlwind. I wound up training in Dayton for six weeks and then working out for NFL teams in Indianapolis in July. I wasn't thrilled with my performance. I had hoped to run the 40-yard dash in the low 4.5 range. The scouts on hand clocked me between 4.57 and 4.64, which was just slow enough to leave them unimpressed. It was a horrible way for me to transition from college to pro football.

It's important for me to make it clear that I loved my time at Ohio State. The coaches there taught the players so much about football that I felt prepared to handle anything the next level threw at me. It didn't matter that we ran the ball forty times a game. If you were a wide receiver sitting in meetings, the coaches still expected you to know everything about what the defense was doing, even if you were just blocking on a play. Playing receiver wasn't just about catching passes in their eyes. It was about doing everything possible to help the offense be successful when you were on the field.

I also felt like I had helped start a long-running tradition for wide receivers at Ohio State. After my All-American year in 1986, we had a number of star receivers come through Columbus. I'm talking about guys like Jeff Graham, Joey Galloway, Terry Glenn, David Boston, Ted Ginn Jr., Santonio Holmes, and Anthony Gonzalez. All those players had strong careers in college and they all became high draft picks in the NFL. As for me, I wound up the Philadelphia Eagles' fourth-round selection in the 1987 supplemental draft.

I knew I wasn't going to be a first-round pick, even though a lot of teams said they liked me. Thirteen teams said they wouldn't participate in that draft because they didn't like the precedent it was setting. There were also plenty of college coaches who viewed me as some kind of criminal. Michigan's Bo Schembechler told *Sports Illustrated*, "I have never heard of [then NFL commissioner] Pete Rozelle doing anything for the benefit of college football. This message says to a college player, 'Go ahead and rob, steal, cheat, and kill. Then as soon as you are declared ineligible, don't worry, because then you get into the NFL.'"

My own college coach, Earle Bruce, even told the Associated Press that "Here you have a young man who has taken money from an agent and done something to ruin his college eligibility and he's rewarded with an N.F.L. contract. I think the N.F.L. has opened up a whole new can of worms with this decision." Still, the hardest criticism for me to absorb came from my mother.

She knew I was on the verge of doing great things as a senior. I was being touted as a Heisman Trophy contender and I could've been the first wide receiver to ever win the award. Once I lost my eligibility, she told me how disappointed she was that I'd jeopardized my college career. I had expected her to be a little more supportive. Instead, her unhappiness created a rift in our relationship that would only grow as my career progressed.

So there I was, stuck between a school I couldn't return to and a league that largely didn't want me. Even with the ample motivation I had to prove myself on the next level, I was starting my professional career in a horrible way—as a pariah.

If the Norby Walters-Lloyd Bloom scandal wasn't bad enough, I was also entering the NFL at a horrible time. I didn't go to training camp. I didn't sign a professional contract until after our first game that season. Once I signed, we played one more game and then the players all went on strike for four weeks.

I had tried to get Melanie to leave school and come to Philadelphia with me, but her parents weren't going for that. When I suggested the idea to them, her mother looked at me like I was crazy.

"Melanie is staying here and finishing her education," she told me that day. "She isn't going anywhere."

Melanie just sat in the room with a look on her face that said, "I guess that's it."

I went back to Columbus to see Melanie a few times during the strike.

There were few highlights once the season resumed. I wound up catching all of 5 passes for 84 yards. The only real positives about that year were: (1) I was earning a decent living playing football (the Eagles had given me a base salary comparable to the last receiver selected in the first round of that year's regular draft, the New York Giants' Mark Ingram Sr., future father of the Heisman-winning running back drafted by the Saints in 2011), and (2) I was learning plenty by watching the veterans I saw every day, both in my own locker room and on opposing sidelines.

The Eagles had Mike Quick and Kenny Jackson as their starting receivers in those days, and both were consummate professionals. They embraced me when I arrived, taught me little secrets to competing at that level, and gave me the kind of support that helped me put my controversy behind me. I also knew I had to play with a huge chip on my shoulder. Nobody was promising me anything when I came into the league, so I learned early on that it was crucial to take whatever you could get.

On my first offensive pass play of that year, I didn't even try to hide my desire to leave a mark on the league. As soon as my quarterback, Randall Cunningham, dropped back to throw, I raced downfield and blasted the cornerback who'd been covering me in the back. When the defender looked up at me in shock, I told him, "You may not know who I am but I'm Cris Carter." I was so wired when I returned to the sideline that it was hard to even sit down. I just wanted people to know that I was going to make plenty of noise in the league, one way or another.

I also noticed other things about the NFL that made me realize how I could succeed as a receiver once my playing time increased. Teams still played plenty of man coverage and there were plenty of big plays to be had. Sure, you had to be mindful of big-hitting safeties like San Francisco's Ronnie Lott and Minnesota's Joey Browner—players who would clobber anybody who crossed their paths—but times were clearly changing for the better. Passing was becoming more essential with each season.

What couldn't be denied by that point was how much Jerry was altering the game. He was one of the few guys whom you couldn't cover man-to-man because he would embarrass you. His ability to catch the ball and accelerate to full speed was unlike anything I'd ever seen before. And it didn't even matter if he was covered when Montana—and later Steve Young—would throw him the football. He'd go up over one or two guys and come down with the ball secured.

I still remember the first time I saw him on the same field. It was September 24, 1989, and we were meeting the 49ers in the third game of that season. It was a big matchup because San Francisco was the defending Super Bowl champ and we had won the NFC East a year earlier. It was a game where we expected to prove how much we had grown as an up-and-coming NFC power. That was before we actually kicked the ball off.

Jerry caught a 68-yard touchdown pass from Montana in the first quarter. He had a 33-yard scoring catch late in the fourth quarter.

Montana got plenty of credit for what he did on that day, throwing for 428 yards and 5 touchdowns in helping his team overcome an 11-point fourth-quarter deficit, but Jerry was just as spectacular in that 38–28 game. On a day when San Francisco scored 4 fourth-quarter touchdowns, he caught 6 passes for 164 yards and 2 scores against one of the league's most vicious defenses.

What stood out most about Jerry in that contest—and throughout his career—was his mental toughness. A lot of our defensive players were talking trash to him before the game and threatening to shut him down, but he never said anything back. He just focused on his pregame routine and what he had to do to prepare for action. I told some of our defensive backs not to mess with that guy because I was certain Jerry would use all that chatter as ammunition once he lined up for real.

That's how he was during that time. People loved to challenge him and he loved to make them pay for it. I think a lot of that attitude by defenders was in response to his build and temperament. Jerry wasn't a guy with great strength and he was always very quiet. That probably made defensive backs think he was a pushover in some way, a receiver who would wilt if you punked him a couple of times.

But the Jerry I knew had a hard edge to him. He didn't speak much to opposing receivers and he didn't strike me as the friendliest dude in the world. He later told me, "If I ran into somebody the night before a game, I was totally cool and into talking. But I was in a zone on the day of the game. I was focused on what I had to do. I remember teammates coming up to me and saying that people didn't want to talk to me then because I wouldn't say anything to anybody. I was thinking more about helping my team win and having fans walk away from the game saying, 'Did you see what Jerry Rice did today?'"

Jerry became the only wide receiver to ever win the NFL's Most Valuable Player award when he had 22 touchdown receptions in 1987. He became the Super Bowl MVP a year later when his 11 receptions, 215 yards, and 1 touchdown helped the 49ers beat the Cincinnati Bengals. And a year after that, in the 1989 season, Jerry helped the 49ers repeat as Super Bowl champions with 3 touchdown receptions in a blowout victory over the Broncos. Jerry wasn't just a star receiver by the end of the 1980s. He was on his way to being the game's best player ever.

"The game changed when Bill Walsh decided to put the ball in Jerry Rice's hands as much as possible," said Atlanta Falcons wide receivers coach Terry Robiskie, who has spent more than thirty years as an NFL assistant. "The 49ers were winning Super Bowls with that approach and that made everybody else want a Jerry Rice. They saw what San Francisco was doing with Jerry and Joe Montana and other teams wanted to win that way."

Added Mariucci: "Jerry took playing wide receiver and turned it into an art form. It wasn't an accident. He was obsessive about it. He trained like a track guy. He was as into his craft as any coach could ever hope. I'm talking about going out early and staying out late. He thought that if he was in better shape than everybody else, he could make plays early or late in a game. He was committed to being the best conditioned player on the field at all times."

Jerry also had a no-nonsense style to his game. I remember him doing the "Cabbage Patch"—a popular dance—on *The Arsenio Hall Show* after one of his Super Bowl wins, but that was the extent of his showmanship. As far as Rice was concerned, he didn't need any flash in his game. "I tried to do that stuff early in my career but then I'd be embarrassed once I saw it on replays," he said. "I'd tell myself that I looked stupid and that I'd be better off just handing the ball to the officials after scores."

Jerry wasn't alone. When you look at that generation of receivers, the biggest names often held their personalities in check. While I liked to talk trash and be demonstrative, future Hall-of-Famers like Seattle's Steve Largent chose to just catch passes and let their play do the talking. Aside from being part of "the Fun Bunch" celebrations in the early 1980s, I don't remember Art Monk doing anything to draw attention to his game. The same can be said of other stars of the 1980s, gifted talents like Lofton, the Buffalo Bills' Andre Reed, and the New York Jets' Al Toon.

The big trend back then was to have tandems. You had "the Three Amigos" in Denver (Vance Johnson, Mark Jackson, and Ricky Nattiel).

You had "the Marks Brothers" (Duper and Clayton) thriving with Dan Marino in Miami. "Air Coryell" (Joiner, Chandler, and Winslow) was a huge hit on the West Coast, while "the Posse" (Clark, Monk, and Sanders) excited plenty of Redskins fans back east.

We didn't have any flashy nicknames for our group in Philadelphia because our team was built around a defense led by stars like defensive end Reggie White, cornerback Eric Allen, and linebacker Seth Joyner. Our offense revolved around Cunningham improvising and getting the ball to tight end Keith Jackson and running back Keith Byars early and often. I won't say that receivers were a complete afterthought on a team led by a defensive-minded head coach like Buddy Ryan. But I also think he wasn't too interested in copying the way other teams were using their receivers to break games open.

During my first three years in the league, I caught a total of 89 passes while scoring 19 touchdowns. Those numbers also happened to be the least of my problems in Philadelphia. I came to that town carrying more baggage than I would've liked and created even more for myself while I was there. I kept thinking of myself as a different kind of receiver, the player who could do anything he wanted, like I did in college. As a young NFL receiver, I found myself struggling to create that same magic and cope with all the distractions that hover around the lives of professional athletes.

I imagine my career would've started much differently if I'd avoided all the problems that plagued the end of my Ohio State career. But I couldn't change my mistakes and I didn't spend much time regretting them. I had to move forward with my life and find a way to produce the kind of impact that Jerry was enjoying in San Francisco. As I later found out, there was a young, brash player in Dallas—a receiver the same age as me—who was striving to accomplish the exact same goal.

CHAPTER 4

Meet "the Playmaker"

I've always felt a strong bond with Michael Irvin, the Hall-of-Fame wide receiver who played with the Dallas Cowboys. He had a swagger to him that was evident from the moment we met as college athletes back in the mid-1980s. We first ran into each other at a preseason All-American photo shoot during the summer prior to my junior year and it was like looking at my reflection in a mirror. We had similar builds, similar speed, and definitely similar egos. Sure, he talked a lot more, but that was fine. You couldn't tell Michael, who was a star at the University of Miami, Florida, that he wasn't the best receiver in the game. I felt the same way about my abilities.

Throughout our lives, it seemed like Michael and I were always linked in some fashion. We knew of each other in high school because we were two of the top receivers in the nation. We knew of each other in college because we played at prominent programs. As our NFL careers unfolded, we also sympathized with each other's problems. We both had our fair share of issues as professionals and mine nearly cost me my career at a young age.

I loved being in Philadelphia when I first entered the NFL. If you played for the Eagles, you earned every bit of respect that came your way. Philadelphia is a blue-collar town with a no-nonsense attitude that runs deep to its core. Eagles fans love hard work, relentlessness, and perseverance. Excuses and inconsistency will get players run out of town before they ever check out the Liberty Bell.

That culture felt like a good fit, because I was eager to clean up my name after arriving in Philadelphia. When I left college in 1987, I had been tainted by my relationship with agent Norby Walters, who eventually wound up in federal prison for illegally interacting with college football and basketball players. Instead of being a first-round pick in the 1988 NFL draft, I had been ruled ineligible for my senior year at Ohio State and forced to enter the league as a supplemental pick (Michael was the eleventh overall selection that season). I found my way, though. I didn't let criticism by others disrupt my ability to focus on being a professional.

I caught only 5 passes as a rookie, but my second year was a different story. Blessed with a full off-season and training camp to hone my skills, I started all sixteen games and caught 39 passes. By the end of my third year, I was really coming into my own. I had become a more polished route-runner, a savvier student of NFL defenses, and a red-zone terror. Of my 45 receptions in 1989, 11 were touchdowns. Only San Francisco's Jerry Rice and Green Bay's Sterling Sharpe caught more scoring passes that year.

If there was one season in the 1980s that typified how far wide receivers had come it was that one. Twenty different receivers surpassed the 1,000-yard mark, a record at that point. Some running backs still caught plenty of passes—like Seattle's John L. Williams or my teammate in Philadelphia, Keith Byars—but the passing game had evolved substantially. The West Coast offense was all over the league by then and most teams either thrived with short passes to receivers or they were throwing the ball downfield with precision (as was the case with the Los Angeles Rams and San Diego Chargers).

Receivers had become so prominent that the days of having teams on which only one pass-catcher could be the star were over. The Washington Redskins had three 1,000-yard receivers that season (Art Monk, Gary Clark, and Ricky Sanders). The Rams had two (Henry Ellard and Willie "Flipper" Anderson), as did the 49ers (Jerry Rice and John Taylor). Sharpe and another second-year receiver, San Diego's Anthony Miller, also were making the first huge steps in what was an obvious youth movement at the position.

I wasn't too concerned with not having phenomenal numbers in those days. I knew I was part of a strong team that could consistently compete for the NFC East crown. Plus, I was enjoying all the spoils that came with life as a professional. I had money, confidence, and, as it turned out, a little too much time on my hands.

The 1989 season was a huge turning point in my career, not only because of my success on the field. It also was the first time I ever failed a substance abuse test in the NFL. Back then the league's testing procedure wasn't as strict or sophisticated as it is today. If a player didn't have any positive tests, he only had to go through the testing process before the start of training camp. Everybody knew what day he'd be tested. I only had to get clean long before my time arrived. It really came down to simple discipline.

Now people who were deep into drugs might have struggled to keep up with that schedule, but I didn't think I had that problem. I'd drink with friends and smoke marijuana. I'd do cocaine every now and then. But I wasn't out of control. I never showed up late for work. I didn't blow assignments during games. I never had a teammate call me out for letting my life fall apart. And believe me, we had plenty of strong veteran leaders in Philly at that time—including Byars, Reggie White, and Keith Jackson—who would set you straight if necessary.

They didn't see me as a hard-core partier because I was far from being that. They didn't even know that I failed that first test. I didn't tell anybody, not even my family. I thought it was a simple mistake on my part, an error that I wish I had the chance to go back and correct. I had been smoking marijuana with some friends and I thought a week was more than enough time to let the drug clear my system. But it turned out that it takes about fifteen to twenty days for that to happen.

I was worried after that first positive test but I wasn't freaking out. That's what you think when your life starts getting away from you. *This isn't so bad. I can handle it.* It's like the first time you get pulled over for speeding. You're not thinking about why you were speeding. You're wondering why that police officer had to pick that day to have his radar gun pointed at your vehicle. In my eyes, it was bad timing that ultimately did me in.

Still, that failed drug test meant I had to enter a more strenuous level of the league's substance abuse program. Instead of submitting to testing once a year, I had to take two or three tests a week. Once you start doing that, you might as well stop doing drugs altogether because your chances of failing another test go up exponentially. Unfortunately, I learned that after failing my second test a few months after the 1989 season ended.

The second one was far more unsettling than the first. Since I was already in the program, I was looking at a thirty-day suspension at that point. The only positive was a sizable loophole in the league rules: any player who failed a second drug test at the time had to serve his suspension immediately. If you got popped during the season, that meant you were automatically out for four games. If you were like me and you tested positive in the off-season, then you served your time when hardly anybody would notice your absence.

I'm sure that my career in Philadelphia might have been a little different if I would've missed four games during the 1990 season. Instead, I only had to stay away from the Eagles training facility and all team functions for a month. The media never heard anything about it—because of confidentiality stipulations—and the only people who knew inside the building were head coach Buddy Ryan and some executives. I was embarrassed and upset, but I also had something going for me that provided comfort: I still felt some semblance of control over the matter.

Even though I was subject to random testing at any time and any place, all I had to do was perform. That's what I did when things got tough. I stepped up my game. I produced. And I didn't worry about who or what I was facing.

In my eyes, I didn't have a drinking or drug problem; I was a recreational user. I'd been drinking and smoking marijuana since I was at Ohio State and I became one of the greatest players in that school's history. I didn't have to convince myself of these facts. It was the truth. I wasn't some bum sitting in the corner of a crack house in some jacked-up part of Philly. I was a wide receiver playing in the NFL. I could handle anything.

The problem, however, was that my life really was falling apart. I was hardly talking to Melanie—we had married in February 1990—and she sensed there were larger problems than I was admitting. I had done a good job of convincing myself that I wasn't struggling with drugs and alcohol but my wife saw more than I ever knew. I was shutting her out in all the little ways that destroy a marriage: awkward silences, superficial conversations, arguments that erupted out of nowhere and only generated more distance between us. I didn't even tell her about the failed drug tests.

The sad part was that I didn't even realize how little I was sharing with my wife. Melanie noticed every bit of it. She was fed up enough with me that she was prepared to leave me only a few months after our wedding. The only reason she stayed was because a good friend, Jerome, pleaded with her to give me another chance. He basically told Mel to stick around until eight P.M. that night and she would hear everything. He wanted me to come clean to my wife about my actions and the failed tests.

Mel loved me enough to stick with me after that conversation. We also went to counseling together so I could work on my problems. That might have been a good thing if I had been honest in those sessions. As soon as Mel sat down with me and heard what I was saying, she immediately knew I was lying my way through that treatment program.

Buddy Ryan also saw plenty of potential problems with my failed drug tests. In the 1990 draft, the Eagles selected receivers with three of their first picks (Mike Bellamy, Fred Barnett, and Calvin Williams). I was a little surprised by that, but I also figured it had more to do with circumstances than my issues. Mike Quick and Kenny Jackson were approaching the end of their careers. We needed more weapons in our passing game.

When training camp opened later that year, I stopped being so dismissive about how the times were changing. I sustained a minor hamstring injury early in camp and something clearly was wrong when I returned to action. Suddenly, I wasn't running with the first team anymore. Williams and Barnett were getting the majority of the reps while I was relegated to backup duty. So I approached Buddy about it and he didn't pull any punches.

He told me that the team couldn't afford to risk having me as a starter when one more failed drug test would've resulted in a yearlong suspension. I could be the third receiver, which would've been fine in a pass-happy franchise like Houston, but meant little in a more conservative offense like Philadelphia's. I could be a major threat on third downs and in the red zone, but I was done as a starter. I felt like Buddy had punched me in the face when I heard that. And I came right back at him.

There was no way in hell that I was going to spend the rest of my career in Philadelphia as a backup. I had spent the last three years fighting to prove myself on the field and I'd just had my best season as a professional. If I had accepted that demotion, I easily would've been out of the league in a few years. People would start wondering why Buddy Ryan gave up on a guy who seemed to be a rising star and then word would get around fast.

I also knew in my heart that I'd be a terrible teammate if relegated to backup status. Never in my career had I been forced to sit behind players who weren't as good as I was. I didn't believe in playing that game and I probably would've made life miserable for everybody around me. It wasn't that I didn't understand Buddy's logic in taking away my job. I just didn't agree with it.

Instead of pleading, crying, and condemning the man, I offered an easy solution to my head coach. "Cut me," I said. I meant it, too. I knew what I could do in this league and I knew what I had done already. Somebody would give me a job sooner or later. As much as I liked being in Philadelphia, I also realized that was the only path I had left. Drugs and alcohol might have put me in that position but they definitely weren't going to keep me there.

So on September 3, 1990—Labor Day of that year—the Eagles put me on waivers. I initially thought I was going to the New York Giants because their head coach, Bill Parcells, had called to say they were claiming me. A few minutes later, my agent told me the Minnesota Vikings had put in a claim as well. Since the Vikings had a worse record the previous year, they had the right to pick me before the Giants.

A day later, I arrived in Minneapolis with no clear sense of where my career was heading. I know Melanie was terrified. She was pregnant with our first child, Duron, and we had just bought our first house. I also hadn't done a great job of managing our money. Even though I was making around $300,000, I did what many young players do in the NFL: I gave it away to the people who were constantly asking for financial help.

I'd been sending $1,000 a month to my mother from the time I received my first paycheck. I didn't even receive a phone call from her the day I lost my job. It would've been nice to hear a "How are you doing?" or a "Can I do anything to help?" Instead, all I got was another reminder of how dysfunctional our relationship had become.

The only positive in all this was the way the Eagles handled my drug problems. When the news broke, the story coming out of Philadelphia was that the Eagles had dumped me because I was limited as a receiver. As Buddy (now famously) proclaimed, "All Cris Carter does is catch touchdowns." Of course, we both knew different factors had been at play. I was grateful that my dirty laundry hadn't been tossed into the streets.

The Vikings didn't even know about my drug tests until I arrived in Minnesota. After checking my file, they sent me to employment assistance and set me up with a counselor named Betty Trilegi. I thought we'd go through some routine introductions and then I'd be off to continue my career. I couldn't have been more wrong about that initial assumption.

If the first three years of my career were frustrating, I can only imagine what Michael was going through in Dallas. We weren't tight during those days but we were in the same division during both the

1988 and 1989 seasons. The Cowboys won four games total over that period and Michael wasn't much of a factor. He caught 32 passes as a rookie and then a torn ACL ended his second season—one that had looked far more promising—after just six games.

I remember a *New York Times* story that referred to a defining moment Michael had prior to the 1990 season. While I was desperately trying to win back my job with the Eagles in training camp, he was testing his surgically repaired right knee during joint practice sessions with the San Diego Chargers. The Cowboys were still a mess at the time, a team coming off a one-win season and not even sure if Troy Aikman was their long-term answer at quarterback. Michael was trying to find his own way as well. At times, that effort was thoroughly frustrating.

One day in camp, Michael fumed because he couldn't dominate the Chargers defensive backs in the way he had abused opponents in college. He couldn't separate from them on pass routes and he certainly couldn't energize his teammates with his customary big plays. By the end of the practice—after constantly talking back to Chargers who had taunted him all afternoon—Michael turned on his fellow Cowboys and challenged them.

"I'm out here by myself," Michael yelled. "You're going to let them get away with this! Are you guys my teammates or what?"

I wasn't surprised to hear a story reporting that Michael cried shortly after that outburst. That's how much he cared about winning and I understood that emotion to the core. Just as I had once threatened my own teammates in a peewee football game, Michael wanted the Cowboys to find the same desire that ran deep within him. He always was the player who motivated everybody around him. Michael didn't know how to do anything else except lead.

That attitude is what separated him from every other receiver during our glory years. You hear about players having "on-off" switches in their personalities, which is basically the ability to increase their energy levels when the games begin. Well, Michael didn't have an "off" switch.

He wanted to destroy anybody who ever lined up across from him. And he wanted to have fun the entire time he was kicking your ass.

Some of that mind-set probably came from growing up in a home with seventeen siblings and eating corn flakes with water for breakfast. Maybe a little had something to do with him losing his father while he was in high school or playing for a college program as defiant as Miami's. But wherever that bravado came from, Michael Irvin had more of it than any big-time receiver I've ever seen in the NFL. That's what allowed him to have such an impact on the league. He took the idea of swagger to an entirely different level.

If Michael caught a touchdown pass, he would point to the sky and prance around the end zone. If one of his receptions led to a first down, he'd lunge forward and hold the ball in front of him as if it were some imaginary sword. He'd pound his chest, shake his butt, and do just about anything else to make people aware of what he'd done. There had been a few flamboyant receivers before Michael ever showed up on the scene. None ever did as much to back up his showmanship. As former NFL wide receiver Keyshawn Johnson said, "Michael might only catch eighty passes a year. But they were an important eighty."

There are stories about Michael showing up at Miami practices when he was just a high school senior, when he'd stare across the field and figure out whose job he planned on taking after enrolling. His signature game with the Hurricanes came in 1987, when he caught 2 second-half touchdown passes and helped Miami to a comeback win over Florida State. The Michael Irvin I knew then was the same talent he'd become in the NFL. He lived for the big stage and the big moment. He even named himself "the Playmaker" just in case there was anyone out there who didn't immediately recognize exactly what he did.

Michael also did something else that was vital to the position: He made it acceptable for receivers to be galvanizing forces on their teams. As great as Jerry Rice was—and he's arguably the best football player ever—he didn't force his feelings onto others. He overwhelmed defenders with consistency, preparation, and a ruthlessness that belied his quiet nature. Rice killed opponents with a sniper's calm while setting a strong example for others to follow.

Michael, on the other hand, was going to challenge his teammates whenever he deemed it necessary. Aikman once said Michael would show up for conditioning drills fully intent on winning every test. If the team was running sixteen 110-yard sprints that day, Aikman said Michael would run thirty of his own *before* the drill. That way everybody else would know how you're supposed to attack one of the most painful aspects of training camp.

Former Cowboys fullback Daryl Johnston said it wasn't uncommon for Michael to go through a team workout with the strength and conditioning coaches and then return later in the day for another session. He'd study the science of what those coaches were trying to accomplish to fully understand how far he could push his body. Before long, he became faster, stronger, and more explosive than he was in his first few years. He also reminded people of the price he was willing to pay to back up his big talk.

"I actually had to change my thinking about Michael when I first met him," said Johnston, who joined the Cowboys in 1989, one year after Michael arrived. "I wasn't a fan of his when he was at Miami because of all the brashness. I thought it was all about him. But he was completely different than what he portrayed on television. Nobody worked harder than Michael. And I never misjudged somebody as badly as I misjudged him."

I always respected the approach Michael brought to the job. He never had blazing speed but he did know how to think his way around a football field. He understood how to position his body and set up defensive backs on pass routes. The man also had unbelievable strength, both in his hands and upper body. If a cornerback came up to challenge Michael at the line of scrimmage, he was taking a huge chance in coverage. Michael could run right through a defender and he never had problems snatching balls in heavy traffic.

Like myself, Michael also was hungry to be the best in the game. We didn't really become great friends until we played together in the

Pro Bowl following the 1993 season, and that's when I discovered his desire. We'd sit around and talk about how much we wanted to write our own names in history. It bothered us that most people only talked about Jerry Rice when they discussed great receivers. We wanted to be recognized as well. We believed we could do things that were also amazing and impressive.

Hell, the first time Michael made it to Hawaii (after the 1991 season), he apparently annoyed everybody by claiming he wasn't getting the football enough. He wound up winning Most Valuable Player honors in that game while reminding everybody of who he was. He was a man with insatiable appetites and an inability to go at anything less than full speed. He used that mind-set to pull himself out of poverty, in much the same way I did. He'd also used it to go as far as the game would take him.

What Michael and I didn't know was that we were both going to have to travel treacherous paths to that level of success. While Jerry's low-key personality made it easier for him to focus on his job, Michael and I had certain character traits that were a little more vulnerable to distraction. Michael didn't fully see the dangers he would face until he was deeper into his career. I discovered mine shortly after I arrived in Minneapolis.

Addiction is one of the hardest challenges in the world to understand. It can attack you when you're weakest. It can sneak up on you when you're on top on the world. It doesn't play favorites, either. It can take anybody at any time, even if you feel you're too strong to ever fall into its trap.

I can't say exactly how painful addiction can be once it has its hands on you. I can tell how it feels to be told that you're going to run head-long into it one day. It doesn't really register at first. You hear that you are on a path to self-destruction, but you can't even see the road that you're supposedly following. You think you're doing the same things you've always done, and yet those very actions are the red flags that deserve the most attention. How do you deal with a hell that somebody predicts you'll be living someday? More important, how do you fight something you can't see?

When I first arrived in Minneapolis and sat down with Betty, I didn't know anything about the perils of addiction. I only knew that I wasn't going to associate that word with my life. When I failed my drug tests in Philadelphia and entered counseling there, they didn't say anything to me about booze. They just told me to stop using drugs. So I started drinking more.

After a few sessions with Betty, I was hearing a different message. We met consistently—by ourselves and together with Mel—and then Betty also would spend time alone with Mel. Betty was far savvier when it came to my lying. At one point, after only a couple of meetings, she openly called me out in front of Mel.

In Betty's eyes, I was trying to manipulate her the same way I had played the counselors in Philadelphia. "Now that you've told me all the bullshit, let's get down to the real stuff," she said one day after I had given her what seemed like a believable explanation of my issues.

"What do you mean?" I said.

"If you don't have a problem, let's see if you can go a week without drinking," she said. "And I'll test you just to be sure."

To be honest, I had never considered giving up alcohol before that day. I had been drinking since I was seventeen years old and that hadn't stopped me from being a top recruit in football and basketball. I'd been doing it at Ohio State and that hadn't stopped me from being an All-American. Until I failed those drug tests in Philadelphia, there hadn't been one single reason for me to think drinking was something I needed to give up.

I also thought Betty's suggestion that I give up drinking was pretty extreme. I understood why something like cocaine could be danger-ous. I first tried it with a few friends on the night I graduated from high school and I didn't use it again until my junior year at Ohio State. Even in the NFL, I only did it recreationally. Once Len Bias died from a cocaine overdose in 1986, within days of being the second overall pick in that year's NBA draft, that drug wasn't nearly as attractive as it had once been.

Drinking was a different story. I wasn't sloppy or slurring my words when I drank, nor was I searching for a bottle of Bacardi after waking up in the mornings. To me, an alcoholic was the derelict with the beer can stuffed inside a crumpled brown bag, the shameless fool who's constantly hitting up strangers for money to buy booze. I had a great-paying job and plenty of loved ones around me. Drinking was simply a way of socializing.

Betty saw things differently. She asked a lot of questions about my relatives and my family's history of drinking. She talked about how alcohol could be a more sinister drug than something like cocaine or heroin. I could function and even thrive while drinking more than I probably should've been consuming. I wouldn't even know alcohol had destroyed my life until it had invaded my home, isolated me from my family, and completely turned my world upside down.

Betty explained that was how it started. It might be as simple as my saying, "I don't have a problem," but the problem would be there eventually. She had no doubts about that. Even when she asked me how long it had been since I'd gone a good month without drinking, I didn't have an answer for her. It had been so long since that actually had happened that I couldn't recall a time when I wasn't comfortably sipping on something.

That's when Betty broke it down for me. "If you can stop drinking for a week, then you can stop drinking for a month," she said. "If you can do a month, you can do a year. And if you can do a year, then you can stop altogether."

Betty had one basic rule in counseling: We always told the truth in that room. It was an important expectation because she knew addicts would say anything to get what they wanted. The critical aspect of our relationship was trust. I didn't do everything Betty suggested but I did believe she wanted the best for me. She encouraged me to lean on my spirituality, to ask for the support of my family. In time, she even became good friends with Mel.

There have been plenty of days when I've thanked God for bringing Betty into my life at a time when I was so low. If I'd been a Pro Bowl player at the time, I might have reacted differently to what she was saying. Instead, I was a reject from the Eagles who had shown up on waivers, a guy who didn't have the luxury of blowing off therapy or the false hope of moving on to a productive life. I couldn't afford to be the macho football player who hides his fears and weaknesses as routinely as he slips on shoulder pads. I had to start accepting that what Betty was saying was vitally useful information.

I later discovered that Minneapolis was on the cutting edge of diagnosing and dealing with addiction problems. There was serious research going on there that allowed people like Betty to feel comfortable with anticipating what might happen to a person with red flags in their personal lives. She never guaranteed that I'd end up being a full-blown addict in dire need of a twelve-step program. But she did make it clear that alcohol might eventually lead to something more difficult to overcome, and in order to beat this problem, I'd have to seek help from others.

That was enough warning for me to hear because I'd had enough by that point. I didn't want to tear my family apart and I was tired of wondering how good I could be. It was time to start finding out how far I actually could go in the game. I had just been learning my craft in the past while enjoying my life along the way. After three seasons in the league, it was time for me to start growing up.

So on September 19, 1990—just two months shy of my twenty-fifth birthday and two weeks after meeting Betty—I stopped drinking. I didn't know what to expect and I didn't think about putting together a plan. I just told myself that I was done, that Betty's prognosis was enough evidence for me to walk down a different path. I already had plenty of other areas to focus on by that point. And it was best to avoid anything that might turn into a potential stumbling block.

People don't realize the temptations you face when you're giving up alcohol. It's hard enough for the average person, but try steering clear of booze as a pro athlete. If I went to a club with my teammates, there would be all kinds of people trying to buy me a drink. I learned quickly to always have a glass in my hand, one that looked like it was filled with some kind of stiff cocktail. Once I sipped on a couple of those during a night, I could tell my friends that I'd had enough for the evening. They pretty much left me alone after that.

That didn't mean there weren't other challenges involved with giving up alcohol and drugs. I know it was hard on Mel because she had to become comfortable with an entirely different person. When we started dating, I was laid-back and accommodating. When I was rehabilitating myself, I was opinionated, blunt, and irritable. As Mel said, she thought I was super-sweet in those early days. She had no idea that I was high.

Still, that decision to give up alcohol turned out to be the major achievement of my first season with the Vikings. I had begged out of Philadelphia because I didn't want to be a backup in that organization. I wound up stuck in the same role in Minnesota and with a receivers coach who didn't see much potential in me. I'll never forget that man, Dick Rehbein, because he told me I'd never start as long as Anthony Carter and Hassan Jones were on that team. Rehbein also told *Sports Illustrated* years later that he didn't know how much I "liked to practice or work out back then."

I had a ton of respect for Anthony and Hassan in those days. They'd been in the league longer and they'd earned their jobs (Carter had been to three straight Pro Bowls prior to my arrival). But it wasn't like I was the only one whose actions could be questioned. Anthony used to leave the facility so fast after practice that I wondered if he ever showered. I'm serious. As soon as the final horn blew to end our sessions, he would jog off and be driving away from the building before I ever even pulled off my shoulder pads. I guarantee you Anthony wasn't thinking about catching extra passes or fine-tuning his routes at the end of a long day.

Still, I wasn't going to let Rehbein write me off. That had nearly happened in Philadelphia and I hadn't come this far to give in to others' doubts. I worked harder in the weight room. I studied more in meetings. I stayed longer after practice to catch balls and work on routes with quarterbacks. I always felt like I'd be a great receiver in the league one day. That fall I started making serious progress toward realizing that dream.

I don't know how much my decision to give up booze played into my increased focus but I have to believe it didn't hurt. After catching 27 passes in 1990, I had 72 receptions as a starter the next season. Rehbein didn't have as much to do with that because Tom Moore—our assistant head coach and one of the game's best offensive minds ever—had seen my potential and growth. For the first time in my career, I was in an offense geared to use my gifts and I was free of distractions.

Unfortunately, I couldn't say the same for Michael Irvin.

Michael and I have always had an eerie symmetry to our professional careers. We both needed about three years to really find ourselves in the league. We both developed a reputation for being candid and uncompromising in our attempts to help our teams win. And we both earned our stripes by doing the dirty work that sets some receivers apart from others. Nobody ever confused us with burners. We had to make our livings running slants and crossing patterns that left us vulnerable to big-hitting safeties and hard-charging linebackers.

One major difference in our NFL experience was the environments we played in. When I came into the league, I played on a Philadelphia team that was competing for the NFC East crown and was filled with respected veterans. When I came to Minnesota, I was playing behind a Pro Bowler in Anthony Carter and another solid pro in Hassan Jones. I couldn't tell you whom the Cowboys had at receiver when Michael first arrived in Dallas. I only know it didn't matter. He was the one who carried the high expectations and he did so on a team that was horrible during his first three seasons.

Michael was playing on the biggest stage in the league. If you played for the Cowboys, people paid attention to you even when the team was losing. Every NFL city has its share of crazy fans, but in Dallas football is comparable to religion. People live to see that blue star on those shiny silver helmets. They love to reminisce about all the great players who've been a part of that franchise, from Roger Staubach and Tony Dorsett to Bob Lilly and Randy White. The Cowboys even talked about having an opening in the top of old Texas Stadium so God could watch His favorite team play. They called the Cowboys "America's Team" for a reason.

When you combine that kind of stage and a player with Michael's personality, there is going to be a strong potential for problems. And the more the Cowboys won, the more issues started to emerge with Michael. They won the Super Bowl following the 1992 season and once again the following year. Troy Aikman became one of the league's premier quarterbacks, while Emmitt Smith emerged as a dominant runner. You also had head coach Jimmy Johnson cementing himself as a hell of a motivator and tactician, a man who won with a dominant defense and an electric offense.

In the middle of all that was Michael. Starting with his breakout season in 1991 he went to five straight Pro Bowls. He played big in the biggest of games, including 6 receptions for 114 yards and 2 touchdowns in his first Super Bowl appearance (a win over Buffalo during the 1992 season). "Everybody on those teams would tell you that Troy was our leader," Johnston said. "But the quarterback has to be cool and calm. Michael was our emotional leader. If he wasn't on the field, you knew there was something missing from our offense."

"You could see he was their Energizer Bunny," said NFL Network analyst Jamie Dukes, who played ten NFL seasons between 1986–95. "Michael once told me that he cared so much about his teammates that he would appear at the summer football camps run by the third-string offensive tackle. He knew that meant a lot to the player. He also understood that was how you commanded respect as a leader."

What few people outside of Dallas knew was how much Michael was doing off the field as well. In March 1996, local police raided an Irving, Texas, motel room and found Michael, an assortment of other guests (including topless dancers), and at least ten grams of cocaine. When the case went to trial, one of the dancers testified that Michael had paid for drugs and bankrolled similar parties before that. The case ended with Michael pleading no contest and paying a $10,000 fine, but the damage to his reputation had been done.

No longer was he just "the Playmaker." Now he also was the brash jock who didn't give a fuck, the dude who once strolled into a court-house wearing a full-length fur coat. The league hit Michael with a five-game suspension after that scandal, which was the most painful punishment he could receive. "When he saw the looks on our faces—and realized that he'd let us down—that was hard on him," Johnston said. "That was the moment when the lightbulb went off for him."

Still, Michael's troubles didn't end there. A woman accused him and Cowboys left tackle Erik Williams of sexual assault later in that 1996 season. Though the story was later proven to be complete fiction, it still tainted Michael in ways that were hard to overcome. His problems only worsened when news broke that several Cowboys used to hang out at a suburban residence called "the White House," where prosti-tutes and cocaine were all part of the revelry.

When Cowboys owner Jerry Jones heard the stories about that place, he asked Michael what was happening. Michael's response was both crazy and comical, as he tried to make the entire operation sound like a way for teammates to hang out together. "Boss," he said, "I was trying to do the right thing but I was doing it the wrong way." Most people around the league thought Michael was out of control by that point. Like a lot of friends who knew him well, I was scared of what might happen next.

That was a strange time in our relationship because I had to be careful about how I approached him. I was close with both Michael's wife, Sandy, and his mother, Pearl, and there was a natural urge to get more involved with helping a friend overcome his drug problems. I didn't know what it was like to have police bust into a thirtieth birth-day party or to have strange women make up stories about you. But I did know how my own counselor, Betty, had come at me. She had been honest and straightforward and it helped me see what I had to do to save my own career.

In Michael's case, I didn't think I could be that candid with him. He seemed to be in so deep that it would've been hard for him to deal with somebody who wasn't going to be empathetic. Don't get me wrong—I called him after every incident and said he had my undying support. But I wouldn't have made excuses for him. I knew he was the only person who could figure out what to do next.

I did tell him plenty of times that leaning on his religious faith was an option he should consider. Both his wife and his mother were devout Christians, and as I told Michael one day, "Religion does help."

There were also times when I think he'd get annoyed by his wife and mother using me as an example of how to recover from such problems. Sandy invoked my name so often—she'd say, "Cris beat this so you can, too"—that he finally snapped at her one day. "You need to stop talking about Cris Carter in my house," he said.

Michael laughed when he told me that story a few weeks later, and I knew he wasn't irritated by how I dealt with my own problems. I'm sure he appreciated that I never judged him for what he had to deal with in his own personal life. Michael's struggles also weren't unique to the league. Being in the NFL exposes players to more things. They've got more money. They're living in bigger cities. If you're a guy who parties and goes to the club, you're just going to go more. Being a professional athlete only enhances what you already are.

The sad part of Michael's career is that his problems coincided with the end of his greatness. We went to three Pro Bowls together—1993 through 1995—but Michael never made it back to Hawaii after that. It wasn't that his production had decreased, because he had two more 1,000-yard seasons before his retirement. It's just that his impact wasn't the same as it was during the height of his career.

Michael's 1996 season ended with a broken collarbone in a playoff loss to the Carolina Panthers. He eventually retired at age thirty-three after sustaining a cervical spinal cord injury following a hit by Philadelphia Eagles safety Tim Hauck four games into the 1999 season. Michael was going over the middle when he caught the pass, tripped over a defensive back's tackle, and felt Hauck crash onto his back. As he lay motionless on the Veterans Stadium turf, Philadelphia fans applauded enthusiastically in one of the saddest displays of fandom that you'll ever see.

I suspect those Eagles supporters were excited to think that a player who had tormented them for so many years might not be doing that again that afternoon. Maybe it was the larger image of Michael that led to their reaction. They might not have cared for his swagger, his bravado, and all the antics that made the cameras follow Michael everywhere he went. But I also know this: Few players in the NFL ever affected people in the way that Michael Irvin did.

He was inducted into the Hall of Fame in 2007, and when I think back on his career, I don't only see a great receiver catching passes and helping his team win Super Bowls. I see an entertainer parading around in spectacular suits, flashy sunglasses, and enough jewelry to make any woman envious of his substantial bling. I see a performer prancing his way into the end zone and shimmying through life to his own personal sound track. Basically, I see a great presence.

"Michael was always very consistent," Johnston said. "The things I'll always remember are the scenes of him with his teammates on the sidelines during games. People will ask me what he was screaming at us in those moments, and I always say Michael never used words like 'I' or 'me.' He always said 'we' or 'us.' He never acted like he was playing hard and we had to step it up to match him. That's a gift. He always thought about the team."

I'll always be thankful my own career dovetailed with Michael's because I was able to understand him in ways that most people couldn't. I also was able to accept what he meant to the game and the position. Before Michael came on the scene, receivers mostly knew only one way to operate. They kept their personalities in check and they did their jobs to the best of their abilities. There was no shame in that, either. It was how the world worked back then.

But the game truly was changing when Michael entered the NFL. Free agency was on the horizon. Television was evolving so much that the game was being marketed differently. It was becoming acceptable, even fashionable, for stars to emerge at positions other than quarterback. The revival of the Dallas Cowboys in the early 1990s—they would win three Super Bowls in four seasons—also added a critical element to the mix. Football was on its way to cementing itself as the most popular sport in America. That meant more opportunities for everybody, especially receivers.

I sensed that my own career was blossoming in Minnesota during that time. The arrival of head coach Dennis Green in 1992 offered an exciting shift in offensive philosophy, and I also was encouraged by the newfound calm I felt in my game. The position was coming easier to me in the NFL because I was making better choices in my life. That's what I always hoped Michael would see, that you could play this game without the drama that comes with substance abuse.

In fact, it's still hard for me to discuss addiction with some people because they often only see it from one vantage point. My life hadn't imploded, but I also have no problem saying I was on the road to addiction when I came to Minnesota. Like Michael, I was too stubborn for my own good. I needed a change of surroundings and a strong, supportive presence like Betty to help put my life back on the right track.

Unfortunately, Michael had some run-ins with the law following his retirement, but I've never thought those issues should change the way people view his career. He left a sizable footprint on the NFL and he had a blast during the majority of his playing days. He also stretched the notion of what a receiver could be and do for his team. As former New Orleans Saints Pro Bowl receiver Joe Horn said, "Michael proved that if you did your thing on the field, you could enjoy yourself at the same time. He was the Muhammad Ali of receivers."

"I might have thought differently of Michael if I played on the Redskins, Eagles, or Giants," Johnston said. "But he was a great teammate. People ask me, 'How can you defend him after what he's done?' And I tell them that they don't know Michael like I did. People who didn't know Michael didn't know how much he really cared."

Of course, nobody could've seen such contributions coming from Michael when people were writing him off following that knee injury early in his career. Even more unpredictable was the impact one of his future teammates had on receivers, all while playing on the other side of the football.

CHAPTER 5

The NFL Goes "Prime Time"

I t's amazing what happens when the right decisions are made. The game comes easier. There's a calmness both on and off the field. Instead of talking about greatness like it's some far-off destination, every day it is within reach. After a while, it's easy to wonder why things couldn't have been so simple from the start.

I knew my game was going to another level when the Minnesota Vikings hired Dennis Green as their head coach following the 1991 season. I had made considerable progress in putting my issues with drugs and alcohol behind me. I had worked so hard that my overall production had improved dramatically. I also had the support of my offensive coordinator, Tom Moore. The first time we met, he sat me down in his office and said, "You're the kind of player a coach needs on the field. You're going to make the quarterback's job easier."

All I needed was a head coach who had the same mentality about my game and that's where Denny came in. He had spent three seasons as the head coach at Stanford before coming to Minnesota, but what really made him attractive was his experience with the San Francisco 49ers. Denny had coached receivers in that organization from 1986–88. The gold star on his résumé had been mentoring Jerry Rice and John Taylor as they became big-time playmakers for that franchise.

Denny made it clear from the minute he took over the Vikings that we were going to be an aggressive passing team in the mold of the

49ers. He didn't want his receivers only catching 10- and 12-yard passes. He wanted them going downfield. He wanted them terrorizing defensive backs. Most of all, he wanted them big. Denny's philosophy was basic: The more size a receiver had, the less a quarterback had to worry about making a mistake with an errant throw.

Denny also wasn't just stuck on the idea of using two receivers to be his difference-makers. He wanted as many playmakers on the field as he could find and that meant we would be using three-receiver sets as long as he had the job. I loved it because he treated me like a basketball player playing football. He wanted me working out of the slot, where I could use my height to ward off defenders and catch balls in traffic. His constant advice to me on the field: "Post up on them."

Now I've heard a lot of people question what kind of guy Denny Green is. They've seen him do some eccentric things in public—usually when he's ranting to the media about something—but he was always a good head coach. One of Denny's greatest strengths was recognizing where the game was going and tailoring those trends to his own vision of success. It didn't take long to see what he valued most in Minnesota. He wanted a strong offensive line to give his quarterback time to throw and he wanted receivers who created all kinds of mismatches.

Denny also didn't believe in letting circumstances dictate how he attacked opponents. I remember one time we were scheduled to play in Green Bay for a Monday night game and the forecast called for rain. Denny didn't care about that. In the practices leading up that game, he just kept saying, "We're going to bomb them." And that's exactly what we did. That kind of confidence made his players want to believe in his game plans. It made us want to believe in him.

What I liked most about Denny was that he wasn't just a good tactician. He also knew how to motivate players. He tapped into the psychology of the men he coached and it meant a lot that he was a black man in a position of power. Denny was only the second African American head coach in NFL history (after Art Shell) and the third ever in pro football history (Fritz Pollard had coached the Akron Pros in

1921). He knew we wanted him to succeed. And he knew how to reach people like me.

Denny always talked about having a plan for everything. It didn't matter if it was the route we took to work or how we managed our days. He'd constantly remind me that being a player was the same thing as running your own business. He'd say, you've got Cris Carter Inc., Warren Moon Inc., Randall McDaniel Inc. It wasn't just you out there playing ball. You were representing something much bigger than that.

Denny encouraged me to lead from the moment he arrived. During our first year together, he pulled me aside in practice one day and told me that I had to be the guy setting the standard in our locker room. Anthony Carter was getting older and Hassan Jones was being phased out, so Denny saw me as a key part of his agenda. "I don't want to see you over there throwing balls around and taking it easy when I walk out here," he said. Denny wanted me to stay on players, to push them and to create an expectation of what the Vikings were supposed to be. The days of just worrying about myself ended when his tenure began.

That didn't mean Denny would let me run wild. If I ever went off on somebody in a way that he didn't approve, he'd let me know in a hurry. One year I exploded on a teammate during a home game and Denny grabbed me immediately. "You need to get your shit together," he told me. "There are too many people out here watching for you to act like that." He'd even do that when I got on somebody for a legitimate mistake. "Don't do that," Denny said to me after one such occasion. "That guy will quit on us if you ride him too hard."

It was still rare to see coaches asking receivers to be such prominent voices in a locker room in the early 1990s, even though stars like Rice, Green Bay's Sterling Sharpe, and Dallas's Michael Irvin clearly had become powerful presences on their own respective teams. What wasn't surprising was Denny's offensive philosophy. It wasn't uncommon to see multiple-receiver sets all around the NFL. The quarterbacks were too good and the rules were too favorable for the offense.

You had the Buffalo Bills running their K-gun system during that time, an attack that kept quarterback Jim Kelly in the shotgun while running a no-huddle offense that utilized receivers like Andre Reed and James Lofton. The Houston Oilers were producing similar numbers in the run-and-shoot offense, while the Detroit Lions and New Orleans Saints had their own versions of that attack. The Atlanta Falcons had also installed their variation of that system, one that featured rising stars like Andre Rison and later Terance Mathis.

But while the Falcons were throwing the ball plenty in those days, it wasn't their offense that had a huge impact on the NFL. Instead, it was a certain cornerback with a shiny Jheri curl, a cocksure grin, and enough raw ability to turn a one-hour *SportsCenter* episode into his own personal highlight film. Most people believe Deion Sanders revolutionized the cornerback position when he became an NFL star in the 1990s. What he did for receivers is something that doesn't get nearly as much attention as it deserves.

I've sat in a lot of offensive meetings during my sixteen-year career. Only once have I ever heard a coach sound frightened by the prospect of attacking an opposing defensive back. It happened early in my tenure in Minnesota and it was repeated anytime we were facing Deion. "The only time we're throwing his way is if we have a clear, open angle," our coaches would tell our quarterbacks. "Other than that, don't go near the guy."

At the time it seemed crazy to think one player—particularly a cornerback—could create so much concern for opponents. Reggie White inspired that kind of fear because he was 6'5", three-hundred-plus pounds, and capable of charging right through an offensive tackle. Lawrence Taylor could do it because he had so much quickness, strength, and malice that he was damn near unstoppable coming off the edge. But Deion scared you with a different set of skills: He could embarrass teams in a heartbeat. All he needed was the opportunity.

There was an aura about Deion from the minute he entered the NFL as the fifth overall pick in the 1989 draft. He quickly became a star with the Atlanta Falcons and he was talented enough to split time as a Major League Baseball player (he ultimately played nine years in that sport, including stops with the Yankees, Braves, Reds, and Giants). There were plenty of days when it seemed as if he was capable of doing anything he wanted in sports. He had speed, intelligence, and, above all else, a penchant for the spectacular. At times, his self-appointed nickname, "Prime Time," seemed to undersell his endless abundance of flair.

I'm talking about a guy who scored on his first punt return in the NFL. There was one year, in 1992, where Deion played a game in Miami against the Dolphins and then flew to Pittsburgh for a playoff game as a member of the Atlanta Braves. They say his 4.27 40-yard dash time at the 1989 scouting combine was the second fastest in history, after Bo Jackson. Oh yeah, he also scored 10 touchdowns in his first five seasons in the league.

"To this day, the two best athletes I've ever seen are Bo Jackson and Deion Sanders," said Jamie Dukes, who played for the Falcons from 1986–93. "When he was playing baseball and football in Atlanta, I know players on both teams loved it. We rooted for him. The only people who didn't like it were people outside of those franchises."

I rarely lined up against Deion because he usually didn't venture inside to cover receivers in the slot. The players who did face him had to earn everything they got. As Warren Moon, a Hall-of-Fame quarterback and my old Vikings teammate, once said, "The thing you always had to respect about Deion was that he backed up whatever he said. If he said he was going to return a punt for a touchdown, he did it. If he said he was going to score on an interception, he did it. If he was talking about doing something, there was a pretty good chance he would produce."

What made Deion especially effective was his ability to control half of the football field from his position. Most times he wouldn't even trot into the huddle to hear the defensive call. He'd just linger out near the sidelines, waiting for his next victim to join him. Few receivers ever had enough ability to escape him in the open field. Even if they were open for a moment, Deion would recover so quickly that he'd scare the quarterback into looking for another target.

Now there were plenty of great cornerbacks in the league when I started playing. You had Albert Lewis and Kevin Ross in Kansas City; Hanford Dixon and Frank Minnifield were stars in Cleveland; Rod Woodson, Mike Haynes, and Darrell Green all ranked among the best in the business. But none of those guys could cover like Deion.

Take Darrell Green, a man who played twenty seasons for the Redskins and became a first-ballot Hall-of-Famer. He was an exceptional cornerback, but he didn't have Deion's length or his gangly arms. Darrell could mirror a receiver as well as anybody in the game. Deion, on the other hand, could smother a wideout anytime he felt the urge.

That ability didn't only come from Deion's vast physical gifts. When you talked football with him, you saw that he really understood the nuances of the game. He studied with the intention of discovering key indicators of a receiver's preferences. He had a keen feel for how to play angles and bait quarterbacks into dangerous throws they'd love to have back. The mistake people usually made with Deion was thinking that he simply showed up on game day and played. He made plenty of people look bad because he knew a thing or two about preparation as well.

Drew Pearson used to talk about the impact that Pittsburgh Steelers cornerback Mel Blount, another Hall-of-Famer, had on receivers because of his size and nasty streak. Blount was so tenacious that he could stand over receivers at the line of scrimmage and literally manhandle them out of their routes. When the league had to start pondering new ways of opening up the passing game, Blount was used as a primary example as to why receivers felt so stifled in those days. Deion had the same impact on receivers in the 1990s.

"Deion was the perfect storm," Jamie Dukes said. "When he came into the NFL, most teams were still using two-back, two-receiver, one-tight-end sets. His ability to shut down half the field meant teams literally had to find other ways to throw the ball."

As much as teams were throwing the football by that point, it wasn't like many franchises had a receiver who could challenge Deion. From what I remember, Rice and Irvin were the main ones who consistently

Posing with Vikings legend and Minnesota associate Supreme Court Justice Alan Page. *From Cris Carter's personal collection*

Feeling blessed to be in the company of two great Vikings wide receivers: Anthony Carter (*left*) and Ahmad Rashad (*right*). *From Cris Carter's personal collection*

My wife, Melanie, and our kids, Duron and Monterae. *From Cris Carter's personal collection*

Posing with my boys from back in the day. *From Cris Carter's personal collection*

A nice shot of Duron, Michael Irvin, and myself at the Pro Bowl. *From Cris Carter's personal collection*

Duron checking out Daddy's locker. *From Cris Carter's personal collection*

Duron visiting Vikings training camp. *From Cris Carter's personal collection*

A quiet moment between father and daughter. *From Cris Carter's personal collection*

Fooling around during practice.
From Cris Carter's personal collection

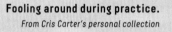

Monterae Carter: Daddy's little girl. *From Cris Carter's personal collection*

One of the best moments of my career: my 1,000th reception. *From Cris Carter's personal collection*

With two Pro Bowls in two seasons, Bengals wide receiver A. J. Green is already one of the game's best playmakers. *Courtesy of the Cincinnati Bengals*

Steelers cornerback Mel Blount was so dominant in the 1970s that the NFL changed its rules to open up the passing game. *Courtesy of the Pittsburgh Steelers*

Randy Moss reenergized his career when he hooked up with Tom Brady in New England in 2007. *Courtesy of ESPN*

No player was more inspirational to young receivers in the 1970s than Pittsburgh's Lynn Swann. *Courtesy of the Pittsburgh Steelers*

Lynn Swann may have been the acrobatic star in Pittbsurgh, but fellow wideout John Stallworth was a Hall of Famer as well. *Courtesy of the Pittsburgh Steelers*

Keyshawn Johnson with then NFL Commissioner Paul Tagliabue after being taken by the New York Jets as the first pick in the 1996 NFL draft. *Copyright © AP/Wally Santana*

Dallas wide receiver Michael Irvin made it fashionable for receivers to be both brash and willing to lead their team in ways never before seen. *Copyright © AP/Tim Sharp*

Deion Sanders only played one season in San Francisco, but his 1994 campaign changed the game for receivers. *Copyright © AP/Tom DiPace*

Buffalo's Andre Reed was one of the most dynamic receivers of his generation. *Courtesy of the Buffalo Bills*

wanted to attack him. Those three would ramp up their competitive juices so much that they'd even go after each other at the Pro Bowl. Whenever we'd have one-on-one drills between the defensive backs and the receivers during the NFC practices, it would only take a few repetitions before Deion would be facing Michael or Jerry.

It would start with Deion trotting out to line up against one or the other. Maybe Michael or Jerry would beat him on one play. Then Deion would come back and shut them down on the next two or three opportunities. Once we got into team drills, Deion would wave off the safety help just so he could continue the battle. That's how much he loved the challenge of facing the best in the game.

The obvious dilemma around the league was that most teams didn't have a Michael Irvin or a Jerry Rice. So if you were playing Deion, you had to assume that your best receiver wasn't going to be doing much that day. "He allowed the other defensive backs and linebackers to do things in coverage that they might not be able to do otherwise," said Drew Pearson. "He took away your best receiver and he took away half the field. Before he showed up, you never heard the term 'shutdown cornerback.' . . . [W]hen I played, everybody was a shutdown corner-back. After Deion, everybody was looking for that kind of defender."

The game was already becoming more situational when Deion arrived, meaning that offenses wanted to exploit whatever matchup they could work to their advantage. After he blew up, the need for doing that only escalated. If you were going to lose your best receiver and half the field for an afternoon, you opened yourself up to all kinds of other problems offensively. The pass rush would be on your quarter-back faster. Running backs would have a harder time finding room to operate because more defenders would be committed to stopping the ground game. Basically, it would be a long day for everybody.

So offensive coaches really had two choices to make at that point. One route was to stick with the belief that everybody would somehow get their hands on a Rice, Irvin, Sharpe, or similar receiver with Hall-of-Fame potential. The other path meant doing more with the players

Deion wasn't covering. If he was going to take away part of the field, then teams had to make better use of their second receivers, their tight ends, and—to my great joy—their slot receivers.

I never felt like my career had reached its peak when success first started arriving in Minneapolis. It wasn't until 1994, my fifth season there, that I really was where I needed to be. I'm not talking about numbers, because I was definitely catching more balls. I'm talking about understanding what it really means to be a professional football player, how deep you have to go to be one of the best in the business.

When Denny Green arrived in 1992, one of the first big-name players who arrived with him was veteran running back Roger Craig. Roger had been in the league since 1983 and he'd been a star with the 49ers during their glory years. He knew what it took to thrive at a high level. He'd done it himself and he'd watched Jerry Rice do it for years in San Francisco.

I couldn't ask Roger enough questions about what he and Jerry did to become Pro Bowlers. His answer was usually the same: They worked harder than anybody else. Roger would tell me about how often he and Jerry would run steep trails in the Bay Area hills during the off-season. He raved about how frequently Jerry stayed after practice to refine routes. The people who worshiped Jerry often only saw the end results of his preparation. His true greatness had plenty to do with how he approached the game from Monday through Saturday.

I didn't need to hear much else after that. I immediately started doing my own things to hone my body for the kind of excellence at that level I'd long coveted. I did more Olympic weight lifting to create more explosive movements. I did more interval training to build stamina and quickness off the line of scrimmage. I also took advantage of the knowledge offered by another veteran who showed up in 1994: Warren Moon.

Before Warren signed, we had never had a top-flight quarterback in my first four seasons in Minnesota. We had Rich Gannon at the start of his career, a decade before he ever blossomed into a Pro Bowl quarterback with the Oakland Raiders. Jim McMahon came in for a season, while Sean Salisbury and Wade Wilson also started at different points. All those players were decent. They just weren't in the same class as Warren.

The minute Warren arrived at our first off-season workout, I felt as if everything was heading to another level. He jogged onto the practice field with the aura of a man who'd done just about everything in football short of winning a Super Bowl. He'd spent the first six years of his professional career becoming a star in the Canadian Football League, mainly because the NFL wasn't ready for black quarterbacks when he left the University of Washington in 1978. After the Houston Oilers signed him in 1984, he used the next ten years to make everyone realize the idiocy of that shortsightedness (and discrimination).

Warren wasn't merely exceptionally talented. He also was an amazing motivator. He made you want to be accountable when you stepped on the field with him. He made you want to do more to help him win games. You never saw me going to minicamps during my first four years in Minnesota. When Warren came in during my fifth year, I was the first to jump in line to catch balls from him. *We're definitely getting ready to throw the football now,* I kept thinking.

Warren loved exploiting the seams in defenses. He had done it for years in college. When he was at his best in Houston, the Oilers used a wide-open system that spread the field with quick, dangerous receivers. The more wideouts Warren had to work with, the more damage he was going to do with his rocket arm.

Like Denny Green, Warren also had a plan for how he wanted to utilize me. He had followed my college career and my brother Butch's basketball career as well. Warren figured that having me in the slot would open up plenty of opportunities for our offense. As he said later, "When you have a guy who plays bigger than his size, runs great routes, and has great hands, you have to like that as a quarterback. It means you can take more chances with the football. You can throw it up there and know that your guy has a pretty good chance of coming down with it."

Now you have to understand what the league was like at that point. Most teams had two good cornerbacks, but it was rare to find many who had three. If you had two good outside receivers and somebody who worked out of the slot like me, then the defense had to make some choices. They could: (1) shift one of their better corners off an outside receiver to cover me; (2) use a nickelback who probably couldn't match me in size; or (3) bring a safety down to try his luck. Out of all those choices, the one that sounded best to me was "all of the above."

The 1994 season was setting up for me perfectly because I finally had the coach, quarterback, and offensive system to generate big numbers. Joining me at receiver were 6'3", 216-pound Jake Reed and speedy Qadry Ismail. Robert Smith was in the backfield, and the offensive line featured studs like Randall McDaniel, Todd Steussie, and Jeff Christy. We also had a young offensive coordinator named Brian Billick. He had replaced Tom Moore in 1993 and his offense led to me producing 86 receptions and my first 1,000-yard season. A year later, Billick had even bigger plans for me.

The NFC Central race was pretty tight that season, so every game was a dogfight. I also was in a zone. I had 14 catches in a loss to Arizona and 10 more in a win over Green Bay. By midseason I had 60 total receptions and the possibility of breaking the league record for single-season catches became real. Green Bay's Sterling Sharpe had set the mark with 112 receptions in 1993. I was already halfway to making history.

The most important thing during that year was maintaining my focus. It wasn't easy at times because so many players around the league were going off. Sharpe was on his way to catching 18 touchdown passes that season, the second-highest total in NFL history. Jerry was once again doing his thing in San Francisco. He'd end up with 112 receptions, while Atlanta's Terance Mathis would grab 111 of his own.

What I always tried to tell myself was that Sharpe's record wasn't the only goal. Winning was the bigger deal. I wanted to shine on a team that made the playoffs because I'd been accustomed to success my entire career. I ultimately was fortunate enough to get the record in my second to last game of that season, and the team earned a playoff spot after a win over San Francisco the last game of the regular season.

We didn't do much in the postseason, but that year was special because I'd finally broken out in my mind. That's what I tell people all the time: You don't come into your own when you have a certain number of catches. You do it when you know exactly what it takes to be an elite player. I'd taken every last bit of advice, encouragement, and coaching I'd received and channeled it into a performance that etched my name in history.

At a time when receivers were catching more balls than ever before, I was taking my game to places I'd never been. In another part of the league, Deion was also showing people things they'd never quite imagined.

In 1994, Deion Sanders enjoyed the most amazing season by a cornerback in NFL history. When his contract expired with the Atlanta Falcons that year, he decided to not return to the only pro football team he'd ever known. Instead, he played ninety-two games in the Majors (forty-six each with the Atlanta Braves and Cincinnati Reds) while teams all over the NFL pleaded for his services. The San Francisco 49ers eventually won out, signing him shortly after baseball concluded its regular season.

By the time Deion arrived in San Francisco, he was something the NFL had rarely seen before: He was his own personal brand. He preened and boasted, danced and dazzled, all while commanding the spotlight in ways that served as educational seminars for future publicists. Anybody who watched football knew who Deion Sanders was because you couldn't miss the guy. He had every bit of personality that Michael Irvin had brought to Dallas except for one key thing: He had even less opportunity to display it.

The common explanation for receivers wanting attention was that we barely had enough chances during a game to showcase our talents.

In Deion's case, he was holding the football in his hands maybe five or six times a season on defense. If he was returning kicks and punts, he might have a shot at another fifty or so opportunities. It wasn't like people were scheming for ways to put Deion in the best possible position to shine. He had to earn everything he got . . . and he relished the idea of becoming a star at a position that was never known for celebrity.

If you were a cornerback, you usually gained attention because of a mistake, like a long touchdown pass or a missed tackle. The cameras followed Deion even when teams weren't throwing his way. He was that exceptional, both at his job and influencing others. When former Falcons defensive end Chuck Smith walked onto the team bus for a road trip to Washington in 1993, he wore a T-shirt. Deion cringed. His advice to Smith: Wear a suit when you travel because people notice how you carry yourself.

That sense of style didn't only endear Deion to other players. His entire personality drew people to him in droves. Celebrities wanted to hang with him. Teammates from both sports celebrated his swagger. Popular culture was changing with the explosion of hip-hop and it felt like Deion wasn't merely a football player. He was an indication of what football players could become if they had enough sizzle.

"Deion was like a walking concert," Smith said. "Master P would come to the stadium just to meet Deion. When Snoop Dogg said he was a fan of Deion, I was standing right there to hear it. Bobby Brown would want to hang out with him. Janet Jackson would invite him onstage if he was at her concert. Deion didn't drink or smoke, but you'd see him around people like [former rap producer] Suge Knight and they would totally be respectful of that."

"I remember the first time I felt like things were changing because of Deion," said Eric Allen, who played cornerback for the Eagles, Saints, and Raiders during his fourteen-year career. "We were at the Pro Bowl in 1991 and you could see the difference. It used to be that guys like Lawrence Taylor, Ronnie Lott, and Mike Singletary were focused on everything happening on the field. When Deion came in— and Michael Irvin for that matter—they brought the entertainment aspect. He actually had a concert with MC Hammer that week. He was wearing a money suit and singing onstage. And this was before he ever became one of the league's top cornerbacks."

The beauty of Deion was that he was changing the game by being himself. And not just the *game* of football, but the *business* of it. The NFL Players Association had started fighting for unrestricted free agency in 1987 and it didn't evolve into its current form until 1993. That was the year Reggie White became the most prominent free agent ever, leaving Philadelphia for the Green Bay Packers. But while the pursuit of Reggie made people see how much a franchise could change with the right acquisition, the pursuit of Deion made plenty of other players see how much their opportunities could change with the right deal.

Now there weren't that many cornerbacks who were capable of demanding the kind of money that Deion warranted in those days. However, there were several receivers who had to be noticing the way teams lined up for his services. What's more, they had to covet the freedom Deion clearly had in his career. He could say whatever he wanted, do whatever he wanted, and still know he was going to get paid at the end of the day.

Older receivers say one of the biggest issues with being too flashy or too brash in the 1970s was the possibility of teams blackballing players to send a message. Free agency was about to end all of those fears. Though many receivers probably didn't know it at the time, they'd been given a free pass to unleash their personalities. They already had one such role model in Michael Irvin. Deion's presence only made it more attractive for wideouts to get in on the game.

"When Deion came onto the scene, a lot of people realized you could have fun and be flashy in the game," said wide receiver T. J. Houshmandzadeh, whose eleven-year NFL career included stops in Cincinnati, Seattle, Baltimore, and Oakland. "He had the do-rag, the headband around his neck, and about twenty pairs of socks on his feet. His confidence translated to every position."

From the moment Deion joined San Francisco, it seemed as if the football universe was changing radically. The 49ers always had been more businesslike in their approach, with stars like Joe Montana, Jerry Rice, and Ronnie Lott setting the tone. Deion's arrival created speculation that he'd have a harder time fitting into that locker room. Instead, he proved to his teammates that his self-promotional impulses stopped the minute he punched in for work at the facility.

Linebacker Gary Plummer once told the *San Francisco Chronicle* that he expected to have a hard time liking Deion that year, especially since Plummer had brought a blue-collar reputation with him to San Francisco after leaving the San Diego Chargers. But Sanders won his teammate over by constantly scouring videotape to find weaknesses in upcoming opponents. The reputation Deion brought to the 49ers was that of a man who would do anything so long as he was paid handsomely. But he signed a one-year deal for only $1.2 million to play for the 49ers, mainly because such a discount offered him the best chance of winning a Super Bowl.

Plummer even told the *Chronicle* that Sanders often used bravado as a way of making opponents underestimate him. One such ploy involved Deion standing away from the huddle before plays. "It made him look arrogant, aloof, cocky when he wouldn't come into the huddle," Plummer told the paper. "But he wasn't just over there to dance and jaw with [the opposing] players and their coaches. He was trying to pick up information. And believe me, even if he wasn't in the huddle, we had hand signals and he was communicating . . . He was as smart a corner as I ever saw."

"Deion understood that his public persona was different than his private persona," said former 49ers safety Merton Hanks. "The biggest transition he had to make was understanding he didn't have to be the whole show with us. He was that in Atlanta but he walked into a locker room filled with Hall-of-Famers in San Francisco. The players who were already there had done things he wanted to do. And to his credit, he did everything possible to blend in with us."

By the time we played the 49ers in the regular-season finale, there was little doubt about where they were going as a team. They had clinched home-field advantage for the playoffs, and I caught 3 passes against their backups as we won the NFC North title. I imagine it would've been a different game if they'd competed. Their offense was a machine with Jerry, Steve Young, and Ricky Watters leading the way. Their defense was even scarier with Deion on the back end of a unit that featured Pro Bowlers like Hanks, Rickey Jackson, Dana Stubblefield, and Tim McDonald. By season's end, Deion had 6 interceptions, 303 return yards, and 3 touchdowns and had won the league's Defensive Player of the Year award.

The 49ers eventually destroyed the San Diego Chargers in Super Bowl XXIX, but that season also was notable for what it did for Deion's image. He suddenly had national commercials with corporations like Nike, PepsiCo, Pizza Hut, and American Express. He produced his own rap album on MC Hammer's label and even released a video. Deion wasn't merely selling himself to the highest bidder in football any longer. He was transforming himself into an icon.

"When Deion went to the 49ers, that's when he really became dominant," Allen said. "But he also changed the atmosphere around there. For so long, that team had been business oriented. After you won the game, you went home and that was it. When Deion arrived, he was showing up in limos, holding after-parties, and having a great time. He made it exciting."

I really have no clue how many receivers Deion upset with his showmanship and success. I do know that one of them didn't like the idea of playing in his vast shadow in 1994: Jerry. News reports claimed that they had an altercation in the days leading up to Super Bowl XXIX because Deion missed curfew one night. When Deion eventually signed a seven-year, $35 million deal with Dallas in 1995, Jerry went off on the local media and famously said, "No one individual won the Super Bowl."

That rift eventually blew over—"Even though he was flamboyant, he also wanted to be a good defensive back," Jerry said—but the impact Deion had on the entire league couldn't be overlooked. He sold his services first to San Francisco and helped the 49ers win a Super Bowl. A year later, he made more money in going to Dallas and helping the Cowboys win that season's Super Bowl. You had to be blind not to see the genius in what he was doing. Deion was marketing the notion that—in the ultimate team sport—the right player could be a game-changer. "Deion was the paradigm shift," Dukes said. "He showed everybody that one guy could make a huge difference."

In many ways, Deion had the mind-set of a receiver. He wanted the ball in his hands as much as possible. He wanted to shine whenever he had the opportunity. He wanted everybody to see how gifted he was and how much he could help a team that invested in him. Deion even played some snaps at receiver during his career, including a 36-catch season in Dallas in 1996.

You'd be crazy to think receivers around the league didn't notice his impact, especially younger ones. Deion had everything they wanted: championships, money, and notoriety. The camera followed him everywhere he went and owners would do anything for his services. Deion also had the liberty to choose his employer in the age of free agency. He understood the newfound leverage that players held in the league and he wanted others to use it as well.

When the Falcons played the 49ers in 1994, Deion watched as Chuck Smith struggled to maintain his stamina in the second half of a blowout loss. Smith was in the final year of his contract, which meant he could earn a huge payday with a brilliant season. Deion knew that as well. During a brief break in that game—as a teammate lay on the turf while trainers tended to his injury—Deion ambled over to Smith with some advice just as powerful as that which he'd offered about Smith's wardrobe selections years earlier. "He told me that wasn't good enough," Smith said. "We were in the middle of a game and he's telling me how much better I have to play to make money."

Plenty of other players also were thinking about how they could enjoy the same benefits as Deion. Dallas Cowboys wide receiver Alvin Harper had the chance to test free agency in 1995 and he found a willing suitor in Tampa Bay. The problem was Harper's work ethic and inability to make plays without Michael Irvin on the other side of the field. He caught 18 touchdown passes in four seasons in Dallas. He had 3 in the last four years of his career, while lasting only two seasons in Tampa.

But Deion didn't just make players see the value of exploiting an open market. He also raised the bar for receivers by being so dominant. Suddenly teams wanted to find more shutdown cornerbacks in his mold and this wasn't good for the growth of receivers. More players who were athletic enough to thrive on offense in high school and college would eventually envision themselves as the next Deion.

Receivers weren't the only ones who had to elevate their games with Deion running around the field. Coaches and general managers also had to think about how to offset the impact he was having. They had to find an answer for a player whom nobody—at least that I saw—could outrun. And at some point, a different breed of receiver had to evolve to deal with both Deion and the sudden influx of talented cornerbacks.

For decades, the NFL had relied mainly on smaller, quicker receivers to fuel their passing attacks. The popular belief was that they could separate from defenders and create better passing windows. The more Deion thrived, the more sense it made for the league to start thinking even bigger about the position. We already had been doing that in Minnesota. A few years later, plenty of other teams were moving in the same direction.

CHAPTER 6

From Hardwoods to a Hard Game

I've been playing basketball since I was old enough to bounce a ball. It's a game I learned growing up in the projects in Middletown, Ohio, where I watched Butch do his thing for years. If he was going to play a high school basketball game that started at seven thirty, I'd be right there with him at the gym around four that afternoon. By the time the players had taken the court to warm up, I'd have probably taken more than one hundred shots. Basketball, regardless of how my life played out, was my love. Football was something that came easily.

Most of those feelings came down to one important fact about basketball: You're always in motion. I thrived off the action of the game from the moment I started playing it. You're only a part-time player in football, because you're only competing on offense or defense once you've moved on to college and the NFL. In basketball, you're doing everything, whether it's dribbling and shooting, rebounding and passing, or locking somebody down from baseline to baseline. It's easy to get bored in football and it happens more than people realize, especially with receivers. Basketball requires a nonstop motor.

When I was in the fifth grade, I loved playing offense and defense in basketball. I'd sit at half court, wait for an opponent to dribble toward me, and steal the ball before he knew what hit him. I once scored 49 points in a game that year, mainly by using that tactic. I also didn't handle it well when my coach pulled me. When he found me sobbing on the bench, I explained that I was hoping to hit 50.

That's another great thing about basketball: It's easier to play when you're younger. If we wanted to play football, we had to find a bunch of guys and then search for a field big enough to accommodate all of us. If we wanted to play baseball—which was boring as hell—we had to find bats, balls, gloves, and some base paths. When it came to basketball, all we needed was free time.

There were many days when I'd grab some friends, pile into a car, and drive to someplace like Dayton or Cincinnati for a game. We'd go out to the suburbs and challenge middle-class kids. Being from Ohio, everybody knew that football was the most popular sport in the state. But in my neighborhood, with all the influences I had around me, basketball was a lot more fun.

My attraction to the game also had plenty to do with Butch's success. He's seven years older than I am and he was always the father figure in our home. Since my mother worked a bunch of odd jobs to support us, he was the one who became the leader when she was gone. He had that same sense of responsibility on the court. A 6'5" shooting guard, Butch made a point of playing the right way all the time, whether it was being fundamentally sound as a shooter, setting solid picks, or moving efficiently without the ball.

Since Butch was a by-the-book kind of player, it made perfect sense that he signed to play for a by-the book coach, Bob Knight, at Indiana in 1976. However, I didn't like the decision one bit. It's not that the Hoosiers weren't good—Indiana was a college powerhouse at the time, a national championship team coming off the last undefeated season in college basketball history. It's just that everything about that squad screamed conservative. Their uniforms were basic. Their style of play was slow. The only thing I did like about the Hoosiers was their waffle-toed Adidas shoes.

Along with looking corny, I also felt like my brother wasn't going to get a fair opportunity to shine at Indiana. He was the best player in Ohio when he graduated, but Knight had also signed the best player in Indiana (Mike Woodson) and two of the best from Illinois (Glen Grunwald and Derek Holcomb). I wanted my brother to continue being the star I'd watched in high school. I didn't want him sitting on the bench for a team I didn't like in the first place.

Butch eventually wound up enjoying a successful career at Indiana—he started his final two seasons—but his time in Bloomington had a notable downside for me: He became an even bigger stickler about the finer points of basketball. Butch was always riding me about my game. He'd tell me to tuck in my shirt, to make the right pass, to stop worrying so much about wearing fancy shoes. One day I got so irritated with him that I asked him point-blank: "Have you actually seen me play?"

That same lack of recognition even extended to Butch's school. When I attended Indiana's basketball camp as an eighth grader, I dominated the competition. I was the best player in the one-on-one drills, the three-on-three competitions, and most of the individual fundamental categories. But when the camp ended and the coaches called all the players together to pass out awards, I didn't get one single T-shirt or trophy from Coach Knight. I was fuming as I sat there in the crowd.

Butch later told me that I couldn't receive any awards for my play because I had attended the camp for free (since I was a player's relative, they found odd jobs for me to do around campus to pay for my attendance). I was done with Indiana after that. I didn't like the idea of Butch being there and I definitely couldn't stand the place after being shafted at that camp. I was so down on that program that my mother wouldn't even let Coach Knight recruit me once I became a high school star. She knew I had way too much mouth to spend four years in a program that rigid.

Butch and I were always different in that way. He wanted structure where I coveted freedom. He was stoic and quiet where I was outgoing and loud. Some of that probably comes down to one guy being the oldest kid in the family and the other being the youngest. Butch constantly felt the urge to give me advice on everything, to basically fill the void created by an absentee father. I always wanted to do my own thing, which meant there was a good chance I wouldn't listen to him most times.

The only good thing about Butch being at Indiana—at least from my perspective—was the exposure I had to some of the greatest players in basketball history. He actually helped recruit a 6'1" super-quick guard from Chicago named Isiah Thomas to the school in 1979. Since I was a high school and college basketball junkie in those days, I knew all about the player whom nobody could check. In fact, I could tell you everything about the stars coming out of Chicago, New York, and Washington, D.C., back then. That's where all the best players seemed to be competing in the late 1970s.

Isiah was so gifted that my brother used him as an example of why I should start thinking about a career in football. Butch said that any guard who was small should use Isiah as a barometer of his talents, and he wasn't sure if I could measure up to that high standard. I thought it was all nonsense.

"I'm bigger than Isiah," I told Butch one day.

"Yeah, well, he's better than you," he responded.

Of course, Isiah went on to be an All-American, the leader of the 1981 Indiana national championship team, a twelve-time NBA All-Star, and a two-time NBA champion with the Detroit Pistons. But I had so much ego and talent that I couldn't imagine not doing similar things. By the time I was midway through high school, all the Big Ten schools were recruiting me, and I also was considering Kentucky and Louisville. I was good enough to earn an invitation to the five-star basketball camp when I was fifteen, which gave me a chance to see all the great players I'd read about in other cities.

I'd be eating lunch and see Michael Jordan working in the cafeteria. Patrick Ewing might be cleaning up or Kenny Smith might be busing a table. Since those big-name players attended the camp for free, they had to work to pay for their entry fees. That didn't mean I lost respect for them. I remember watching Jordan play and then coming home to rave to my family about "this super-dark black guy who was the greatest player I'd ever seen."

What I didn't know was that my own brother was talking me up to some of his friends. The Los Angeles Lakers selected Butch in the second round of the 1980 draft. He wound up playing on a team that had won an NBA championship the previous year with Magic Johnson—who played against Butch while at Michigan State before becoming the first overall pick in the 1979 draft—and sharing my exploits with his teammates. When I met Magic for the first time, during Butch's rookie season, he immediately said, "So you're the guy I've been hearing about for years."

I was so stunned that I didn't know what to say. "Yeah," Magic continued. "Your brother has been telling me how good you're going to be for the last couple years."

What Magic didn't know was how much I was using Butch as my own standard for my career. I never really wanted to be my older brother because I didn't think it was possible. I wanted to be better than him. I saw all the great things he was doing in his career and I realized how much competition was out there. If I was going to be special, I had to have a mean streak to my game. Thankfully, I never had a problem with being tough.

Whenever I played in high school, I'd drive people crazy because of my love for physical contact. I'd pick a guy up on the opposite baseline and stay in his face all the way down the court. I'd drive into the lane with no fear of taking shots, just to take on bigger defenders. And I had no problems fouling people. More than once, I heard an opponent say, "You're not playing football out there."

The hell I wasn't. I knew toughness—both physical and mental—was something players either have or don't have. I just didn't know that it would be more valuable to me in football.

I have to believe most NFL receivers grew up with a similar love of basketball. If you're talking about black receivers, I'd argue that it would be hard to find somebody who wasn't attracted to the game. If you're blessed with a body that is long and angular, you're already well suited to compete in basketball. Add in other qualities that many receivers possess—such as quickness, body control, and explosiveness—and you're going to be a natural.

In fact, it's easy to take the skill set of a basketball player and apply it to football. Butch used to tell me that all the time when I was in high school. He'd say, "You can be a small guard and try to be Isiah Thomas, or you can be six-three and play like somebody much bigger in football with your leaping ability." When I thought about it that way, it made a lot more sense.

A 6'2" or 6'3" athlete is small on a basketball court. Put that same person on a football field and he becomes one of the biggest players out there. The only hurdle for basketball players making that transition to football is learning how to be more physical. Most guys who spend their lives playing basketball generally don't like getting touched.

When you find a top-flight athlete who has that combination of physical and mental toughness, look out. It's hard to find a defense that can actually deal with him. It's just impossible to produce enough defensive backs who have the height, speed, and quickness to keep up with him. I've been around football for more than thirty-five years and I can count on one hand the number of defenders who've had that rare skill set.

"I'll always take a good basketball player who plays receiver," said Brian Billick. "A receiver with straight-line speed is limited. But a guy who understands basketball has a feel for how to use his body in space. That's a huge asset when you're asking guys to find holes in zone coverage or make tough catches in traffic. It's like the old adage in basketball. 'Do you want a good small guy or a good big man?' I'll take the big man every time if everything is equal."

That's why I've always said that somebody like LeBron James would've been a terror on the football field. He was about 6'6" and 225 pounds during his junior year at St. Vincent–St. Mary High School (in Akron, Ohio) and he was a two-time All-State receiver. A broken wrist was the only reason LeBron didn't keep playing as a senior. If he had wound up in the NFL instead of becoming a 6'8", 250-pound NBA star, who knows what kinds of problems he would've caused across the league.

The fact that you can rise so quickly in basketball is what also makes it so appealing to future football players. I was playing basketball with my brother Butch and his college friends by the time I was in ninth grade. LeBron was probably playing with adults even earlier. There's no way you could do that in football. There simply aren't that many teenagers who have the physical maturity to take on older guys.

It's also easier to prepare for basketball. You can get in tremendous shape if you play three or four hours every day of the week. When it comes to football, you have to lift weights and work on specific drills. Talk about boring. In football you spend your summers slaving away in intense heat so you can handle the physical demands of the sport come fall.

When I was preparing to attend Ohio State, I remember the training staff sending me a list of workouts I had to follow in the summer before my freshman year. My routine included lifting weights on certain days of the week, running on most others, and also an assortment of fundamental drills. I'm not talking about one sheet of paper, either. I'm talking about an oversized binder that would cover the three months between my high school graduation and the start of training camp.

I would've been overwhelmed if I hadn't peeked at the last page of that booklet. That's where I found the information about all the conditioning tests we'd have to perform before we started practice in Columbus. So I thought: (1) I could follow that routine every day because that's what they told me to do, or (2) I could train for those tests because that's how they were going to evaluate me. It wasn't a difficult choice. I didn't catch a ball. I didn't do any drills. I just got myself ready for those tests and enjoyed the rest of my summer.

What I knew even then was that I wasn't going to thrive by having the best bench press or the fastest time in the 800-yard shuttle run. My job as a receiver was to be a difference-maker. If I could use all the qualities that made me a top high school basketball recruit—and not be intimidated by older athletes looking to take my head off—I could make a name for myself. My suspicion is that plenty of other bigger receivers were thinking the same way as they were coming up in the 1980s.

If you looked at the NFL in the 1970s and 1980s, you saw a common denominator among many receivers: They tended to be on the shorter side. Future Hall-of-Famers like Charlie Joiner, Steve Largent, and Lynn Swann were all 5'11". Dan Marino rose to prominence in Miami by largely throwing to two 5'9" targets (Mark Duper and Mark Clayton), while Joe Gibbs built his potent offense in Washington with the help of diminutive targets like Charlie Brown, Gary Clark, and Ricky Sanders. Once a handful of teams installed the run-and-shoot, you saw a need for even smaller receivers.

The rationale behind shorter receivers in those days was simple: The smaller they were, the quicker they were. Nimble receivers had a better chance of separating from slower defenders, and that meant quarterbacks had more openings to throw into on-pass plays. It was hard to argue with that logic. There were plenty of productive receivers in the 1980s, many of whom didn't stand a shade over six feet.

What was easy to miss, however, was the way basketball was influencing an entire generation of younger receivers. People who follow college basketball and the NBA realize that there is no more critical era to the popularity of either sport than the 1980s. March Madness blew up during that decade, with nearly every NCAA tournament featuring games that ended on buzzer-beaters and dramatic championship finals. The Big East conference was prime-time, must-see television, and dominant programs like Georgetown, North Carolina, and Louisville excited fans nationwide.

The NBA was even bigger. The emergence of Magic Johnson and Larry Bird helped the game explode as the rivalry between the Lakers and Celtics captivated people across the country. Nearly every team had a charismatic superstar, including Detroit (Isiah Thomas), Philadelphia (Charles Barkley), and Atlanta (Dominique Wilkins). Of course, the Chicago Bulls had Michael Jordan, who was well on his way to becoming an icon.

I liked watching the NFL but I loved following the NBA. Pro basketball just seemed to have far more personality. Magic would come out for a Lakers game and it wouldn't be his 6'9" size that would blow you away. It would be his energy. The man was always smiling, laughing, and apparently having the time of his life on that court. You couldn't tell me that he didn't make that sport more appealing.

If you turned on a game between the Oakland Raiders and Pittsburgh Steelers back then, all you saw were oversized men running around with helmets on. If you watched the 76ers taking on the Lakers, you'd probably see Dr. J dunk on somebody or James Worthy soaring through the lane. Once the dunk contest became the signature event during the NBA's All-Star weekend in the 1980s, that league had young black athletes in its back pocket. It was only a matter of who would be gifted enough to actually make it all the way to the highest level of the sport.

That was always the lone rub of basketball, as Butch reminded me in my high school years. There simply weren't enough jobs in the NBA to accommodate all the players who ultimately would chase that dream. Football was always the more practical sport for somebody with my dimensions. The longer I competed, the more I realized that other players had given up on their own hoop dreams for similar reasons.

It would be hard for players to admit it today, but I'd bet there are plenty who wish they could be in the NBA. If you went into any NFL locker room and posted a sign-up sheet for a b-ball charity contest, you'd have people lining up to add their names. Most of those players probably either grew up with the sport or admired those who played it at a high level. They know how the game revolves around energy and athleticism and that it's an easy sport to love for a lifetime.

When I came into the league in the late 1980s, it was common for many teams to have a group of veterans who would play basketball together in the off-season. The New York Giants had a squad that traveled around New Jersey. The Dallas Cowboys were so into their team that they chartered a bus to roam around Texas for games that paid $700 to $800 per man. We weren't that sophisticated in Philadelphia but we had a damn good squad of our own. We also didn't waste any time in the off-season getting out to let people see our talents.

Tight end John Spagnola was the player who organized our games, and our team usually consisted of our best veterans. We had massive defensive linemen like Clyde Simmons, Reggie White, and Jerome Brown working the frontcourt. On the wing we'd have receivers like Kenny Jackson and Mike Quick, along with defensive backs like Eric Allen and Wes Hopkins. I'd work out of the backcourt and we'd also have running back Keith Byars and tight end Keith Jackson in the mix.

We had size, quickness, confidence, and no shortage of teams to challenge. We'd drive to Harrisburg for the night to take on a bunch of police officers. We might head over to Kutztown the next day to compete against some teachers. We always put the word out for towns to round up their best talent. The better the games, the better we were paid in the long run.

On average, we'd get about $500 a night back then, which amounted to $8,000 to $10,000 a summer. It doesn't sound like much by today's standards but it was plenty good for a twenty-four-year-old man who was rolling like I was in those days. When you're trying to buy drugs, it always helps to have some spare cash. I wasn't paying any taxes on it and the dealers weren't interested in taking credit cards. I also had a sporty little Nissan 300 back in the day.

My week was pretty simple back then. We'd go through our off-season workouts from Monday through Thursday and then we'd travel for basketball on Fridays and Saturdays. There weren't any issues with the coaches or the team, either. They knew we were more talented than anybody we were playing. They realized we wouldn't take unnecessary risks with our bodies.

When I look back on those days, I can see why the teams started to find bigger receivers. There were many players who surely saw the obstacles involved in pursuing basketball careers. It's pretty difficult to make an NBA roster, unless you are insanely talented. As I learned from my own experience, there are far more opportunities to stand out on a football field if you have size and athletic ability.

By the early 1990s, you started to see a greater demand for bigger receivers. The first two wideouts taken in the 1991 draft were 6'4", 210-pound Herman Moore (by Detroit) and 6'3", 210-pound Alvin Harper (by Dallas). Four years later, two of the three receivers taken in the first round of the 1995 draft were 6'3", 220-pound Michael Westbrook (by Washington) and 6'4", 218-pound J. J. Stokes (by San Francisco). You also had other young talents—players like Cincinnati's Carl Pickens (6'2"), Houston's Haywood Jeffires (6'2"), and the New York Jets' Rob Moore (6'3")—emerging as stars.

"Bill Walsh used to say the perfect receiver for his offense was six-two and 215 pounds," said former 49ers safety Merton Hanks. "He wanted somebody who could take the hits on all those inside routes they ran in the West Coast offense. As the nineties progressed and the passing game opened up, every team had to take a position on receivers. If they couldn't find that guy with exceptional speed, they were looking for that basketball-player type who could box out and go get the football. Most of the first-round picks at receiver taken from the mid-nineties on were averaging six-three or six-four."

This trend wasn't just coincidental, either. Taller receivers such as myself, Michael Irvin, and Jerry Rice were producing huge numbers. Deion Sanders also had been such a dominant defender that it was becoming impossible to find receivers who could separate from him or other elite players like Eric Allen, Darrell Green, and Rod Woodson. Great size was the only thing cornerbacks didn't have in abundance. Kansas City's Albert Lewis was one of the tallest at the position and he was 6'2".

It is simple logic. As much as coaches and quarterbacks valued separation in the 1980s, many receivers in the 1990s would be defined by the same skills that characterized players in basketball. Bigger wasn't just better. It was vital to some teams who understood a basic principle about football: The easier the job is for the quarterback, the more productive an offense becomes.

Suddenly, a receiver didn't need to blow by a cornerback to make a big play. It also didn't matter if the coverage was tight. A savvy receiver knew how to position his body against the defender to create room for the catch. Even though I didn't have exceptional speed, I understood that football is a game of lines and angles. If you can manipulate those aspects to your advantage—and you have the sense of anticipation that you develop playing basketball—you can impact games without being a burner.

Drew Pearson once said that Michael Irvin was a master at using his long frame to ward off defenders for receptions. "Michael brought so much physicality to the position because of his size," Pearson said. "The defense knew what routes he was going to run. He was going to run a deep in, an out, a slant, or he was going deep. But he was so physical that it was hard to stop him. If a defensive back came up to jam him, he relished the opportunity. And he knew exactly how to shield himself to make a catch over the middle. Sometimes, he'd take the hit and use it to propel himself up the field."

"You could really see how basketball influenced guys at that point," Allen said. "Players like Michael Irvin had such big strides when they ran that they had to find another way to be dominant. So they basically started rebounding. Once you got into the red zone, they'd box you out and go up and get the ball. That's where you really saw them exploiting their basketball skills. Everything used to be about speed with receivers and it was all about how fast a guy could run. When all these big receivers started coming into the league, it wasn't just about forty times anymore. The big question became how high a guy could jump."

If there was one season that really exemplified the push for bigger receivers, it was 1995. It was a crazy season statistically because a league-record nine different players caught at least 100 passes. I actually caught 122 passes for the second consecutive season, but Herman Moore broke my record with 123 receptions of his own. Of the top five receiving leaders that season, four were 6'2" or taller. Of the top ten receivers that season, nine were wideouts and only two (Atlanta's Eric Metcalf and Detroit's Brett Perriman) were shorter than 6'.

We had a great thing going in Minnesota because I was playing at my highest level and Jake Reed had caught 157 passes between 1994 and 1995. The only downside was that my basketball days ended when I signed a long-term contract in 1993. The Vikings pretty much told me that they knew I played a lot of basketball in the off-season. They assured me that I wouldn't be receiving certain guarantees in my contract if I continued doing that.

That is the price of being a true professional. I'd given up basketball when I knew football was the best way for to me to earn a living in sports. I gave it up again so I could continue enjoying the life I'd created for myself. It wasn't so bad. I learned to appreciate other ways of staying in shape in the off-season.

I also soon realized that size wasn't the only thing that was starting to separate receivers from one another. The world around us was also changing in ways that seemed subtle at first but ultimately proved to be substantial.

The mid-1990s were significant for receivers for one key reason: Television changed. More specifically, the NBA changed. The NFL had been America's most popular sport throughout the 1980s, but pro basketball had given it some serious competition. The presence of Magic, Bird, and Jordan brought more eyes to that sport than it had ever known.

We need only look at the numbers. No NBA finals game had a rating above 10 from 1978–81. The public interest in the sport was so weak in 1980 and 1981 that CBS aired the league finals for both years on tape delay. It wasn't until Bird and Magic ignited the Celtics-Lakers rivalry that the NBA's popularity exploded. And when it blew up, plenty of people couldn't get enough of it.

What NBA commissioner David Stern realized then was something the NFL really had yet to embrace: Stars matter. If you had enough players like Magic, Bird, Jordan, Isiah, and Barkley, you could appeal to a younger audience. The speed of the game was mesmerizing, the sheer physical ability of the top stars mind-blowing. The NBA, more than any other sports league, was fresh, exciting, and most definitely hip.

When I left Ohio State and joined the Eagles in 1987, I thought there was tremendous freedom in the NFL compared to college. Guys would spin the ball in the end zone when they scored. Others would spike it if they felt the urge. You definitely got to be more of yourself in the NFL, but the NBA was an entirely different level. You watched those dudes and it seemed like they were rock stars.

The perfect example of that was the Dream Team, the squad that featured the NBA's greatest players at the time competing in the 1992 Olympics. Those guys were so beloved that they literally had opponents begging for autographs and photos before and after games. They had throngs of fans following them wherever they went and surrounding their buses in Barcelona. That team proved that basketball had a growing global popularity that football couldn't match. People generally had an easier time connecting with the players in that game.

The problem, however, was that the NBA couldn't sustain the crazy popularity it enjoyed forever. When Bird and Magic left the league in the early 1990s, Jordan was still there to drive fans' interest. But when he abruptly retired from 1993–95, the NBA's appeal dipped as well (although it instantly surged upon his return). That also happened to be the same time that Fox Sports was making a huge push into pro football. Its timing couldn't have been better.

Fox first had tried to purchase NFL broadcasting rights in 1987, when ABC was waffling on whether it wanted to renew its contract to carry *Monday Night Football*. But Fox didn't have enough clout at the time to sway the NFL into partnering with it. When 1993 rolled around and the league was negotiating new TV deals, Fox wasn't going to be denied. It bid $1.58 billion for the rights to air NFC games on its network. The offer was approximately $100 million more than what CBS had been willing to pay to continue carrying the same games.

Fox wasn't just bold with its cash, either. Once it ripped the NFC away from CBS, it immediately created a new approach to broadcasting pro football. Rupert Murdoch, the media mogul who owned Fox, hired David Hill to run his sports coverage, and Hill decided that the NFL's entertainment value needed to increase. While other networks had been more conventional in their coverage of pro football, Fox was going to make the game more fun.

Fox didn't do that solely with gimmicks, special effects, and the hiring of big-name broadcasters like John Madden. It did it with the same model that drove the NBA to such great popularity: It started focusing on individuals. "There was a concerted effort to put the emphasis on stars," said Fox sideline reporter Pam Oliver. "It was discussed. It was premeditated. And the approach was that the glamour guys got the attention. Our boss [Hill] didn't know American football that well, but in his mind, you made stars and you kept them in the spotlight. That was how you covered football."

It already helped that Fox was connected to a conference that featured huge media markets like New York, Chicago, Dallas, Washington, D.C., and San Francisco. It also meant plenty that the NFC was stocked with powerhouses at the time, as the Giants, 49ers, Redskins, and Bears had accounted for the last nine Super Bowl winners before Fox bought into the league in 1993. What also couldn't be denied was the star power in the NFC when Fox began broadcasting in 1994. Even if Fox solely focused on the Cowboys (Michael, Troy, and Emmitt) and the 49ers (Deion, Jerry, and Steve Young), there were plenty of capable celebrities for the cameras to follow.

Fox was so into promoting Deion that it actually ran a weekly series early in the season that followed him and Eric Allen. The idea was to determine which cornerback was the best in the league and it drew some legitimate interest. When the 49ers finally played the Eagles during week three of that 1994 season, a picture of Eric and Deion graced the cover of *TV Guide* (yeah, I know: *TV Guide*).

"It was great for the top one or two percent of the league," Allen said. "Fox didn't only care about telling people who was going to win the game and why. They also wanted the fans to be able to interact with players in a different way. You had people coming to the facility to do interviews and ask questions leading up to the game. They wanted to know how you grew up, what you did in your spare time. We were never doing that before. Nobody cared about what was happening during the week."

That's because, as Oliver pointed out, "there was an arrogance to [how networks covered pro football] back then. People had their nose in the air about it and they believed it had to be driven by important talk. A lot of guys would go on television and use all sorts of jargon to make themselves look smart." Fox, on the other hand, wanted as much personality as it could find.

"My network definitely contributed to that mentality," Oliver said. "There was such a fabulousness to our shoots. They were glitzy and they were expensive, and we weren't afraid to spend fifteen thousand dollars on one shoot. That was a lot of money for something like that, but the mind-set was that these things were going to be well produced and well edited. We wanted to make these guys look good."

It seemed natural that quarterbacks would demand the bulk of the attention with such a push toward celebrity. But you can bet that plenty of receivers saw the value in what Fox was selling as well. No position was better suited to play to the cameras, especially because of the combination of speed, acrobatics, and big-play potential. Add in some of the growing personalities in the sport and it was a no-brainer as to which group of players would eventually steal the show.

As Fox drew larger audiences to its coverage, reporters like Oliver eventually noticed a change in how athletes prepared for potential interviews. "You would get notes from public relations people before we came to town," Oliver said. "They wanted to know when we were coming so the players could get a haircut or look better than they normally would. It became a big deal for some guys."

Fox wasn't the only network looking to make a big splash. ESPN had become a bigger player on television in the late 1980s and early 1990s, and its signature show, *SportsCenter*, was a huge hit by that point. Driven by sensational highlights and entertaining broadcasters like Chris Berman, ESPN had a view similar to Fox when it came to showcasing the NFL. The scores only mattered so much. What fans really cared about were things they couldn't keep their eyes off.

Instead of focusing solely on the game of football, players suddenly had a broader platform to express themselves and build their own reputations. "If you look back at guys like Jerry Rice, Mike Quick, or other receivers from the eighties, they basically went about their business," Allen said. "They weren't focused on what was going to happen post-career. That all changed in the nineties. When guys like Michael Irvin came along, they were thinking about what was going to happen while they were playing and when they were done with the game."

Added Warren Moon: "Once TV really started to take off [in the nineties], receivers had more opportunities to be spontaneous and expose themselves more to a larger audience. And once some players saw how much attention certain guys were getting, it made other people want to get in on the act."

I could see that happening across the league. Though Michael Irvin and I were the first receivers to start celebrating receptions that led to first downs—we'd both lunge forward and extend our arms to mimic an official's signal to move the chains—there were more receivers trying to pump themselves up. I doubt any of it was planned or rehearsed in practice. More often, it seemed like receivers doing what they usually do—enjoying the chance to do something productive on the field.

That spontaneity was a nice addition to the game and it had to make all the TV networks feel good about where the entertainment aspect of the game was heading. By the end of 1995, the NFL had reached a critical point when it came to marketing the game. It had more broadcast money than ever and more networks lining up to get in on the action. What it needed—even if the league didn't openly say it—was more stars. In a couple of years, it would have more than it had ever imagined.

CHAPTER 7

A New Breed

was thirty years old heading into the 1996 season, and some huge changes came with leaving my twenties behind. My family—Melanie and my children, Duron (who was four at the time) and Monterae (two)—had grown. I had been maintaining my sobriety. My faith in God had deepened after everything I'd been through before that point in my life. I also had the comfort that comes with financial stability in the NFL.

When I came home at night, I generally didn't have to fret about my contract. I could enjoy my time with my family and I often did. Wednesdays were the only days that were especially hard because the team had its longest practices of the week that day. But whenever I came home, my kids waited until I was asleep on the couch, and they'd curl up with me. Duron would shimmy his way between my legs. Monterae would crawl on top of my chest and lie quietly.

I cherished those moments because so much stress comes with a job in pro football. It's not like the NBA or Major League Baseball, where guaranteed contracts and larger salaries ensure that players make their money regardless of what happens. It also isn't like golf, tennis, or some other individual sport that allows any accomplished player to reap huge endorsements. NFL players can be here today and gone tomorrow. Your employment status can swing dramatically on one bad game and an irritable head coach.

I'd seen it happen plenty of times. I'd be playing cards with a guy in the Vikings locker room one day and then I'd come in the next and his locker would be empty. Somebody across the room might ask, "What happened to Bob?" and I'd say, "Bob got cut." That's when you'd probably hear somebody else say, "He did? He owed me fifty dollars."

In Minnesota, we dealt with the uncertainty of the game by keeping our locker room as structured as possible. If you were a veteran guaranteed to make the team, then you had a locker on the edges of the room. If you had enough clout—such as myself, Randall McDaniel, or John Randle—then you had access to a second locker where you could house all the stuff that overflowed out of your original space. After that, everybody else was stuck in the lockers placed in the middle of the room. You didn't want to be there very long.

We called that space the mobile home unit and that's where all the unknowns wound up. You had rookies, undrafted free agents, and assorted special teamers all camping out in that part of the room. If the team brought in a group of players for tryouts, they'd dress in that area as well. The main reality of being there was that you could be dumped at any time. The closer a player moved his locker to the edges of the room—the area we called the suburbs—the better he felt about his future in the league.

One such player who started in the mobile unit was a wide receiver who eventually became a major weapon on our team: Jake Reed. Jake stood 6'3", weighed 216 pounds, and had phenomenal straight-line speed. The Vikings selected him in the third round of the 1991 draft, and the hope was that he'd blossom into a big deep threat in our offense.

There were only two problems with that dream: (1) Jake didn't have much sophistication to his game, and (2) he didn't have a ton of confidence. The first issue was easy to deal with. Jake hadn't played in a complex offense at Grambling State. Like a lot of receivers with superior skills, he was good enough to beat defenders mainly off his physical ability. It was hard enough to find players with his combination of size and speed at the top levels of college football. He clearly had domi-

Duron enjoying
his time with the
camera on him.
*From Cris Carter's
personal collection*

49ers fans surely got used to this
sight when Jerry Rice was dominating
the NFL in San Francisco. *Courtesy of the
San Francisco 49ers/Terrell Lloyd*

Jerry Rice only knew how to
play one way: all-out. *Courtesy of
the San Francisco 49ers/Terrell Lloyd*

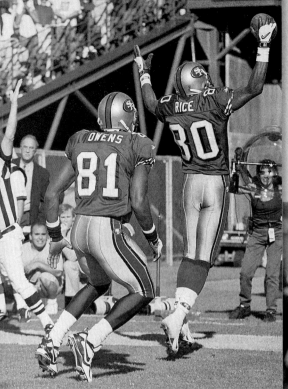

The 49ers were lucky enough to have Terrell Owens blossom at the same time Jerry Rice was entering his final years with the franchise. *Courtesy of the San Francisco 49ers/Terrell Lloyd*

Terrell Owens became better known as T.O. in 1999; the NFL was never the same after that. *Courtesy of the San Francisco 49ers/Terrell Lloyd*

Chad Johnson turned the Bengals into must-see TV with his natural talents and his passion for showmanship. *Courtesy of the Cincinnati Bengals*

This is me going against Tennessee in the 1998 season. *Courtesy of the Minnesota Vikings*

Randy and me doing our thing during our years in Minnesota. *Courtesy of the Minnesota Vikings*

Seattle's Steve Largent went from being an unheralded fourth-round pick in 1976 to being the leading receiver in NFL history upon his retirement in 1989. *Courtesy of the Seattle Seahawks*

Art Monk and the Fun Bunch helped define a new age in football, one where touchdown celebrations became more creative. *Courtesy of the Washington Redskins*

Washington's Art Monk waited so long to make the Hall of Fame—he was passed over seven times—that he received the longest ovation ever upon his induction. *Courtesy of the Washington Redskins*

Randy Moss doing what he usually did in Minnesota—making the difficult catch look easy. *Courtesy of the Minnesota Vikings*

Philadelphia's Harold Carmichael thrived in an era where receivers were happy to catch fifty balls a season and rarely cracked the 1,000-yard mark. *Courtesy of the Philadelphia Eagles*

Houston's Andre Johnson has been a scary sight for defenses since arriving in the NFL—big, fast, and consistently productive. *Courtesy of the Houston Texans*

Atlanta valued the potential of wide receiver Julio Jones so much that the Falcons traded five picks to select him in the 2011 draft. *Courtesy of ESPN*

Lions wide receiver Calvin Johnson has become the NFL's most dominant receiver because of plays like these. *Courtesy of ESPN*

Arizona's Larry Fitzgerald and I doing what we do every summer: finding ways to improve his game. *Courtesy of ESPN*

Calvin Johnson took his game to another level in 2012, when he set an NFL record for receiving yards in one season. *Courtesy of ESPN*

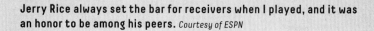

Jerry Rice always set the bar for receivers when I played, and it was an honor to be among his peers. *Courtesy of ESPN*

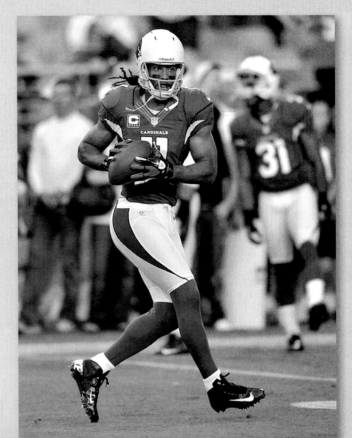

Larry Fitzgerald is widely considered to have the best hands in the business. *Courtesy of ESPN*

San Diego's John Jefferson was the most exciting receiver in football in the late 1970s and early 1980s. *Courtesy of the San Diego Chargers*

nated people during his tenure at Grambling and his strong work ethic gave him great potential at the next level.

The lack of confidence was the harder problem to remedy. Jake caught 11 passes in his first three seasons and the coaches constantly let him know he wasn't living up to expectations. It didn't even matter that he excelled as a gunner on our coverage units. The guy was a third-round pick. They didn't take him that high to chase down punt returners on fourth down.

I know that pressure got to Jake, because there was only so much time for him to actually start producing as a receiver. If he didn't make it happen within his first three years, the team would definitely search for somebody else who could deliver. Denny Green wanted a team that could attack through the air consistently. He couldn't do that if his second-best weapon couldn't overcome his own self-doubt.

I empathized with Jake because there are so many receivers—and players, for that matter—who struggle to find their niche. When that happens, pro coaches will ride players in a way that doesn't come close to what happens in college. A college coach might yell at a player, but he isn't going to strip him of a scholarship that day. A pro coach will say, "I'll send your ass home," and make it happen twenty-four hours later. That's the kind of threat Jake heard on a daily basis.

Jake was also going through the same dilemma many other receivers face. He knew he could play football. He just didn't know if he could play in the NFL. We all go through that when we're making a jump in competition. I still remember how I was stumbling around the field at Ohio State during my first practice as a freshman with upperclassmen.

What Jake had to learn was that there is only one temperament that keeps you in the league: You have to be ready to take somebody else's job. If teams are keeping five or six receivers—typical amounts at the start of a season—then you have to believe that somebody other than you is leaving town during the cut-down process in training camp. It's not cruel. It's not cocky. It's simply survival.

So instead of watching Jake's career evaporate before he ever had a chance to showcase his potential, I decided to do what Denny always asked me to do: be a leader. I spent countless hours talking to Jake about splits, route adjustments, and simple techniques to beat a defensive back off the line of scrimmage. We went through drill after drill to refine his footwork and improve his hands. One day, I also noticed that Jake needed even more help off the field to become a better receiver.

We were in practice before the 1994 season when Jake ran a go route on a defender. Warren Moon dropped back and unleashed a long pass, a throw that seemed destined to hit Jake in stride. But when Jake turned his head to find the football, something about the motion looked awkward. He eventually extended his arms too late and watched the ball glance off his fingers for a drop. When he jogged back to the huddle, I turned to a coach and said, "I don't think he ever saw that football."

I've always had excellent vision, so it's hard to imagine how anyone could catch footballs for a living with bad eyesight. I definitely believed that's what Jake had been trying to do for the first three years of his career. Tom Moore, the Vikings' assistant coach from 1990–93, and I always believed that Jake could be a productive NFL receiver. Now everybody literally could see what had been holding him back.

It's an amazing thing when the light goes on for a receiver that way. One minute he's struggling to get off the line or consistently catch the football. But once he finds himself, he can't wait to attack a defense. As soon as Jake started meeting with specialists and improving his eyes, he started becoming a different player. Once that happened, his entire career shifted in another direction.

Jake caught only 5 passes for 65 yards and started one game in 1993. A year later, he had a career-high 85 receptions and the first of four straight 1,000-yard campaigns. We also developed so much chemistry that we'd switch spots on the field during games to capitalize on a potential matchup. We called it "chasing the ball" and we'd do it whenever one part of the defense was softer in pass coverage than another.

There's little question that my career wouldn't have gone to the next level if Jake hadn't raised his own game. I also felt it was important to help him because of the support I received from Mike Quick, the former Eagles star receiver, when I first came into the league with Philadelphia. Back then, Mike wasn't threatened by a cocky, young receiver with a chip on his shoulder that could've been seen from the Goodyear Blimp. Instead, he saw somebody who needed serious guidance.

Mike used to always tell me, "Cris, just wait—you're going to be a great receiver in this league." He tried to help me realize that goal by teaching me the finer points of the position. One of the first things he said was that I'd never get away with the things I did in college. NFL defensive backs were too quick and too savvy for me to beat them with the same routes that worked at Ohio State. I immediately bought into what Mike was saying because he was too accomplished to ignore. The man had played in five Pro Bowls and earned a reputation as one of the most dangerous playmakers in the game.

Mike offered so much advice on and off the field that I had to pay it forward with Jake. Even when my career exploded in Minnesota, Mike would call and say, "I told you it was going to happen. I told you." Messages like that made me understand how fortunate I'd been early in my career. I couldn't have asked for a better mentor and I could've learned more if injuries hadn't limited him to thirteen games in my final two years with the Eagles. Along with winning a Super Bowl and playing my entire career in Philadelphia, back then my wish was to have the chance to play a full season with Mike.

I don't know if Jake felt the same way about me, but he became my closest friend on the Vikings. I also remember how excited he was when he finally had the opportunity to move from the middle of the locker room to the suburbs. It happened during the 1994 season, when our combined number of catches (207) set an NFL record for receptions by teammates. Jake had taken a huge step forward in his career and earned the same security I felt.

It was satisfying to see a young receiver find his niche in a league where more ambitious wideouts were arriving every season.

Jake may have been open to being mentored, but not all receivers in the NFL were as interested in seeking guidance around that time. I met one such player, New York Jets wide receiver Keyshawn Johnson, in week thirteen of the 1997 season. We had opened that year by winning eight of our first ten games, so there was plenty of excitement about what could happen in the postseason. I also was in the midst of another strong individual year—I'd finish with 89 receptions and 13 touchdowns, so consistency was really defining my career at that point.

Jets receivers coach Todd Haley wanted me to meet Keyshawn before that game in order to help the second-year receiver develop (it was common for opposing coaches to seek out veterans from other teams for such guidance). Keyshawn already had made quite a name for himself off the field. He'd been the first player taken in the 1996 draft and he'd written a book entitled *Just Give Me the Damn Ball!* in the offseason before his second year. The dude had as much bravado as any player to ever line up at the position. His problem was that people knew more about his mouth than his game.

When Haley found me during pregame warm-ups that day, I immediately knew he was frustrated with Keyshawn. "I've got this young knucklehead that won't listen to me," Haley said. "I need you to talk to him." A few minutes later, I watched Keyshawn trudge across the field like a high school student being dragged into the principal's office. I learned later that he'd scoffed at the idea when Haley had suggested it. "That old motherfucker can't teach me shit," Keyshawn told his coach.

At least Keyshawn was more respectful when we finally stood across from each other. Since he was another big receiver—he was listed at 6'4" and 212 pounds—I explained that the toughest challenges for him in this league would be escaping the line of scrimmage and separating from defensive backs at the top of his routes. Smaller receivers had the quickness and shiftiness to shake cornerbacks in tight spaces. Taller wideouts had to work extremely hard to perfect the art of separation.

Now I don't know how much Keyshawn used that information after our brief talk. I also imagine that Haley had him meet a few other veterans whom the coach referred to as "real receivers." The one thing that was becoming more apparent about young receivers during that time was their heightened level of self-confidence. While somebody like Jake had to work himself into a comfort level at the position, a player like Keyshawn arrived with no doubts about what he could do for the game.

In fact, the 1996 draft that featured Keyshawn as its marquee talent would go down as one of the most notable moments in the history of receivers. Along with Keyshawn, four other wideouts went in the first round and eventually became future stars in the league: New England's Terry Glenn, St. Louis's Eddie Kennison, Indianapolis's Marvin Harrison, and Buffalo's Eric Moulds. The next four rounds of that draft produced five more players who would enjoy productive careers, including Amani Toomer, Muhsin Muhammad, Bobby Engram, Terrell Owens, and Joe Horn.

Every one of those players caught at least 500 passes in his career. Four of them (Keyshawn, Harrison, Muhammad, and Owens) had at least 800 receptions. Those are benchmark numbers for the position. You leave the league with that much production and people know that you did some serious damage.

"There were so many guys in that class who went on to become Pro Bowlers and enjoy Hall-of-Fame careers," said Joe Horn. "Being a receiver was the thing to do because there were so many great players at the position. You had Michael Irvin, Cris Carter, Jerry Rice, Andre Rison. I felt blessed to be a part of that class because we respected what the receivers had done before us. And we wanted to take the position to another level."

As great as that class was, I did have some issues with it. First off, I never put much stock in Keyshawn being the first player taken that season. It was a big deal in some circles—he joined New England's Irving Fryar as the only receiver to be taken that high—but the honor had more to do with circumstances than anything else. There wasn't any other player in the draft who was dominant enough to impress teams that year, which is something that rarely happens.

This is no knock on Keyshawn because he had a great career. It's just that a receiver should never be the first pick in the NFL draft. Quarterbacks make plenty of sense because they handle the ball on every play and lead their franchises on and off the field. There was a point where exceptional defensive tackles and left tackles were in such short supply that teams had to select them so early. But receivers? Taking one first overall was like playing with fire, especially one with Keyshawn's skill set.

Once you got past Keyshawn's size and physicality, you realized he didn't have the speed to really devastate NFL defenses. He and I were actually about the same speed and I had always wanted the ability to run faster. My hands, route-running skills, and leaping ability helped me thrive in the league. Blazing speed would've put me in an entirely different category.

I also didn't see Keyshawn as an amazing college player. He had a couple of strong seasons at USC (catching 168 passes during that time) before he came into the league. But it wasn't like he was doing the things Jerry Rice did in college, where his dominance and his numbers blew people away. Keyshawn was an above-average player with a great upside. Those aren't the kinds of guys who end up as the first overall pick in the draft.

The same thing was true of Irving Fryar. There's no way in hell he should've been the top player in the 1984 draft, even if it was great for receivers. The dude caught 40 passes in his senior year at Nebraska. That could've been the result of bad scouting. It could've been connected to the rise of the USFL, which featured Nebraska's Heisman Trophy–winning running back Mike Rozier as its top overall pick that year. All I know is that it made no sense. Fryar wasn't that impressive.

But that's proof of how much the position had evolved. General managers and coaches could make the argument that a receiver belonged at the top of the draft because the state of the game had changed so much over the last two decades. It had reached the point where front-office types were probably sitting around and thinking one of two things: (1) *I have a big-time receiver,* or (2) *I've gotta get one.* Suddenly, receivers were extremely vital to a team's chances for success.

As much as I questioned Keyshawn being taken at the top of that draft, I didn't dispute the talent in that group. I had met Terry Glenn when he was still a star at Ohio State, and he was as good as it got. The concern around Columbus during that time was whether the Buckeyes could replace Joey Galloway, the star receiver who became the eighth overall pick in the 1995 draft. Once Terry started playing, all those questions stopped. He was easily a better college player than Joey was at that stage.

Terry actually reminded me of Henry Ellard, the old Los Angeles Rams star receiver. He had breathtaking speed and incredible body control, and he was a precise route-runner. The only concern I had about Terry was his background. He had a lot of demons, especially since his mother had been in and out of prison and murdered before he was thirteen. I don't think Terry could even talk about some of that stuff until he was in his thirties.

But Terry also got lucky when he came into the league. He wound up playing for Bill Parcells when he went to New England, and he caught 90 passes as a rookie. That didn't just happen because Terry was an exceptional talent. It happened because Parcells is a master at reading people and motivating them. "That's what made Bill special," Haley said. "He was able to coach players hard and let them know he cared about them. And Terry needed to have people who believed in him and supported him because he'd been through hell and back in his own life. If he felt like you were behind him, he was good."

Still, the receiver who impressed me the most from that class was Harrison. At 6' and 175 pounds, he had the speed and the ability to mystify defenders anytime he wanted. Some of that surely came from his basketball background, because Marvin was a dominant player during his high school days in Philadelphia. He used to say that he could make every route look exactly the same when he was on a football field. That efficiency of movement is precisely what enables basketball players to blow by opponents on the court.

Marvin was also a different kind of guy. Being in Indianapolis with a quarterback like Peyton Manning helped him become a special player, but Marvin never cared about the rewards that came with such success. I remember interviewing him once after my career had ended, and he wouldn't even go on camera. It was like the dude was in a witness protection program.

"Marvin didn't even like the spotlight in his own locker room," said former Colts general manager Bill Polian. "We used to joke that he could disappear in plain sight. He'd be there one minute and then the next he'd be gone. When we asked where he went, we'd find him on the field catching passes or running routes or doing something to get better. He didn't want or care about attention."

That definitely wasn't the case with Keyshawn. The Jets quickly learned what they were dealing with when his agent, Jerome Stanley, was negotiating his client's rookie contract. "The negotiator told us the team couldn't pay a wide receiver more than the franchise quarterback," Keyshawn said. "My agent's response to that was that the quarterback wouldn't be a franchise quarterback without this particular receiver. The whole culture of the game was built around the idea that a wide receiver was supposed to catch passes and be quiet and grateful. The quarterback was the only focal point of the team."

When Keyshawn wrote his controversial book, he'd played only one season and caught 63 passes as a rookie. He blasted his head coach (Rich Kotite), ripped a fellow receiver (Wayne Chrebet), and even suggested that his quarterback (Neil O'Donnell) faked a season-ending injury. I actually never read the book, but I will say the title spoke for what a lot of receivers felt around the league. You can bet I was thinking, *Just give me the damn ball*, in Minnesota. Michael Irvin surely felt the same way in Dallas and so did a bunch of other top wideouts. We all felt winning would be an easier goal with the ball in our hands.

What was unique about Keyshawn's bravado was that he put it out there before his production could match his personality. He also did it on a stage where the entire world could hear what he was saying. It wasn't like he had the clout of an Irvin or Rice, both of whom had won championships and made multiple Pro Bowls when that book came out. But here's the key point: Keyshawn carried himself like he expected to reach that level sooner rather than later.

It was a lesson he'd learned from watching Michael Irvin. "I always admired Michael's game, but he was a different cat," Keyshawn said. "Being from the West Coast, I had my own thought process. We weren't wearing mink coats to court because that's something that was probably considered cool in the South. But I saw what he did and decided that I was going to do things my way. If people didn't like it, they could hit the highway. I was the first guy to say, 'Fuck you. Give me the ball or trade me.'

"My thing was that I wasn't going to sugarcoat anything for anybody. I had to be myself. If you draft me and try to turn me into something I'm not, that's going to be a disaster for everybody. The people who got it right had success with me. As for the people who got it wrong, it didn't work out so well for them."

Kotite was one of the first coaches to realize that much. Keyshawn had scored his book deal before the 1996 season ever began, meaning he was going to write something. His perfect scenario would've been a personal diary that chronicled every step the Jets took toward a Super Bowl. Instead, Keyshawn was left to make sense of a 1–15 record that year.

It was taboo to think that a player so young could be so outspoken about so many subjects. The unwritten rule in the NFL was that what happened within the team was supposed to remain private. You might have players or coaches who spoke to the press anonymously, but Keyshawn had a different mind-set. As he said, "Nobody else would say [negative] things even though they were thinking them. They thought you should take the money and shut up."

"There was no fallout to me [for writing the book]," he continued. "Kotite was going to get fired. Bill Parcells was coming in and he didn't care about what had happened the year before. And people were going to write whatever they wanted about me. The one thing the book did for my career is that it made people take notice. They said, 'Who the fuck is this guy?'"

Parcells had some similar questions about Keyshawn after taking over the Jets in 1997. When Parcells agreed to move Haley from the personnel department to receivers coach that year, Haley wasn't exactly thrilled with the opportunity. Haley thought he'd be coaching the quarterbacks. Instead, Parcells told him, "If you can handle the receivers room, you can do anything in this league."

Parcells and offensive coordinator Charlie Weis also were more enamored with Terry Glenn. The Patriots had watched Terry shine as a rookie and they loved his quickness and explosiveness. Keyshawn didn't come close to having Terry's speed. As a result, the Jets weren't sure what to do with him.

"[Parcells] wanted to trade for Terry," Haley said. "He had already gotten [running back] Curtis Martin in a deal with New England and they wanted Terry just as bad. I had to battle for Keyshawn to get opportunities because I knew he'd make me look good. He wound up winning everybody's trust because he was a willing blocker."

Once Keyshawn won the trust of his new coaches, his career took off. Haley convinced quarterback Vinny Testaverde that Keyshawn would make plays in games even if his lack of speed didn't lead to great separation in practice. The Jets wound up running successful toss-sweeps with Martin because Keyshawn was willing to block down on massive defensive ends. Even when the Jets coaches questioned whether it was worth letting Keyshawn run a reverse, he found a way to make it work. He actually scored a touchdown on the first carry of his career.

What was clear about Keyshawn was that he needed to talk and draw attention to himself. "Keyshawn had borderline speed, so he got charged up by running his mouth and putting himself in crisis situations," Haley said. "I think that's how he got his adrenaline going. He wanted that pressure and—like a lot of receivers who come from rough backgrounds—he needed to know he could trust you. I knew Keyshawn would run through a wall for me because I was in his corner. I always tell people that Keyshawn never lied. He just didn't have a filter."

Keyshawn also drew attention from other people around the league. When one of his former college teammates, Chicago Bears wide receiver Curtis Conway, saw Keyshawn wearing a diamond-studded ear-ring during a game, Conway was blown away. The next thing you knew, Conway was calling Keyshawn to see how he got away with it. "Damn, dawg," Conway said. "I'm going to start rocking my shit."

Before long, Keyshawn had endorsement deals and reporters hang-ing on his every word as if he were an A-list celebrity. He also had spawned a cultural shift in his own way. "When I came into the league, you weren't supposed to challenge the coach," he said. "People weren't really doing that. But if you looked at the NBA, it was happening all the time. It wasn't strange to see somebody like Derrick Coleman tell his coach, 'Shut your apple head up and sit down.'"

Now, I've always looked at Keyshawn as a big, goofy kid from Southern California who likes to have a good time. He's not trying to intimidate anybody. He just likes to say whatever's on his mind. I can relate to that candid approach because I'm exactly the same way. And the more I spoke my mind in Minnesota, the more I realized that some people couldn't handle that delivery.

I was the most prominent voice on the Vikings once we reached the 1997 season. We had Pro Bowl–level stars like John Randle and Ran-dall McDaniel, but I was the highest-paid player on the roster. I also had the most juice with our head coach, Denny Green, and our general manager, Jeff Diamond. I was so close with Jeff that we'd play golf on Tuesdays, which was the regular off day in the NFL. Instead of being a player trying to make a name in the league—as had been the case in my early and midtwenties—I was the type of veteran that management approached for feedback on ideas.

While such clout was good for me, it also made some teammates uneasy. I once walked into the team lounge and a handful of younger players immediately stopped their conversation. When I left, I heard one of them say, "You better stop talking when Cris is around. He'll run upstairs [to the coaches and executives] and tell them what we're doing." I had to laugh when I heard that nonsense. As I told them then,

"If you think I'm going upstairs to tell on you, then you're fools. Because they already know everything that you're already doing."

There was another day when I went out to run a steep hill behind our training facility and a couple of teammates looked at me like I was crazy. It didn't make sense to them that an accomplished Pro Bowl player would spend part of his off day sprinting uphill, so they called me "an Uncle Tom." My response to that slight? I told them, "Talk to me when I stop making this money because I know the bank likes dealing with me."

Even today, I hear people talk about how I wasn't close with my teammates and I don't agree with that at all. I pushed my teammates because that's what my role was on the team. Anytime a player is in a leadership position and is as outspoken as I have always been, he's going to rub some people the wrong way. But I didn't know how to do it any differently. Results always come faster when you tell people exactly what you're feeling. On top of that, I trusted my teammates to respond when I needed them.

For example, there were plenty of times when I'd hear other teams' defenders talking about hurting me. Former Denver Broncos linebacker Bill Romanowski said as much before a game once. He kept telling me in warm-ups that he was going to take me out, that I'd better be ready to see my career end. So I didn't hesitate to act. I went over to my offensive linemen and told them to blast his ass whenever they had an opportunity. Anybody who followed through could expect a cash reward afterward.

In today's world, they'd call that a "bounty." The way I came up, it was called "self-preservation." I'd give my teammates a little money to make sure I didn't sustain a serious injury and they made sure I stayed intact. They knew I was an important part of our team's success. And when the games started, it didn't matter that I was tough on players when I felt it was necessary.

My teammates also knew I'd do the same things for them if somebody went after one of my guys. If Deion Sanders came off the edge and took a cheap shot at my quarterback, he knew that I was coming after him at some point. That's what leaders do. They recognize what a team needs and find a way to provide it.

So as much as people might not have liked my style—and even my own wife jokes that I "wasn't nice"—I believed in its effectiveness. I knew the game and I understood the mind-set of players. The average person thinks that everybody in the NFL is trying to win. That's not true. A lot of guys are only concerned with keeping their jobs. And after everything I'd been through early in my career, I took it upon myself to make sure younger players weren't stumbling into the same mistakes.

If I came to practice and smelled alcohol on a teammate, I'd call him out. If we were lining up to run a play and somebody didn't know his responsibility, I'd lay into him. I'd see the same guys playing video games, fooling around at their lockers after meetings, and basically acting like they'd done all the appropriate preparation before screwing up on the field. They had to understand that it wasn't enough to merely show up and go through the motions.

I'm sure some players didn't like that I was so hard on them. Others probably didn't like my devotion to Christianity or my disinterest in hanging in the strip clubs. Some of them didn't realize that I'd had my fair share of running the streets early in my career and it nearly cost me my livelihood, that I came to work every day with an unrelenting commitment and a belief that I was constantly fighting for respect in this league.

There was one thing that didn't go away with the stable family life, the unquestioned financial security, and the increased fame: my desire. Even though I'd reached my early thirties, I still remembered the em-barrassment of entering the league as a fourth-round supplemental draft pick. I still recalled the pain of having Buddy Ryan place me on waivers because he couldn't count on me in Philadelphia. The time I spent with Betty Trilegi was just as motivating. Every day of my life was a battle to stay sober.

More than anything, winning was at the forefront of everything I did. I wanted to do the things Jerry Rice had done when I came into the game, and by 1997 he had three Super Bowl rings. Michael Irvin had been my peer since our high school days and a close friend in the NFL. He had three titles as well. I had even played for a championship-caliber team in Philadelphia, so I knew how a Super Bowl contender looked. We were assembling the pieces in Minnesota, but it felt like we always had major hurdles.

The biggest issue was money. We didn't have the ability to open up our checkbooks like the Cowboys and 49ers were doing back in the day. We had to pick up a role player here or a quality backup there. The marquee franchises threw huge dollars at Pro Bowl–level talent. We built mainly through the draft and prayed that everything came together at the right time.

That reality made it critical that I stay on guys to remind them of how slim our margin for error really was. I didn't have a problem with that role because I've always been fine with being a leader. I also understood that certain players would hold success and consistency against others. I've seen that happen all the time and it will always be part of the game.

I also realized we could only go so far in Minnesota with our talent at that point. We'd had quarterbacks come and go. We'd had different running backs step into the lineup. We'd also had a defense that never became consistent after defensive coordinator Tony Dungy left to become head coach of the Tampa Bay Buccaneers, one of our NFC Central rivals, in 1996. The Bucs were going to improve with Tony in charge and we knew Green Bay, the best team in the division, wasn't going anywhere. They'd won the Super Bowl during the 1996 season and had been upset in the same game by Denver a year later.

If that 1996 draft showed me anything, it was that more young receivers were coming into the league and they could have an immediate impact on their team's success. Some didn't need two or three years to hit their groove. They came in expecting big things and producing them faster than people anticipated. A couple years later, we added a player who would do exactly that in Minnesota.

CHAPTER 8

A Year to Remember

When the 1998 draft approached, the Minnesota Vikings needed two important things if we were going to become serious championship contenders: a pass-rushing defensive end and an accomplished cover cornerback to help our struggling defense. Not once did the idea of selecting another wide receiver cross my mind. I was a perennial Pro Bowler by that point and Jake Reed had blossomed into a dangerous playmaker. We just had set an NFL record by being the only teammates with four consecutive 1,000-yard seasons.

So when Denny Green called on the morning of the draft, I couldn't believe what was going through his mind. We had the twenty-first overall pick that year, which meant it would be hours before we'd know what scenarios we'd be facing. But Denny already had his sights set on one guy. "Randy Moss is the best player in the draft," Denny said in a way that sounded like a kid fantasizing about a long-awaited birthday wish. "And he's going to fall to us at twenty-one."

I told Denny there was no way that was happening, so he might as well not even tease himself. Moss was so supremely gifted—he'd been an All-American receiver and a Heisman Trophy finalist at Marshall University—that somebody was going to draft him before our selection arrived. Denny thought that Randy's reputation as a problem child who'd been dropped by Notre Dame and dumped by Florida State would scare people away. Even if that were the case for most teams, I figured Dallas would snatch Randy with the eighth overall selection.

Cowboys owner Jerry Jones loved to take those kinds of gambles. Plus, he needed to reenergize his team. Dallas had lost its swagger in the late 1990s, long after head coach Jimmy Johnson left town and Barry Switzer had bottomed out as his successor. The Cowboys' biggest stars—quarterback Troy Aikman, running back Emmitt Smith, and wide receiver Michael Irvin—also were all in their thirties. The infusion of a supreme talent like Randy would give Jones plenty of hope for the team's future.

The problem, as Jones told me years later, was Irvin. Michael had been involved in so many off-field issues that Jerry didn't like the idea of having another questionable character learning from him. The way Jerry saw it, it was hard enough to keep Michael out of trouble. If Randy followed in his footsteps, there'd be no telling how shaky the Cowboys' image would be in the aftermath.

Of course, nobody on the Vikings knew any of this that morning. We only knew Randy was special. He was taller than Michael, faster than Jerry Rice, and a gifted basketball player who could've easily played that sport in college. He was far more skilled than Irving Fryar and Keyshawn Johnson—the only two receivers ever taken first overall in the draft—and he had a fierce personality. You could see that in his college tape. Randy Moss wasn't a punk.

The people who watched Randy as a high school star in West Virginia talked about him being the best pure athlete to ever hail from that state. He had the familiar edge of a poor kid who grew up with a single mother and no real relationship with his father. Even when Randy was entering the NFL draft, he projected a standoffish aura. After skipping the NFL combine—his agent claimed that an abscessed wisdom tooth had required immediate dental surgery—some league decision-makers questioned whether his college issues suggested deeper problems as a pro. As then New Orleans Saints coach Mike Ditka told the *Sporting News* after the combine that year: "You create suspicions and doubts as to why [he was not there]. I think he should have come—but that's his business. He's a big boy."

I actually never put too much stock into what happened to Randy at the college level. He certainly wasn't the first young person to do immature things. I'd made plenty of mistakes at the same juncture of my own career. I understood how easily a gifted player could find trouble without the proper guidance.

For one thing, Randy never should've signed with Notre Dame. It's hard enough for African Americans to be at a school like that and Randy, well, let's just say he was a strange fit for that environment. When Notre Dame denied his enrollment after he was sentenced to thirty days in jail for his involvement in a high school fight, he went to Florida State, where he violated his probation after testing positive for marijuana. By that point, Randy was on the slippery slope of becoming an urban legend. As extraordinary as he was supposed to be, nobody had seen him do anything in his first two years of college.

It wasn't until he landed at Marshall that we all saw the range of his talent. The last time I'd seen a college player that dominant on a college football field, the back of his jersey read RICE and he was roasting opponents for Mississippi Valley State in 1984. Moss was also facing Division 1-AA talent during his transcendent junior season for the Thundering Herd, but that didn't matter. As he raced by defenders and out-jumped others for receptions, he was every bit a man among boys.

Those images are what excited Denny so much. And as the 1998 draft unfolded, it became quite clear that several other teams cared less about those memories of Randy and more about his troubled past. Though Randy was a top talent, the first four selections that year were two quarterbacks (Peyton Manning by Indianapolis and Ryan Leaf by San Diego), a defensive end (Andre Wadsworth by Arizona), and a cornerback (Charles Woodson by Oakland). When it came time for Dallas to pick, the Cowboys made the move that supported Denny's hunch: They chose defensive end Greg Ellis.

Once I saw the Tennessee Oilers take Kevin Dyson with the sixteenth pick, making him the first receiver drafted, I knew Denny was smiling somewhere. A few minutes later, he called again. "We're going to get this kid," he exclaimed. "Will you take care of him?"

"Of course I will," I said. "I just need to know all the issues up front. I need to know what I'm dealing with. If there are any issues with his personality, I have to know about it before we get started."

Denny assured me that I'd have all the necessary information. My phone rang again a few hours later, shortly before the end of the first round. This time it was Randy. "Mr. Carter," he said, "I want to work with you and learn from you. I really want to be good." We talked for a few minutes about his coming into the NFL and then we discussed off-season plans.

The first thing I asked Randy was where he planned to be before minicamps started. When he said he'd be in West Virginia until heading to Minnesota, I explained that I didn't train in Minneapolis during the off-season. I brought a group of guys down to work near my home in Boca Raton, Florida. If he wanted to train with me, then that's where he'd have to do it.

Before we finished our conversation, I also let him know that I was serious about helping him be the player he hoped to become. "I don't know how much longer I'll be playing because I'm in the last year of my contract," I said. "But I do believe this will be a lot of fun and hard work. If you listen to me and do everything I say, I'll also make you two promises. First, in about three to four years, you'll be the best receiver in football. And second, all that money you just lost in the draft? I'll make sure you make it all back."

Randy wasted no time in accepting my offer. His agent helped him find a condominium near my home in Boca Raton a few weeks later. He arrived early to the first day of workouts with myself, Jake, and a few other teammates in the sweltering heat of southern Florida. When that morning started—and I had my first glimpse of Randy—I knew exactly why Denny had been so giddy. They had nicknamed Randy "the Freak" a long time ago. When people saw him in person, they saw why that label fit.

Plenty of players claim to be taller than they actually are in real life. Randy was a legitimate 6'4" with hands so large they seemed capable of palming an oversized watermelon. A lot of players have impressive speed when a stopwatch is on them. Randy didn't need somebody clocking him to blow people away with his legs. For a man so long and angular, he had the quickness of a receiver who stood 5'9". He glided in and out of breaks and exploded when he had to go to another gear.

On top of all that, Randy worked as hard as anybody I'd ever known. We did all sorts of routines during those sessions—interval training, explosive training, weight lifting—and he never wilted. We'd have him jumping on boxes and over hurdles and he kept coming back for more. He even committed himself to the weights in ways that he clearly never had before. One day we put him on the bench press and asked him to lift 185 pounds. He couldn't even do one repetition, but he kept trying to improve.

Still, nobody was concerned with Randy's muscles. We all understood that would come in time, that his upper and lower body would thicken the longer he stayed in the league. I just wanted him to feel as comfortable as possible and as prepared for the season as he could get. Denny and his assistants were too excited about his potential to have the game overwhelm him once he arrived in Minneapolis.

The more time I spent around Randy in those early days, the more I sensed that he wasn't going to disappoint. When our offensive coordinator, Brian Billick, called to tell me how great Randy could be, I told him he had no idea what was coming to minicamp in a few weeks.

When Randy worked out in his first minicamp, Billick saw exactly what I meant. "Randy ran a go route and he did it in such a way that I wanted to correct his form initially," Billick said. "But then he ran right by the defender. I was saying, 'No, you can't do it that way,' at first. By the time he was done, I was thinking, *I guess you can.*"

The only hard part of dealing with Randy on the field was managing the expectations he created with his talent. My bigger goal away from the field was building a solid relationship with him. It didn't take a PhD in psychology to know that Randy had serious issues with trust, especially when it involved relationships with men. Like a lot of professional athletes before him, he didn't have any bond with his father and his disdain for authority figures was impossible to ignore.

When I dealt with Randy, I made it clear that I wasn't trying to be his father. I didn't even use the word "mentor" when we started our relationship. I wanted to be more of a big brother to him. I focused on talking to him instead of at him.

It helped that I had a family life that Randy found appealing. When we finished our workouts in Florida, we'd go back to my house, and he immediately embraced the environment. My wife, Melanie, would cook for him. My son, Duron, would play video games with him. Most important, he knew I didn't want anything from him. I had all the stuff that young players crave—stability, success, and peace—and Randy certainly saw the benefits of those rewards.

We also forged our relationship in other ways. Randy was a phenomenal basketball player, so we'd play games whenever possible (and I often reminded him that those activities should never get back to the Vikings because of our contractual restrictions). One day I asked him what he loved to do, and he said fish. So we started catching bass in the waters near my home, and I later bought a boat to take on the nearby lakes in Minneapolis. We'd be out fishing, smoking cigars, and having some good old country fun for hours.

The most important thing I wanted Randy to know was that I was giving him a clean slate. Randy wasn't a bad kid and he wasn't out to hurt anybody. He was simply trying to grow up in a world where he'd always been singled out for his gifts. It's hard to be structured and disciplined when people have always changed the rules to accommodate you.

The longer I was around Randy, the more I saw his dedication and desire to improve his game increase. And the longer I watched him, the more I only worried about two things. My first concern was how Randy would fare once he felt the real glare of NFL life, since rookies often wilted under that kind of pressure. My other concern was how quickly I could get my agent to negotiate a new contract with the Vikings. If this kid was half as good as he looked come fall, I needed to ensure my money was straight before he ever got rolling.

There was no disputing that Randy's talent was going to make up for the team's decision to ignore our defensive needs in the first round of the draft. As soon as training camp opened, he was as smooth and explosive as he had looked in our workouts. What made his skills all the more impressive was a little known fact: Randy had sustained a high ankle sprain while playing basketball earlier that summer. It was an injury that wouldn't heal all season but it still never slowed him down.

I'd never seen a player that big who was so comfortable tracking the football in the air. Randy would run under a deep pass with the same grace a veteran center fielder displays when chasing down a fly ball. He knew exactly when to explode or slow down, when to time his leap to snatch the ball from a defender. Once we taught him to catch the ball with one hand, he pulled off even more moves that would shock anybody who watched him practice.

"Everybody was a little in awe of what was he was doing," said former Vikings center Matt Birk, who now plays for the Baltimore Ravens. "Even in practice, you could tell you were watching something you'd never seen before."

At one point, Billick actually had to alter his offensive rules to account for Randy's skills. Billick always told his quarterbacks that any go route had to meet the 45-and-5 standard, meaning the ball had to travel at least 45 yards downfield and be within 5 yards of the sideline. The idea was to give the receiver enough room to catch up to the football while keeping the throw far enough from the safety, who would be coming from the middle of the field.

Once we had Randy, the 45-and-5 rule became the 55-and-5 rule. A few weeks later, it became the 60-and-5 rule. No matter how far the quarterbacks threw the ball, Randy was too fast for their arms. There were many days when our quarterback, Brad Johnson, would come back to the huddle and say, "I can't believe I underthrew Randy again."

Randy's presence also meant our offense had to make some adjustments. We had been primarily a three-receiver team during Denny's tenure, but Billick had wanted to use a variety of formations in his system. That meant the third receiver had to become accustomed to fewer touches on a weekly basis. Given Randy's talent and my seniority, Jake was the most logical person to suffer in the transition.

I feared that his confidence might be shaken with a demotion, so I pulled Randy and Jake aside one day to offer a suggestion. "We can all stay on the field together if we block," I said. "If we can get in the way of those three defensive backs who have to be on the field with us, we can make this work. I know we all like catching passes, but this is what we have to do. We can do this with blocking."

We knew in training camp that we weren't going to start Randy right away. Along with his tender ankle, Billick also wanted to keep his role as simple as possible. The last thing we wanted was for a player that blessed to be thinking too much about his responsibilities. The entire thought process within the offense? Just let Randy do what he does best.

That worked well throughout the preseason because Randy caught 10 passes for 148 yards and 2 scores. With him and Jake working on the outside, I was able to spend more time in the slot, where I felt most comfortable. In the two previous years, I'd been asked to play more outside in the two-receiver sets. Now we had exactly the arsenal we needed: size, speed, and versatility.

"I looked at the receivers we had in the same way you'd look at building a basketball team," Billick said. "You don't want a whole bunch of guys doing the same things. You want somebody to be your point guard. You want somebody to be your power forward. You want somebody to play on the wing. That year we had a big, physical receiver in Jake, a Pro Bowl talent in Cris, and a guy like Randy who had more speed than the other two could ever hope to have. We knew [Randy] could take the top off the defense."

The closer we came to the season, the less I worried about Randy dealing with the high expectations that followed him. I watched the way he met the challenge of training camp. I noticed how veteran hazing never rattled him. I always tell people that Randy was his own man from the moment he entered the NFL. He also was very thoughtful. He understood how important that first season was for him. Like they say: You never get a second chance to make a first impression.

Randy was so confident in his talents that he even unnerved the coaches with his easygoing nature. On the morning of our season opener that year—a home game against Tampa Bay—our wide receivers coach, Hubbard Alexander, approached me in a panic at the team hotel. We normally checked in for breakfast in the morning, and you had to sign your name in no later than nine A.M., even if you weren't eating. Hub, also known as "Axe," was concerned because Randy never showed. I told Axe that Randy was playing video games in his room when I'd last seen him and he probably just lost track of time.

In truth, I had no idea where Randy was that morning. I didn't run into him until I drove into the Metrodome parking lot. We were supposed to be at the stadium by 10:00 and I saw Randy pull up at 9:58. I joked that he should never be the last player to arrive at work and then I asked if he'd eaten breakfast. He said, "Yeah, I had a Coke and some hot tamales." As soon as he told me that, I knew this kid was a rare breed. A Coke and some tamales before his first NFL game. I'd never heard that in my life.

The only thing more astonishing than Randy's admission was his performance that day. There was no doubt that he had come into the season in tremendous shape; he probably had less than 5 percent body fat on his 210-pound frame heading into week one. The motivation was there as well, as Randy made it clear that he was out to torch any team that hadn't believed in him during the draft. Once the game kicked off, it was also apparent that the Bucs simply weren't ready for a receiver like Randy Moss. The entire NFL wasn't.

We were up 7–0 in the first quarter when Brad Johnson dropped back from the Bucs' 48-yard line. The play had called for Randy to run a post-corner route and he was wide open as soon as cornerback Floyd Young bit on his fake inside. But that wasn't the most impressive part of the play. When Brad underthrew the pass, the defender caught up quickly enough to tip the ball into the air, where Randy snatched it before running through the end zone.

The Dome exploded after that. Randy was running so hard that he jumped into the end zone stands and I sprinted over to hug him. On the replay of the game, you could hear the broadcaster saying, "There are going to be nightmares for cornerbacks in the NFL when they [go] up against Randy Moss." By the time Randy caught his second touchdown pass of the half—this one a 31-yarder—that prediction felt like an understatement.

The Bucs had one of the league's best defenses and they'd always given us fits because Tony Dungy, our former defensive coordinator, was their head coach. On that day that advantage meant nothing. We torched their cover-2 defense up the seams and on the edges, and we did it all because Randy was on our side. He caught 4 passes for 95 yards in that 31–7 win. I'd never seen a guy do so much with so few opportunities.

That obviously wasn't Randy's best game of the season, but it was a definitive moment for wide receivers. Jerry Rice may have been the greatest player at the position, but Randy Moss looked every bit like the perfect weapon for the position. He was too fast to catch, too big to out-jump, and too focused on being as great as he could become. He was what Deion Sanders had been to cornerbacks and Lawrence Taylor had been to linebackers.

Randy was simply once in a lifetime. And the scariest part of all? We were barely making the most of his capabilities.

Whatever people had thought about our team that year, whatever expectations had been placed upon us, they all didn't matter after that season-opening win. In the course of one week, we'd become the most dangerous team in the NFL. Every concern we'd had before then paled in comparison to what we could do. In the blink of an eye, we could blast teams through the air. If Randy wasn't doing it, than Jake and I would make it happen.

We were so good that we didn't even have to worry about who was playing quarterback. Brad breaks his leg in week two? No problem. Randall Cunningham dusts himself off, recharges his career, and sets career highs for passing yards and touchdowns. Our defense isn't strong enough to stop anybody? So what? We'll score enough points that it won't matter how many points they give up.

That actually was our team strategy on offense. Denny wanted us to pile up as many points as possible so every opponent would have to play from behind. The whole idea was to play up-tempo—like a fast-breaking basketball team—and not worry about making mistakes along the way. We knew few opponents had the weapons to match us point for point. Most didn't have anybody who could deal with Randy.

That was never more apparent than when we prepared for a Monday night game at Green Bay in week five. The Packers were the dominant team in the NFC, a squad that had won the conference the previous two years and the Super Bowl during the 1996 season. We were 4-0 and averaging more than 30 points a game. To say there was plenty of hype leading up to this game would be an understatement. We were about to find out how good we were . . . and how great Randy could be.

Our game plan all week was to attack the Packers in the air. We were going to go deep as much as possible and unleash Randy on their secondary. The only problem was the weather. The forecast called for rain, and it poured all day in Green Bay as we wandered around the team hotel. Still, none of that mattered when we had our offensive team meeting during the afternoon. "Check the field when you get out there and make sure you're wearing the right cleats," Billick said. "Because we're still going to bomb these guys."

Randy's first touchdown came on a 52-yard pass from Randall Cunningham. The play called for Randy to run up the left sideline, but he was covered stride for stride by Packers cornerback Tyrone Williams. That didn't frighten Randall, though. He stepped up, hurled the ball downfield, and Randy simply jumped over the top of Williams for the catch. After Williams stumbled to the ground, Randy stepped over him like he was a pile of trash and raced right by Packers safety Darren Sharper to the end zone.

If you saw Williams's reaction after the play, his body language said plenty. He seemed to be wondering how he was supposed to stop that kind of talent. The fact was that he couldn't. Randy was too good and too hyped. At one point, I told him to calm down on the sidelines, to catch his breath and relax in between possessions. He looked at me like I was crazy and then strolled closer to the field. "That's Brett Favre out there, man," he said. "I'm going to watch this."

Randy ultimately caught 5 passes for 190 yards and added another touchdown—a 44-yard score—in that 37–24 win. If the NFL had merely gotten a glimpse of him in the season opener, then the effort in Green Bay that day revealed what was coming the remainder of the year. The more Randy played, the more dangerous he became. It was like watching a great scorer in basketball. You couldn't wait to see what he was going to do next.

The impressive part about all of this was how little Randy was affected by the craziness surrounding him. There were plenty of number 84 jerseys popping up all over Minneapolis, but he never seemed to care about his rising cult status. He was only focused on keeping the promise he'd made the day he'd dropped in the draft. By the end of that season, nobody was ever going to doubt Randy Moss again.

I loved playing with somebody that talented and driven. Whenever I stepped onto the football field, I always committed myself to being the best receiver out there. With Randy on the roster, I had to work harder every day just to keep pace with him. At that point, it was rare for me to find a teammate who forced me to raise my level of play. Randy made the game look so easy that you had to bust your tail to avoid being overshadowed.

Randy was on such a roll that people couldn't wait to see what he would do against Dallas on Thanksgiving. It was no secret that he'd wanted to play for the Cowboys coming out of college. It also had been a major surprise when Jerry Jones passed on him in the draft. Of all the teams that had questioned Randy's future in the league, Dallas was the one he loathed the most. In that entire season, I'd never seen him more ready to play than when we prepared for that contest.

Randy wound up with 3 receptions for 163 yards and 3 touchdowns in that 46–36 win. We ran a flea-flicker on our first offensive possession and Randy raced by everybody for a 51-yard touchdown catch. We came back to him toward the end of that quarter, when Cowboys cornerback Kevin Smith was running with him stride for stride. It didn't matter. Randy outran him for a 56-yard touchdown catch on that play.

Still, it was another 56-yard score that became the play of that game. Randall hit Randy on a quick hitch in the third quarter, a play that should've been nothing more than a short gain. After grabbing the pass, Randy raced down the sideline as if he'd been shot out of a cannon. The only defender who came close to him was rookie cornerback Terry Billups, who had a decent angle to at least push Randy out of bounds. Instead, Randy stutter-stepped quickly—almost a lazy-leg-type move—and then went to another gear before coasting into the end zone.

Now, the scouting report we'd received before the game said that Billups ran the 40-yard dash in 4.3 seconds. Randy made him look as nimble as a sumo wrestler. I'd seen Randy do plenty of amazing things before that point, but that was the first time I realized how fast he actually was. The only player I'd ever seen with that much suddenness was Deion Sanders, who didn't play in that game.

I remember watching Randy after that game and thinking that he was like a runaway train. He munched on a turkey leg awarded to him by Fox as the player of the game. He joked with broadcaster John Madden about how easily he'd torched the Cowboys on national television. This was a rookie playing with a sprained ankle in an offense that was adding more dimensions to his role every week. Those factors alone should've made it obvious to anybody who'd seen Randy by then: The kid was a star.

"We had a great offense that year but Randy opened up so many things once teams saw what he could do," Birk said. "He opened up the run game. He opened up opportunities for other receivers. Every team we played had to pay attention to him because nobody wanted to give up a one-play touchdown drive."

The rest of that regular season felt like a blur after that Dallas win. We were on a pace that would eventually allow us to break the NFL record for points scored in a season. Defenses became so wary of Randy that they'd try desperate acts to defend us. They'd put two defenders on him, then two on me in the slot. At some point, they ran out of personnel to cover all our other weapons.

Of course, we also kept winning. The only loss we sustained during the regular season came in our rematch against Tampa. Aside from that, we rolled through each week so consistently that I had to constantly remind myself of the reality of the NFL. No opponent could be taken for granted. If we went into games without understanding that we could lose, somebody would surprise us. Even the lamest team in the league can pull an upset every now and then.

What scared me most was the state of our defense. We went against them every day in practice, so I knew how suspect we were on that side of the ball. There was a reason why we needed a pass rusher or cover cornerback when we selected Randy in the draft. Those were the kinds of players that made an impact on a defense. And if any team was ever fortunate enough to slow our offense, we would find out whether our defense could handle the challenge of helping us.

I'd never played in an NFC championship game until the 1998 season. There's something to be said for being that close to the Super Bowl. One victory and you're literally living the same dream that every NFL player covets. You control your own destiny. Your chance to stamp your name into history is well within your grasp.

When we walked onto the field to meet the Atlanta Falcons in that year's championship game, I knew this was my best chance to reach the Super Bowl. Most people who followed the league thought highly of our team as well. We were 11-point favorites entering that contest. The

Falcons, while balanced and physical, simply didn't have the firepower we were bringing into that game.

Atlanta knew the only way to stop us was by using any means necessary. "Going into the game, we talked about taking out Cris Carter," said former Falcons defensive end Chuck Smith. "We said that if anybody gets close to him, Randy Moss, or Robert Smith, we had to put a good shot on them. It wasn't like we had money on it but it was a bounty of a different kind. We knew we had a better shot if those guys were out of the game."

When I look back on that game, I always remember two key moments more than any others. The first significant play came late in the first half, when we led 17–7 and called a crossing route for Randy near the Falcons' end zone. Randall put the ball on the money but it simply skipped off Randy's fingers. It was a catch Randy could've made a million times without even a bobble. Instead, his error led to us kicking a field goal on that drive when a touchdown would've put us up by 17.

Later in the half, we had an even worse gaffe. Chuck Smith beat left tackle Todd Steussie around the corner, sacked Randall, and forced a fumble that Atlanta recovered at our 14-yard line. A few minutes later, Falcons quarterback Chris Chandler hit Terance Mathis for a touchdown pass to make the score 20–14 at halftime. Suddenly, the Falcons weren't trying to avoid a blowout. They were thinking about an upset.

Later in the game, we had a hard time staying healthy. We lost two linebackers in the second half while one of our guards, David Dixon, also was injured. If that wasn't bad enough, it seemed that everything that could go wrong did. Gary Anderson, a kicker who hadn't missed a field goal or extra point all season, blew a 38-yard attempt that would've iced the game with three minutes left. Dwayne Rudd, an athletic linebacker, dropped a sure interception late in the game that could've clinched the win. Atlanta also drove 71 yards, with Chandler hitting Mathis on a 16-yard touchdown pass that tied the game at 27 with forty-nine seconds left. Just like that, we had wasted a 10-point fourth-quarter lead.

When a Morten Andersen field goal gave Atlanta a 30–27 overtime win, I trudged off the field with my arm around my older brother Butch. I could barely speak in the locker room, and I sat quietly in my stall for what seemed like forever. Reporters strolled by while equipment managers and other team personnel tried to stay out of my way. I'd never felt so hollow after a game in my entire life. As Chuck Smith said, "I was happy we won but sorry to see that team's season end. They had a great squad. People should've seen that team play in a Super Bowl."

All the excitement of that season—all the great memories—had simply vanished. I knew we still had plenty of talent in that locker room, but I also understood something else: There were no guarantees that we would make it back to that point again. I'd known too many friends who'd gone through similar experiences in their own careers. There was no reason to think, at age thirty-three, that I was promised a return engagement merely because I wanted another shot.

As I tried to deal with my sadness and anger, Randy slowly walked toward me. He quietly sat down, as if unsure of how to say what he wanted to express. Finally, after a few seconds, he spoke. "Thanks, dawg," he said. "Thanks for everything that you did for me."

At that point, I knew whatever I was feeling would pass eventually. I also realized that everything that happened before that loss had been special in its own way. Though I'd never be on a team that had as good a shot of winning a Super Bowl, I'd also never be around a talent like Randy at such an important point in his career. I could've been selfish and only seen that season in terms of what I'd lost. Instead, Randy's words helped me view it in terms of what I'd helped a friend gain.

That year had started with me not even expecting to play with this kid and it ended with him lifting me out of my doldrums. I had spent most of my career focusing on what I could do, how I could help the team, why I needed the ball in my hands. Now I understood that as my time was coming to an end, it was important to make way for a new breed of receiver. Randy Moss's time had arrived, along with a much higher bar for the position.

I reminded Randy of that when we traveled to Hawaii for that year's Pro Bowl. Even though we had missed our opportunity to play in the Super Bowl, it was important that he not let his drive wane. I told him there were probably still people out there who might not believe in him after a rookie season that included 69 receptions, 1,313 yards, and 17 touchdowns. It was up to him to continue making believers out of the doubters. "I got you, old man," he said. "I got you."

To this day, I still tell people that Randy was the most phenomenal talent I ever played with on a football field. People talk about the difference between Jerry Rice and the rest of the receivers in NFL history being vast. Well, the difference between Randy and everybody else that year was that big. I'm talking about the size, the speed, the body control, the hands, and the ferocity.

After one season in the NFL he already looked like the best receiver in the league. Jerry Rice was in his fourteenth season by that point. Michael Irvin was one year away from being knocked out of the game. I was wondering how much longer I'd be playing. At the very least, Randy was capable of breaking any record Jerry would set. Anything less would've been a disappointment.

What I didn't know then was how rare that 1998 season would be in the end. The Randy Moss I'd watched and mentored had seemed destined for bigger and better things, but life doesn't always work out so easily. I learned that by going through my own ups and downs in the NFL. And as Randy eventually proved, he was going to walk his own distinctive path in a league where receivers now reigned supreme.

CHAPTER 9

Randy, T.O., and the Points of No Return

always tell people the same thing when they bring up my four seasons with Randy Moss: I never saw him play bad football during the time we spent as teammates. He kept himself in tremendous shape. He devoted himself to improving his craft every year. He also never stopped producing jaw-dropping numbers or game-changing plays.

What I did notice after Randy's spectacular rookie season was a shift in how he conducted himself. Case in point: An NFC divisional playoff game held in January 2000, the end of his second year. We were playing the Rams in St. Louis and everybody expected an exciting contest. We still had most of the key components from an offense that set a league record for points scored a year earlier. The Rams were doing amazing things of their own during that 1999 season, so much so that their aerial attack had been dubbed "the Greatest Show on Turf."

The game didn't disappoint, either. They hit us with a couple of long touchdown passes to go up 14–3 in the first quarter. We came back with two scores of our own to lead 17–14 at halftime. After that, the game got away from us, with the Rams building a 35–17 lead heading into the fourth quarter. That's when frustration got the best of Randy.

Randy was already on his way to a monster game—he would finish with 9 receptions for 188 yards and 2 touchdowns—but he kept complaining that the Rams defensive backs were holding him. Since the officials never threw any flags in those situations, Randy's anger simmered as the game went on. Then, after a pass play in the fourth quarter, Randy jogged to the sideline to take a break. I knew he was tired because he'd been running long routes all game. I just didn't realize he'd reached his limit.

As Randy sipped on a water bottle, he noticed one of the officials sprinting by him on the field. Instead of simply accepting that he was having one of those days, Randy took things a step further: He pointed the water bottle at the official and squirted it at him. Randy did it so quickly that most people probably didn't even see it happen initially.

Unfortunately, it didn't take long for the evidence to appear. I was jogging off the field when I saw the incident on the video screen inside the Rams' stadium. At that point, I knew this wasn't going to be good for Randy and I'm not talking about the ramifications on that one game only. I was thinking about his reputation at large.

Randy had spent his rookie season trying to prove how much his character issues shouldn't have impacted the way teams thought about him entering the 1998 draft. With one ill-fated decision, he had given his skeptics all the ammunition they needed to say, "I told you so." It really didn't matter that the officials didn't penalize Randy in that particular moment. The NFL hit him with a $40,000 fine (which was later decreased to $25,000), with the court of public opinion weighing in shortly thereafter.

It was a huge mistake for Randy to open himself up to such predictable criticism but he didn't care. His job was to catch passes and make big plays, not earn points for congeniality. In Randy's eyes, that official was keeping him from doing his work. Given how vicious a competitor he was, he probably felt justified in "attacking" somebody who stood in the way of his goals.

The most disconcerting aspect of Randy's disinterest in public perception was that he didn't understand how it could hurt him. Randy Moss was literally the biggest, baddest wide receiver on the planet by the end of the twentieth century. There were plenty of other standouts at the position, including Indianapolis's Marvin Harrison, Buffalo's

Eric Moulds, and St. Louis's dynamic duo of Torry Holt and Isaac Bruce. But nobody had the ability to draw cameras to him like Randy did in the late 1990s.

Part of his appeal was obvious: The man had breathtaking ability. The other factor was easier to miss if you weren't paying attention to how the league was changing at the turn of the century. The 1990s had been filled with future Hall-of-Fame quarterbacks like San Francisco's Steve Young, Denver's John Elway, Buffalo's Jim Kelly, Miami's Dan Marino, and Dallas's Troy Aikman. All those players—and other notable signal-callers—would be out of the league by the end of the 2000 season. Green Bay's Brett Favre was the lone holdover from that golden age of passers.

It would be impossible for the league to lose that much star power at its premier position and not feel the collective impact of it. The networks still needed offensive stars to build their broadcasts around every weekend. The coaches still needed playmakers to make life easier on the younger quarterbacks who were coming up in the game. The stage for receivers had never been more wide open. Regardless of whether players like Randy wanted to embrace celebrity, it was coming in ways that no one could have ever predicted.

I could sense the shift in our own locker room when it came to Randy's power. Things really started to change once we made Daunte Culpepper, our first-round pick in the 1999 draft, the starting quarterback. Randy and Daunte immediately formed the kind of close bond that was predictable for two young men living their dreams in the league. At thirty-four, I saw them as the future of that franchise, the players who wielded the most influence in the locker room.

"A lot of people on the outside thought Randy was a bad locker room guy, but he was a great teammate," said former Vikings defensive end Lance Johnstone. "He had a lot of charisma. He was funny. A lot of young and old guys would follow his lead. People had no idea how hard he prepared. I'm talking about a star who you would see in the offseason working on speed drills when nobody else was around."

Randy was very instrumental in getting Daunte up to speed with the offense. We both helped Daunte understand the concepts that Denny had preached for years, and Randy did a great job of not whining about the football when it didn't go his way. That's something I always impressed upon him when he first came into the league. If you're going to beg for the football, make sure you do it with some detail.

From my experience, the easiest way to get passes called in your direction was to speak to coaches conceptually. I would go off at times, but I wouldn't simply scream about the quarterback missing me. Instead, I'd tell the coaches which plays might work against whatever coverages the defense was using. Randy usually operated the same way. If he was demanding the football, he was often talking to the quarterback or the coaches in a language they understood.

"Randy's football IQ was very high," Johnstone said. "I remember the coaches telling me how they'd prepare all week for an upcoming game but they never really knew what would happen with Randy. He'd always have at least two guys around him and sometimes it would be three. But we wouldn't know that until the game started. Randy was a big part of the adjustments the offense made after the first quarter and at halftime. He'd come back, tell the coaches what he was seeing, and help them figure out how to attack it."

Randy also wasn't afraid to speak his mind more, regardless of whom he was addressing. I remember a moment during that 2000 season, when I ran a route near the sideline while trying to catch a pass from Daunte. At the last second, I saw the safety flying toward me and the ball skipped off my fingers as I went to the turf. When I returned to the huddle, Randy said, "We needed that play. We needed you to make that catch."

I could feel my body tense before he even finished that last sentence. In my mind, the ball wasn't catchable and the defender easily could've decapitated me. I calmed down a few moments later after realizing Randy was expecting the same accountability from me that I'd asked from our other teammates. I was as open to being called out as anybody else, so I eventually said, "You're right."

Randy would've had a different image if more people had seen that side of him. He didn't carry himself like a conventional leader but he knew how to lead in his own way. His problem was perception. Whenever people start looking for bad in you, they're bound to find something. In Randy's case, the hunt had been on from the moment he entered the NFL.

The 2000 season should've been one more brilliant year in what was becoming a Hall-of-Fame résumé for Randy. Daunte's presence gave us a strong-armed, accurate passer who would fit perfectly with Randy's ability to go deep. Randy became the youngest player in league history to reach 3,000 receiving yards and 45 touchdowns in his career. Even though the New York Giants destroyed us in the NFC championship game that season—we lost 41–0—it was hard to argue against Randy being the most dangerous offensive weapon in football.

Instead, it became the year when everything changed for Randy. People remembered that water bottle incident. They remembered how brutally the Giants manhandled us that season. What those same people often ignore is how quickly Randy became linked to another rising star wide receiver in the NFL . . . and how the entire image of the position pivoted on their electrifying talents and enigmatic personalities.

I first met Terrell Owens following the 2000 season. We ran into each other at a celebrity basketball game and I immediately extended my hand to introduce myself. I'd never met the wideout who had become such a talented receiver in San Francisco that the team decided against re-signing Jerry Rice after that year. I also had no idea how vindictive Owens could be whenever he felt slighted.

As soon as I offered to shake his hand, he smirked and lowered his gaze. At first, I didn't know what to say. Then I shrugged my shoulders and kept on walking. It wasn't like my feelings were hurt. If Owens didn't want to be respectful, I didn't need to make nice with him.

It wasn't until a few minutes later that the organizer of the event explained what had happened. Apparently, Owens was still miffed about a postgame interview I'd done after the 49ers beat us in a playoff game back in 1998. After the loss, I'd told reporters that our defense had let us down that day. The 49ers had played without Jerry—he was sidelined with a knee injury—and we still let Owens and J. J. Stokes, another young receiver, make plays against us. "I can understand if it was Jerry out there," I said that day. "But those other guys doing that doesn't make any sense."

From that point on, Terrell Owens—who eventually became known as "T.O."—and I were never meant to be friends, which was fine with me. He wasn't that good when I made that comment after that 1998 playoff game, and he became even more problematic as his star rose. He deserves all the credit in the world for turning himself into a Pro Bowl–level talent after entering the league as a lightly regarded third-round pick in that famed 1996 draft. But no other receiver did more to taint the position than Owens did in the prime of his career.

It wasn't like he gave any indication of being that way, either. When he joined the 49ers, he was a shy, hardworking kid from the University of Tennessee, Chattanooga, a player who called his coaches "sir" and longed to follow in Jerry's footsteps. Owens excited most people back then with his size (6'3" and 226 pounds) and athleticism (he also played on his college basketball team). "He really had humble beginnings," said Steve Mariucci, who coached the 49ers from 1997–2002. "He didn't get recruited much out of high school and he was a late bloomer in college. He was a third-round pick mainly because he had some qualities that made him intriguing."

Still, Owens's potential was undeniable from the start. "I remember [former 49ers safety] Tim McDonald and myself pulling T.O. aside after his first minicamp," said Merton Hanks. "We told him he needed to get with Jerry and mimic everything he does. We told him he was going to be great and that he needed to prepare for what that would be like."

Owens surely dreamed about what that stature could do for his life. His grandmother had isolated him from other children while growing up in Alexander City, Alabama. He didn't know his father lived across the street from him until he was eleven and that was only because Owens had befriended a girl who turned out to be his half sister. Other kids also teased Owens because of his skinny physique and dark complexion. In other words, this wasn't a well-adjusted child who was destined to play nice with others once he grew up.

In fact, the most noteworthy aspect of Owens's background wasn't his brutal experience with loneliness and poverty. It was his relentless desire to be a celebrity. When he was a young pro, you'd hear stories about Owens perfecting his dance moves and chiseling his body in the 49ers weight room during late-night workout sessions. He knew exactly how he wanted to address the world once the spotlight eventually found him.

Owens's first big break came when Jerry sustained a severe knee injury in the 49ers' season-opening loss to Tampa Bay in 1997. Suddenly, the no-name kid who hadn't played much was starting—and producing—for one of the NFL's glamour teams. When Jerry returned the next season, there were questions about how Mariucci would accommodate him and his two younger receivers, Owens and Stokes. They had done a decent job of compensating for Jerry's absence, but Mariucci had only two starters on his offense.

Owens ultimately eased the burden on his head coach with an impromptu conversation in training camp. "He came up to me and said he was okay with being the third receiver," Mariucci said. "He said Jerry could have his old job back and that J.J. had been starting longer. He was good with being the third guy even though he'd caught around sixty passes the year before. He said he'd get his touches. That's the kind of guy he was. He was still Terrell Owens then."

Owens made such steady progress in his first four NFL seasons that the 49ers knew they faced an important decision. Jerry was nearly forty years old and Owens clearly had Pro Bowl potential. So after the 1999 season, the team tried to lock Owens into a long-term deal while he was a restricted free agent. He was making $280,000 in the final year of his rookie deal and he was due a hefty raise. The problem was Owens's sense of what a fair pay increase was at that time.

The 49ers never got anywhere with the initial negotiation because

Owens made such outlandish demands for his new deal. The team responded by using a franchise tag on him, a move that was rarely used on restricted free agents but still guaranteed him a salary based on the average pay for the five highest-paid receivers in the league. In other words, Owens would go from making $280,000 to somewhere around $6 million. But as Mariucci said, "Apparently, that wasn't going to be good enough."

"To me, that's when all the problems started," Mariucci continued. "When we couldn't get the deal done, that's when he started banging heads with everybody: me, the owners, the executives. I wasn't in the room when he signed his deal but I was told that he wasn't happy. He just signed the contract, pushed the papers across the table, and walked out. He didn't say thank you. He didn't shake hands. He was just angry. I really think that's when he became T.O."

Whatever anger T.O. felt that day, he didn't let it impact his play on the field. In 2000, he had career highs in receptions (97) and yards (1,451), as well as 13 touchdowns. He set a league record by catching 20 passes in a game against Chicago. He also produced one of the most bizarre touchdown celebrations in the history of the NFL.

Now I'll be the first to say that I had no problems with trash-talking or demonstrative antics on a football field. Having fun was supposed to be part of the game. But when Owens scored 2 touchdowns during an early-season win at Dallas, what I saw wasn't a player having a good time. Instead, it was a receiver crossing a line in ways that could've touched off a brawl.

When Owens scored his first touchdown on a short pass from Jeff Garcia in the second quarter, he raced out of the end zone and straight to the star at midfield inside Texas Stadium. Once there, he raised his hands to the sky, leaned his head back, and peered through the hole in the ceiling that was supposedly designed so "God could watch His favorite team play." That moment so enraged the Cowboys that running back Emmitt Smith retaliated in his own way. When he scored later in that quarter, he raced to midfield as well, slammed the football down, and glared at Owens.

I'd seen a lot of crazy things in my career. What was happening in Dallas that day ranks right near the top of the list. It became even more surreal when Owens caught a short fade from Garcia on another score and then returned to the star for an encore. This time Cowboys safety George Teague charged behind him and blasted Owens. Niners guard Derrick Deese then tried to hit Teague but stumbled and whiffed. While all this was going on—with Teague's teammates holding him back—Owens strolled back to the star, raised his arms again, and posed briefly before officials pushed him back toward his sideline.

If you know anything about football, you know what Owens did was uncalled for and extremely bad for the game. A matchup between the Cowboys and 49ers used to be must-see television in the early 1990s. Now it looked like something that belonged on a late-night episode of pro wrestling, all because of the ego of one misguided receiver. It took a lot of nerve for Owens to pull that stunt. Even worse was the fallout afterward.

I'm not talking about the $8,000 fine Owens received from the NFL. I'm talking about the perception of the position. That day started a serious shift in the way people thought about receivers. It used to be that one mention of the 49ers resulted in fond memories of Rice catching passes from Joe Montana and Steve Young. After Owens's antics in Dallas, a new image of receivers was forming in the public eye. The message Owens was sending at midfield of Texas Stadium that day couldn't be ignored: He was saying the moment was all about him.

The display angered Mariucci to the point that he suspended Owens a game without pay and banned him from the team for the week. "That was when all communication between us ceased for a while," Mariucci said. "I was the enemy." It wasn't hard to see why Mariucci stumbled into that position. Normally, the owner or the general manager punishes a player for crossing the line. In this case, the 49ers' John York and GM Terry Donahue discussed their decision with Mariucci and then left him to give the news to T.O. Making matters worse, Donahue lessened the suspension after rethinking the issue a few days later, and Owens only lost half a week's pay while sitting out the next contest.

Not only was Mariucci left to play the bad cop after all was said and done, but he also was part of a franchise that now was unwilling to take a hard stance with its biggest star. Owens surely was smart enough to see the advantage he had gained in the midst of that controversy. In a profession where toughness is considered the most valuable of commodities, Owens had recognized how soft his bosses could be when forced to take action.

"Some of what happened with T.O. goes back to the NFL encouraging guys to get attention," said former 49ers offensive coordinator Greg Knapp. "After T.O. ran to the star, he actually started reaping benefits from it. It got replayed over and over and people noticed him. It went from being a negative to being a positive."

The sad part about all that was Owens was only getting started. The 49ers were going through a major transformation that season and Jerry knew he was on his way out. He would wind up in Oakland a year later, where he hoped to continue his career working alongside another aging star, Tim Brown. Meanwhile, the 49ers—the most storied franchise of the previous two decades—were about to be placed in the hands of a destructive force.

I knew plenty about transitions during that time because, like Jerry, I was going through my own in Minnesota. I would enjoy my last winning season in the NFL during the 2000 season. I also would be facing my own tough choices about where I took my career after that point. After all those years of fighting for respect, I didn't have to tussle any longer. I only had to savor what was left of my ride in what seemed like a rapidly changing world.

The 2000 season may have ended on a sour note—especially after we started the year 11–2—but it was special for me because of one significant achievement: my 1,000th reception. It came on November 30 of that year, when we faced the Detroit Lions in the Metrodome. The team had made a point of getting me the record as soon as possible and it happened exactly that way. Daunte hit me with a 4-yard touchdown pass in the first quarter, making me the second receiver after Rice to have 1,000 career catches.

The game stopped at that point as teammates mobbed me. A camera crew followed me to the sidelines, where I found Melanie, Duron, Monterae, and other family members. The sheer number alone didn't make that milestone meaningful to me. It also was special because catching that many balls took a lot of hard work and good fortune.

As much as teams were throwing in my day, the NFL still hadn't reached the point where 40 to 50 attempts in a game were common. The most aggressive teams were passing about 30 to 35 times a game, meaning there were fewer opportunities for everybody who made his living catching passes. If you played on a team with as many talented receivers as we had, the odds didn't favor your chances of making that kind of history.

To be honest, I never saw myself catching that many passes. I thought my career would be great and I believed people would see the depth of my talents. But it was impossible to see such numbers coming over the course of a career. Just to say I shared the same company as Jerry Rice—who was light years ahead of everybody statistically—made me proud to know I'd been that consistent during my time in the NFL.

The writing was pretty much on the wall for me by then. I'd enjoyed my thirty-fifth birthday only five days earlier and I had a couple of years left on my contract. When we lost the NFC championship game to the Giants two months later, I was even more aware of how fast the door was closing on my career. I'd had two shots at the Super Bowl in a three-year window. There was no way I was going to get any closer to a title than that.

Walking away from that defeat, I had far more peace with that reality than I expected. It was just a bad game, one that got away from us the moment it started. That was the hard truth of it. We'd done our best and we had to live with it. By that point in my life, I'd accepted that you have far less control over things than you'd like to believe.

Unfortunately, that was a lesson Randy hadn't yet learned. The 2001 season started with him earning his own place in history: He became the highest-paid wide receiver ever when owner Red McCombs gave him an eight-year, $75 million contract extension. Randy's agent had hoped to break the trend of quarterbacks being the highest-paid players in the game and he definitely got his wish. Randy's contract told the world that receivers could be the most important weapon in anybody's offense.

The problem was that 2001 turned out to be a terrible time for Randy to back up that message. The first big blow to our high expectations came during training camp, when Korey Stringer, our right tackle, died of complications related to heat stroke. Randy and I had actually just finished catching balls from a Jugs machine when Korey passed out after a morning practice. He had been working on some blocking techniques a few yards away from us and had seemed perfectly fine as we walked toward the locker room.

The next thing we knew, we were at a local hospital in Mankato, Minnesota, praying for Korey's survival. It was a crazy time because we were concerned about Korey and also trying to reach his wife, Kelci, at their home in Atlanta. Since Randy was extremely close to Kelci, he spent most of his time tracking her down. He eventually arranged for a private plane to pick her up and fly her to Minneapolis.

None of that mattered in the end, though. Korey died that night and it devastated the entire team. Korey was easily one of the most popular players on our roster. He often invited teammates over to his home to play video games, enjoy a barbecue, or just hang out. You couldn't even walk past his locker without seeing his trademark smile creep across his face.

Korey's death was especially painful for Randy, because he suddenly found himself in a rare position: He had to explain the tragedy to the team and the media. Denny had been asking Randy to be more of a leader, and dealing with something like this came with the job. The problem was that Randy wasn't equipped for a moment as traumatic as that. I had dealt with a teammate's death early on in my career, when a good friend, former Philadelphia Eagles defensive tackle Jerome Brown, died in a car crash in 1992. And I had dealt with deaths since. But Korey was one of the few close friends Randy actually had in the league.

Randy's bond with Korey made it all the more difficult when Kelci filed a $100 million lawsuit against the Vikings for not doing enough to prevent her husband's death (that suit started a long legal battle that end in 2009, when the NFL reached a settlement with Kelci). "Randy has never told me this, but I believe that entire situation affected how he looked at management," Johnstone said. "He started to put up a wall at that point. Korey was Randy's best friend on the team and a lot of things were said after he passed. It was alleged that the Vikings could've done better when he started complaining about his [health] problems, and I know his wife wasn't happy about how the team responded after his death. Randy wound up in that camp as far as fighting the team."

Korey's death started a major downward spiral for us that season. That moment was emotional enough, but then terrorists attacked the World Trade Center in New York City a few weeks later. We eventually went 5–11, with McCombs firing Denny before the season finale. Randy also missed the Pro Bowl (despite catching 82 passes and scoring 10 touchdowns) and gave the world a quote that would follow him the rest of his career.

It was in late November of that season when Sid Hartman, an iconic, old-school reporter in Minneapolis, asked Randy some questions about the season. By that point, people had been criticizing Randy for not playing hard on every down. I never had a problem with Randy's effort—nobody goes all out for an entire football game—but I sensed the controversy building over the issue. Randy, on the other hand, seemed oblivious to the entire matter.

From what I heard, the conversation between the two didn't only focus on Randy's effort. It also included references to the roles Denny and I had played in his early success in the league. I don't know if Sid asked Randy if we were responsible for helping Randy blossom or if Randy simply heard it that way. Regardless, Randy took the line of questioning as a subtle slap in the face. And whenever he felt slighted, he was going to come back at somebody full force.

This is what ultimately ran in Sid's column in the *Minneapolis Star-Tribune* on November 22, 2001:

> "I play when I want to play," Moss said. "Do I play up to my top performance, my ability every time? Maybe not. I just keep doing what I do and that is playing football. When I make my mind up, I am going out there to tear somebody's head off. When I go out there and play football, man it's not anybody telling me to play or how I should play. I play when I want to play, case closed."

Randy made other comments in the story, but all anybody heard were those first seven words. "I play when I want to play." On a sheet of paper, the quote wasn't as visually disturbing as Terrell Owens preening on the star in Texas Stadium, but it definitely played that way in some circles. Randy already had one major strike against him because of his background. The second one came when he squirted the official with a water bottle in that playoff game. Once he gave Sid that statement, it was game on. Randy, to many people, was becoming exactly the person teams feared on draft day back in 1998.

Of course, I saw the problem immediately, as did Denny. We knew Randy was just irritated by the perception that he wasn't getting ample credit for his own success. In his eyes, he was thinking the media assumed that Denny and I had propped him up and made him a Pro Bowler. What Randy was trying to say was "I did all this work. Don't take what I did and give the credit to those guys." What people ultimately heard him articulate was "I can do whatever the hell I want around this place."

If Randy was more media savvy—or actually cared about the media at all—he could've clarified what he was trying to say. If he was a little bit older, he could've hidden his disdain for the question and diplo-matically said that he wouldn't have gotten where he was without the help of others. Instead, Randy did what he usually did when he sensed a challenge. He dug in and vowed to fight it until the end.

I tried talking to him. Denny tried talking to him. The more we explained how bad the situation looked, the more he refused to take it back. Once Randy saw it as a reason to prove people wrong, I gave up. This was a huge turning point in his career, one that everybody recog-nized except him.

Even our owner—the same man who'd made Randy the wealthiest receiver ever—was aghast. "When I heard Randy's words, I was angry, hurt, sick to my stomach," Red told *Sports Illustrated*. "I knew he'd get tagged with it forever, because that's the way it works, and that's the way it should be. It will never go away, and Randy understands that. He's paid for it, and he'll pay for it the rest of his life."

What most people outside of the Vikings franchise didn't realize was that Red had another reason to be upset with Randy. Two weeks before that interview with Sid, shortly after a loss at Philadelphia, we had boarded our team buses to head back to Minneapolis. We usually have sponsors—or guests of the franchise—travel with us, and on this day, some decided to sit in seats reserved for players. I don't know if they consciously did that but Randy didn't care. He apparently cursed them out, telling them to find a different bus to ride.

This time, Denny had to do damage control since I hadn't been around when the incident happened. As soon as the story leaked to the press in December, Denny was on his radio show to explain his percep-tion of the incident. The team had fined Randy $15,000 for his behav-ior, but Denny also clarified that this was a two-way street. Though Randy could've been more respectful, the sponsors also shouldn't have been on the bus.

Not that it really made a difference. The public was getting a dif-ferent view of Randy, one that was becoming ever harder to change. He always had an edge to him, but the longer he played in the league, the more blatantly disrespectful he became in certain situations.

In some cases, like the Rams game, it had more to do with him being in a foul mood at a lousy time. It other cases, it was simple defiance that caused him so much trouble. "I always thought the effort thing with Randy was overblown, but he does have some real issues with authority," Brian Billick said. "It's not that he's a bad guy. I think it's more that he's misunderstood. He's always been the best whenever he's stepped onto a field or a court. That's going to give you a unique perspective on life."

"Randy didn't do himself any favors," said Matt Birk. "That's what always upset me. I knew he was a better guy than what he was showing. We loved having him on the team, but the public would kill him. I felt bad about that, but he made it clear that he didn't care what people thought. That's admirable but it also can be a detriment."

It's unlikely that many people outside of Minnesota gave Randy the benefit of the doubt after his comments to Sid. The situation with the sponsors only added to his growing reputation. What was obvious was that Randy had reached a point of no return. Great stats or not, he would be a bad boy for life. The only question—in the eyes of many critics—was who was apt to become the bigger headache: Randy Moss or Terrell Owens?

A lot of people have talked about the "rivalry" between Randy and Terrell Owens in those days. I never thought of it as a rivalry. When Randy was focused, he was the best receiver I'd ever seen. I doubt he even thought he had any rivals when he was in his prime. I'm sure he looked at Jerry Rice and me as old-timers. As for everybody else, he really couldn't have cared less what anybody was doing.

It wasn't like the days when I came into the league, when you knew everybody was fighting to be the best receiver not named Rice and keeping track of other receivers' stats. All Randy knew was that he could take over a game whenever he wanted. He'd been doing it for four years once the 2001 season ended. He didn't need to compare himself to anybody else if people looked closely at his full body of work.

On the other hand, T.O. clearly had a strong urge to prove himself to the world. He couldn't wait to replace Rice in San Francisco. He carried himself as if everybody was against him, both on and off the field. He also had no discernible grasp of how teams operated. The guy was a walking powder keg. "Since he was under contract, he knew we couldn't trade him or cut him," Mariucci said. "No matter what he did or said, we had to deal with him."

Randy may have been creating controversy in Minnesota, but at least you could understand some of his actions. He'd been frustrated in that St. Louis Rams game and irritated after that loss in Philadelphia. The "I play when I want to play" comment had more to do with misunderstanding than outright disrespect. With T.O., his drama defied explanation. The celebration on the Dallas star revealed his personality to the entire nation, but there were plenty of other issues happening behind the scenes. As Mariucci said, "His mood swings weren't week to week or day to day. They were minute to minute."

Owens became known for his defiance around the team facility. Instead of participating in weight-lifting sessions with the team during the season, he would train after hours with his own personal trainer. He also would constantly park his car in places that he knew were off-limits, like handicapped spots or Bill Walsh's space (Walsh was serving as general manager at that point). Mariucci eventually got so tired of telling Owens to move his car that he created a new policy: Any player who made the Pro Bowl got his own parking space. Not surprisingly, even that didn't keep Owens under control for long.

The head coach had watched his relationship with Owens deteriorate after the Dallas incident and it worsened in 2001. After the 49ers blew a 19-point lead in a 37–31 overtime loss at Chicago that season, Owens publicly blamed the loss on Mariucci in typical T.O. style. The day after the Bears defeat, the entire team had gone to a funeral for Jeff Fontana, the son of a longtime team employee and a police officer who had been killed in the line of duty. T.O. was one of a handful of players who didn't attend the funeral. That same day, when he ran into reporters at the facility after receiving treatment for an injury, T.O. offered his assessment of the loss in Chicago.

At no point did he mention that he dropped the pass that Bears safety Mike Brown returned for the game-winning touchdown. Instead, it was all about Mariucci's lack of a killer instinct. In T.O.'s mind, Mariucci didn't want to embarrass his good friend, Bears head coach Dick Jauron, by running up the score even more. In Mariucci's mind, his star receiver had crossed a line that was worthy of a suspension without pay.

"It pissed me off because instead of being at the funeral or talking about how he didn't catch the ball, he's claiming that I threw the game," Mariucci said. "So I go up to my office after hearing this and tell my secretary to find T.O. Right at that moment, I look down and I see him getting into his car. I run downstairs, bang on his window, and ask him point-blank: 'What did you say about me and my friend?' He just looked at me with this big smile and says, 'Oh, it was nothing.'"

T.O. feuded with Mariucci for a couple of weeks until they settled the matter. But the entire story wasn't lost on the public. The more valuable T.O. became to the 49ers, the more destructive he seemed capable of becoming. This wasn't like Keyshawn Johnson ripping teammates in a book after his rookie season with the Jets. This was an undeniably talented player acting like professionalism had no place in professional football. The drama between T.O. and Mariucci reached such a boiling point that local reporters kept track of how often they spoke to each other in practice.

The scary thing about T.O. was the same thing that was scary about Randy: Neither player understood the growing scope of his influence. When I came into the NFL, I looked up to players like Jerry Rice, Mike Quick, and Henry Ellard. More than that, I respected them. They had earned their stature in the game through hard work, dependability, and steady play.

Nobody could ever doubt the work ethic of Randy or T.O. Their numbers spoke for themselves as well. But when it came to respect, both players had issues showing much of that to people outside of their inner circles. In T.O.'s case, he allowed that attitude to infect everything around him. Randy wasn't destructive in that way, but he did harm to his own reputation with his dismissive actions. Regardless of how they dealt with their issues, the effect was unmistakable and lasting: They created an entirely different image of NFL receivers.

That's ultimately how it works. The elite players at the position set the standard for the rest of their peers. When Jerry was at the top of his game, receivers were expected to be classy and consistent. Younger stars like Andre Rison, Michael Irvin, and myself brought more brashness to the position. By the turn of the century, once Randy and T.O. were thriving, people were throwing around a term that had never before been associated with football: "diva."

The cameras couldn't get enough of either player. They were lightning rods for fans who either loved or hated them. They also had as much leverage as any stars could want. If you had a Randy Moss or a T.O. on your roster at that point, you had a chance to do phenomenal things offensively. They were so huge that they overshadowed their own coaches and quarterbacks.

When the Vikings named former assistant Mike Tice as their new head coach heading into the 2002 season, the first major strategic goal he announced was "the Randy Ratio." Tice wanted the ball in Randy's hands as much as possible, which meant that 40 percent of the passes were going Randy's way that season. The idea proved to be a disaster—Tice scrapped it midseason because defenses were too focused on stopping Randy—but Randy made other noise that season for what happened off the field. He wound up getting arrested in September after a traffic cop stepped in front of his car to prevent him from making an illegal turn in Minneapolis—and he pushed her back for half a block.

The 49ers were also trying to get the ball to T.O. more often in 2002, and he wound up with a career-high 100 receptions in just fourteen games. All that success did was embolden him even more. When the

49ers played the Vikings in a 2003 regular-season game, it was hyped as a matchup between the game's two best receivers, Randy and T.O. That's probably how T.O. saw it as well, because he had one of his most notorious meltdowns in that contest.

The 49ers were facing a third-and-1 situation in the first half of that game when Knapp asked head coach Dennis Erickson what he wanted to do. When Erickson said run, Knapp called a play that the Vikings stuffed. Once fourth down arrived, Knapp figured his head coach would consider a pass, given how the last play had gone and because Knapp wanted to throw it as well, but Erickson wanted to send a message. The 49ers wound up gaining nothing on a run and turning the ball over on downs.

It was bad enough that the 49ers couldn't convert in that situation. T.O. only intensified the issue as he spent several minutes berating Knapp on the sidelines. "I knew I wouldn't make things better by responding to him and I also didn't want to sell out the head coach," Knapp said. "So I sat there and took it as he jumped me on national television."

T.O.'s frustration no doubt also had plenty to do with how that game was playing out. Randy was on his way to 8 receptions for 172 yards and 3 scores in that 35–7 San Fran loss. T.O. would end up with "only" 5 catches for 55 yards. You could bet T.O. was thinking this would be his moment to prove who was the best receiver in the game. He left town being known only as the most controversial one.

It was a reputation that T.O. enhanced almost every other time he opened his mouth. When that season ended, T.O. insinuated during a *Playboy* interview that 49ers quarterback Jeff Garcia was homosexual (Garcia, who has four children with his wife, Carmella DeCesare, denied the allegation). It wasn't a remark that came out of nowhere, either. The relationship between those two had deteriorated from the moment that Garcia had succeeded Steve Young as the team's starting quarterback in 2000.

"The relationship between T.O. and Jeff was definitely bad," Knapp said. "When T.O. came in, Steve Young was the quarterback. That meant T.O. had to listen and do what Steve said. When Steve retired and Jeff took over, [T.O.] was thinking, *Who's this guy? I'm T.O. and I'll run the routes any way I want.* He had more leverage. And if you asked Jeff about T.O. today, he'd tell you he can't stand the guy.

"If this were the old days, a veteran quarterback would've put somebody like T.O. on ice. They wouldn't play that game because they wouldn't throw the ball to a receiver acting that way. They'd basically say, 'You want publicity? Then do what I say.'"

The stuff T.O. pulled wasn't just bad for receivers. It was bad for the game and it went way beyond complaints like "I'm open—throw me the ball." At least with Randy, you knew most of his problems resulted from situations away from the field. With T.O., you could have drama at any place at any time.

T.O. actually made so many provocative comments to the media that Mariucci met with him once to discuss the nonstop controversy. "I asked him why he said certain things and he said, 'Coach, I'm just being honest,'" Mariucci said. "I told him there's a saying: 'Some things are better left unsaid.' Somewhere along the line, he got it in his head that honesty is in the best policy. Honesty is good, but sometimes you can hurt people with it. Sometimes you have to hold your tongue. It was constant maintenance with him. You never knew when he was going to blow up."

However, there were also moments when T.O. would reveal a different side to his personality. One day he came to work with one of his children, a three-year-old boy whose mother couldn't care for him that day. When Mariucci saw the child in the building, he asked T.O. what he was planning on doing with the kid. The team had meetings and practice, and a toddler couldn't be brought into those settings. In the end, Mariucci's secretary literally babysat the boy all day because Owens wanted to ensure his son was all right.

Mariucci was just as stunned by Owens after the coach was fired following the 2002 season. Mariucci was cleaning out his office when T.O. appeared in the doorway. All the other players had left for the off-season but T.O. had stuck around to say farewell. "He said, 'I just want to wish you the best and tell you I appreciated everything you did,'" Mariucci said. "That was T.O. I wish there were more opportunities for him to show his good side because he actually did have one."

As a result of people like T.O., the league had shifted so dramatically by the start of the 2000s that I was thankful my career was ending. I could've stuck with the Vikings after the 2001 season—I had an option in my contract that would've paid me another $6 million for my final year—but it was time for me to go. Minnesota had been good to me and I didn't want to play on a team in the process of rebuilding. I also wanted to start focusing on my broadcast career. HBO had given me a three-year deal to join *Inside the NFL*.

The best part of ending my career was the treatment Red Mc-Combs gave me on my way out the door. He promised that the Vikings would retire my number 80 jersey once my retirement was official. After playing five games in Miami in 2002 (the Dolphins were a playoff contender looking for a veteran receiver), I finally sent the league my papers. A year later, during halftime of a week-two Sunday night game, Red made good on his promise.

The Metrodome had always been an electric atmosphere for football, but I'd never fully appreciated that as a player. I was too caught up in doing my job. On that night, I took it all in: the deafening crowd, the number 80 jerseys in the stands, the teammates I'd no longer play with again. I knew it was an honor for that number to hang in the rafters. There are only so many players who mean that much to their organizations.

I also understood the game was inherently different from when I came into the league. People used to judge receivers solely off performance and production. But when you looked at what Randy and T.O. were doing—and all the attention that came with that success—you knew there would be a ripple effect. It might have been different if they were losing money or killing their futures. Instead, they were making serious loot and generating more buzz with practically every move they made.

The bottom line was that stardom mattered more than ever to many receivers once my career closed. Few people cared about the price involved in acquiring it, and many likely believed it was well within their grasp. It was easy to see the appeal of celebrity. What was harder to recognize was the common denominator affecting the actions of the game's biggest stars: a complete lack of trust.

CHAPTER 10

Chaos, Controversy, and Control Issues

I don't have much of a relationship with my mother. We had been close during most of my childhood, but a series of events drove us apart over the years. She wasn't in my corner when I lost my eligibility at Ohio State. She didn't call when the Eagles waived me in 1990. Every time we did speak, it always seemed like I couldn't please her.

Our troubles only increased as my relationship with my wife, Melanie, grew stronger. As soon as my mother saw that she wasn't the most prominent woman in my life anymore, she felt threatened about being replaced. One reason Melanie is my best friend today is that she's always had my back. I didn't make it easy on her, but she stuck with me through everything we faced.

That doesn't mean I don't have anything positive to say about my mother. She was there in the beginning. She didn't abandon us like my father did and that was vital to our survival. There's no telling what might have happened if both my parents had checked out. I probably wouldn't be where I am today—in a position to understand some of the same demons that have plagued other receivers over the years.

Wideouts obviously aren't the only NFL players who struggle with being fatherless. You can go all around the league and hear that story a hundred times over. I do think being fatherless played a huge role in what you saw happening with receivers as we moved into the 2000s. If there was one group—more than any other—that brought major issues onto the field, it was the people catching passes for a living.

In other words, receivers need to have trust. And trust is a strange concept for someone whose daddy ran out on his family. It's even more foreign for someone who has seen his world collapse as a child or watched his mother working three jobs to keep food on the table. Those types of circumstances can harden the most optimistic of people. I know it created an edge in some of the game's most prominent wideouts.

Randy Moss had that edge. So did Terrell Owens and Keyshawn Johnson. The list went on and on from there. It's the one thing I definitely had in common with those receivers and countless others. As we found our way in the NFL, we all had to face one basic question: Who could we trust? It's likely a question we'd all been dealing with since the first time we stepped on a field to play football.

In high school, kids know they can trust their coaches because they don't want anything. They just want to educate and instill some positive values in their players. Then everything changes as you get older. College coaches want you to help their programs win. Pro coaches will dump you the minute you can't help them succeed. The natural instinct of players who come from rough backgrounds is to become more skeptical about every person who ultimately views them as assets.

That's why I've always believed that God has a plan for everybody's life. I can see that in how my own career played out, especially in the people who've helped me along the way. Almost every wide receivers coach I had taught me something valuable about being a man. I imagine other assistants have done the same with other star wideouts. For all the talent and bravado that has become common in the position, you're still talking about a whole bunch of emotionally scarred men running around on that field.

I'm not making excuses for them. I don't believe in that and it definitely happens way too often. I do believe there is something about playing receiver that intensifies some of the demons inside NFL players. I've seen that story enough times to know there definitely is some truth to it.

"Wide receiver is an emotional position," said Cincinnati Bengals head coach Marvin Lewis. "You can't dictate when you get the football, even though some guys think they can. You have to know there will be days when you're not getting many balls and you still have to help your team win. If you're blowing up because you're unhappy, then you're causing problems within the team. You have to be able to handle the ups and downs of the job."

By the start of the twenty-first century, Randy Moss and Terrell Owens were the two most prominent receivers in the game and both had their share of bad press. They weren't alone, though. It seemed that any player who was clashing with a team around that time was catching passes for a living. Like Randy and T.O., they all had a reluctance to back down when the public controversy intensified.

When the New York Jets traded Keyshawn to Tampa Bay in 2000, then Jets head coach Al Groh rationalized that the team made the deal because Keyshawn was demanding a new contract. Keyshawn saw things differently. He felt like Groh was trying to run him out of town because of personality conflicts. Keyshawn's suspicions grew even more when Groh publicly intimated that the receiver's reaction to the team's stance was comparable to that of a spoiled adolescent pouting after being declined an allowance by his father.

Keyshawn was so angry that he shot back at Groh in a *Sports Illustrated* article, saying, "I knew then that I couldn't play for the guy. In the conversations we had, he wasn't at all appealing to me. He was questioning me, asking me if I can be a star for him, saying, 'I need you to be a star on this team next year.' What the f— did he think? Who the f— did he think I was, some nobody? He acted like I hadn't done a f—— thing for the last four years, like I haven't been in the league at all. I'm not a kid, begging for money."

When talking about that controversy today, Keyshawn is just as candid. "I didn't need somebody smiling in my face and pissing down my back," he said. "Plus, I knew I had protection. I went to USC. I understood the way the league worked and how I could blow up their cap if they got crazy with me. They also knew I saved my money. I had enough to hold out if it came to that."

Keyshawn felt comfortable going after Groh and owner Woody Johnson publicly for two reasons. First, it suited his personality. Second, he was a big deal in New York. All the noise he made in that city produced a major effect. He received endorsement deals, gained A-list status, and had plenty of people who admired his bravado.

When Tyra Banks celebrated her twenty-fifth birthday with a party in a lavish New York City club in 1998, actors and rappers were lining up to chat with Keyshawn when he walked in the door. "He was a big part of a cultural change for football players," said former NFL offensive tackle Roman Oben, who played for the Giants when Keyshawn was with the Jets. "In New York City in the nineties, it used to be that football players hung out in the bars with regular people and the NBA guys were out with the celebrities. You'd hear guys talk about how they wanted to roll like the NBA players. It was different when Keyshawn came along. The quarterback wasn't the only star of the team anymore. The receivers could be out there, too."

Still, receivers didn't need to be in New York City to run their mouths. A few months after Keyshawn's clash with the Jets, former All-Pro wide receiver Carl Pickens was squaring off with the Cincinnati Bengals. He publicly bashed that franchise so viciously—even questioning the team's decision at the time to keep Bruce Coslet as head coach—that the Bengals deleted his name from the depth chart, removed his nameplate from his locker, and ordered him to skip that year's minicamp because of his toxic attitude.

That controversy ultimately led to the Bengals setting a new precedent in NFL contracts. The "Carl Pickens Clause" gave Cincinnati the right to withhold bonuses to future players if they made inappropriate public remarks about the franchise. Pickens was once known for being one of the top wideouts in the game. Today many people probably remember him more for his squabbling with the Bengals.

The New England Patriots didn't resort to legal tactics when dealing with Terry Glenn, who was the second receiver drafted after Keyshawn in that glorious 1996 class. Instead, head coach Bill Belichick brought the hammer down during the 2001 season. By that point

Terry had annoyed coaches by skipping off-season workouts and also had earned a four-game suspension for failing to take a scheduled drug test. After learning of the suspension, Terry vanished from training camp and never returned.

Clearly, all those demons I saw in Terry back when he was an All-American receiver at Ohio State finally caught up with him. The Patriots thought highly enough of him to give him a six-year, $50 million contract a year earlier. Yet he was so combustible that he couldn't handle all the off-the-field problems mounting in his life. Even Belichick took personal time off after the 2000 season to help Terry through his issues.

Belichick eventually grew so frustrated with Terry's dysfunctional behavior that he placed the receiver on the reserve/left squad in 2001. That rare move meant Terry was deactivated for the year without pay and couldn't be traded or waived. When Terry fought and won the right to return to the field, Belichick fined him $4,000 for refusing to run on a StairMaster after Terry sustained a hamstring injury. A few weeks later, Terry went on local television and insinuated that he was faking the injury because of Belichick's tactics.

Though Pickens's problems likely had plenty to do with playing on a lousy team, I don't think it's surprising that both Terry and Keyshawn had issues after working for Bill Parcells. Parcells knew how to motivate players, whether it was being brutally honest with Keyshawn or calling Terry "she" as a rookie. Parcells also had the credibility that comes with two Super Bowl victories. Players respected success and Parcells had that in abundance.

But I also didn't have a problem with how any of those teams dealt with their players in those situations. One thing you should never do with any receiver is give him too much leeway. Most of us will run wild with any kind of power we acquire. The sooner a coach squashes a public squabble, the more likely he is to maintain some semblance of control.

———

I was fortunate to have the relationship I had with Denny Green because we never had any personality clashes. He trusted me enough to be a leader for the Vikings. I trusted him enough to take that responsibility seriously and push his cause. The Vikings took care of me as well. I never had to worry about respect during my last ten years with that franchise.

Some coaches didn't have that luxury once we entered the twenty-first century. The problem many faced was an issue of supply and demand. Everybody wanted a big-time receiver but there simply weren't enough special ones to go around the league. In some cases, coaches and franchises had to gauge how much they could tolerate from the stars who were stepping out of line. If those same teams decided to give up and move on, then those players were likely to find somebody even more willing to acquire them.

For example, Keyshawn signed an eight-year, $56 million deal with Tampa following his complaints about the Jets and subsequent trade to the Bucs. Three years after his squabbles with Groh, he had an even more intense clash with Tampa Bay head coach Jon Gruden. Those two had helped the Bucs win the Super Bowl during the 2002 season. By 2003, Keyshawn was bashing Gruden every chance he got after Tampa started the year with a 4–6 record.

To hear some of Keyshawn's teammates tell it, his problems in Tampa stemmed from inconsistent expectations. Keyshawn had a certain way of doing things and Gruden didn't like it when the Bucs stopped winning consistently. "Key used to check into the team hotel on the night before games and then go stay in a condo down the street," said Oben, who played in Tampa from 2002–03. "Gruden was cool with that during the Super Bowl year but he was fining Key for it the next year. Key used to fly back to Los Angeles and take a redeye back on Wednesday mornings. That became an issue when we were struggling. There were two sides to that story, but it definitely divided the locker room."

"We had problems from day one," Keyshawn said. "My routine in the off-season was that I didn't train in Tampa during OTAs [off-season training activities]. [Former Bucs head coach] Tony Dungy was cool with that because I gave my word that I'd stay in shape. Gruden saw it as a dis. He thought I was blowing him off, that I didn't like him. Everybody told him what I did, but we butted heads over that from the start. He had to take his medicine during the Super Bowl year, but then everything changed after that."

The relationship between Keyshawn and Gruden—who declined to comment on the topic—became such an issue that Keyshawn stopped talking to his head coach altogether. Keyshawn literally told Gruden to pass messages to him through assistant coaches. When Gruden asked why, Keyshawn was even more provocative. "Because I can't trust you," he said one afternoon.

One night both men found themselves at a team fund-raising event at a local golf course. Keyshawn claimed Gruden stood near him for most of the night without ever acknowledging his presence. The next day at practice, according to Keyshawn, Gruden strolled over to ask about his whereabouts. "He said, 'Where were you last night?'" Keyshawn said. "'I wanted to have a beer with you and powwow.' I wanted to throw up when I heard that. I'm six-four and as dark as all outdoors, and he couldn't find me? That's when I knew I couldn't deal with him."

Keyshawn didn't only think Gruden was a phony. He also thought Gruden didn't want to utilize him. "I'd bust my ass all week and then he would throw me two balls," Keyshawn said.

There was one game in 2003—a home contest against New Orleans—when Keyshawn caught 10 passes, but even that didn't help. "Key always felt like he had to be used more," Oben said. "He had ten catches in that game against the Saints and it seemed like Gruden was getting him the ball just to shut him up. We threw something like fifteen slants to him."

"I knew something was going to happen between them because the tension was so high," said former Bucs receiver Keenan McCardell. "There were certain things said in meetings that should've been let go. But Key was fed up. Even though we won the Super Bowl the year before, I don't even know if Key was happy with that [because of Gruden].

Key wanted the football but Jon wasn't just going to give it to him because Key demanded it. Jon was in a tough position. We had other people producing and he wanted to keep us all involved."

"We were really only together for one full season [2002]," said Gruden in the only comment he offered on his relationship with Keyshawn. "That year Keyshawn had over 1,000 yards receiving, and we won the Super Bowl. But to be honest, I didn't think Keyshawn was our best receiver. Our go-to wide receiver was Keenan McCardell, and I looked to him in a lot of key situations. Also, I really felt Joe Jurevicius was a dominant red zone receiver. Not all coaches and players see eye to eye all the time, and some never do."

The feud between Keyshawn and Gruden ended in epic fashion. They agreed that Key would be deactivated for the final six games of the season, with the Bucs paying him the remainder of his salary. "I was doing what I was supposed to do, which is why they had to pay me," he said. "They tried to say my conduct was detrimental to the team, but that wasn't the case. The only thing I did was agitate the situation."

But once the Bucs eventually banished Keyshawn, guess what happened? Bill Parcells and Jerry Jones arranged an off-season trade to bring him to Dallas in exchange for Joey Galloway. Keyshawn wasn't vilified or scorned by the league. As soon as he was available, another team stepped up quickly to grab him.

The same thing happened with Pickens. He signed a five-year, $20 million contract with Tennessee five days after the Bengals released him in 2001. Even Terry—who so angered Belichick that he didn't even receive a Super Bowl ring after the Patriots' championship run that same year—managed to find suitors despite his growing baggage. Green Bay gave up two fourth-round picks to acquire him in 2002, then traded him to Dallas in 2003. Once again, Parcells had offered a rescue line to another troubled wideout.

All those situations added to the perception that times were changing. "As guys got more money, teams had to cater to the people making the big check," Oben said. "It wasn't like it was even as early as the mid-nineties, when you had to be grateful to be drafted. That was the old sixties mentality. Once receivers started getting big, you saw more coaches—especially younger ones—trying to figure out how to deal with these players. Teams started thinking that if a receiver wants to act crazy, that's fine. We just want him to make some plays for us."

There was another common belief growing around that time: that a change in scenery could bring out the best in disgruntled receivers. There were a few teams that bought into that mind-set. One was the Oakland Raiders. The other was the Philadelphia Eagles.

People talked a lot about friction between Randy and myself shortly after I retired from the NFL. I never sensed there was any of that. The only indication came in a *Sports Illustrated* article when Randy supposedly said the Vikings could be better without me on the roster. The quote that generated the most attention involved Randy saying, "We've had a lot of b.s. the last two seasons that messed this team up and kept us from competing for a championship, and we got rid of some of that b.s. over the off-season. I never experienced anything like last year, and I can't imagine anything worse."

Plenty of people claimed I was part of the problems that Randy was referring to in that article. I took that statement to mean Randy believed in an offense built around him, quarterback Daunte Culpepper, and some other talented players. It wasn't like I was expecting him to say, "We'll be worse." Randy would never underestimate his chances for success.

When I saw Randy during my visits to Minneapolis, I always gave him his space. The Vikings were his team and he certainly didn't need me getting in the way of any of that. I also suspected there were far more things happening behind the scenes than most people knew. That's just how it works in the NFL. When you're on the outside, you're never hearing everything that is really happening inside an organization.

Still, it was becoming clearer by 2004 that the Vikings were growing more frustrated with Randy. A hamstring injury sidelined him for five games that year, resulting in him producing only 49 receptions and 767 receiving yards. Randy did have 13 touchdown catches, but numbers didn't define him that season. Instead, controversy once again was his undoing.

Randy made national news when he walked off the field before the Vikings attempted a last-ditch onside kick in the final minute of a loss to Washington. Daunte Culpepper and Pro Bowl center Matt Birk were so angered by the act that they confronted Randy in the locker room afterward. "I was the first to get to him and we definitely had words," Birk said. "It was a symbolic thing. You just don't do that. Football is the consummate team sport and his frustrations got the better of him in that situation. Now would we have won the game? No. But he was thinking more about himself than the team in that moment."

A week later, Randy drew more scrutiny after scoring a touchdown in a playoff win over Green Bay. After catching a long pass from Daunte, Randy jogged to the goal post, turned his back to the Packers fans, and pretended to pull his pants down in a fake mooning gesture. The incident in Green Bay cost Randy a $10,000 fine from the league. His early departure in Washington cost him his credibility with the Vikings.

By March 2005, Minnesota had structured a trade that would send Randy to the Oakland Raiders in exchange for linebacker Napoleon Harris, a first-round pick in that year's draft, and a future seventh-round pick. The move wasn't surprising given that Daunte had publicly talked to reporters at that year's Pro Bowl about the franchise's frustration with Randy. "He's my good friend, but you almost get to thinking that maybe enough is enough," Daunte said at the time. "And maybe the Vikings organization has had enough."

Said Birk: "It was a surprise when they traded him because of who he was. But it wasn't like it came out of left field. He was becoming frustrated and his career seemed to have run its course. It was probably best for everybody that he moved on."

There probably was a time when nobody could've imagined the Vikings giving up Randy Moss. He had made them relevant on the national scene from the moment he arrived, and his talents were undeniable. But the Vikings also had a serious void in leadership. Given the sequence of problems and the seven years Randy had spent with the organization, it seemed like the only logical resolution.

The Raiders had always been a team willing to take "rebellious" players, especially because former team owner Al Davis prided himself on being a maverick. Oakland also loved throwing long, which meant Randy would've fit in perfectly. Davis also had to believe Randy could instantly ignite a franchise that had imploded just two years after reaching the Super Bowl. There already was plenty of proof across the country as to what a gifted receiver could do to boost an organization.

The 2004 season may have been the year that Randy finally pushed the Vikings past their limits, but Terrell Owens had been the bigger story before that campaign ever began. The 49ers were frustrated enough to let him walk when he had the option to void the final year of his contract following the 2003 season. When T.O.'s agent botched that process and ruined his client's right to become a free agent, the Baltimore Ravens traded a second-round pick in return for him. When T.O. complained that he'd already negotiated a deal with the Philadelphia Eagles under the pretense that he was a free agent—one who didn't want to play in Baltimore—an arbitrator eventually ruled that he could be traded from the 49ers to the Eagles.

The feeling at the time was that Philadelphia had hit a home run. They'd finally found an elite receiver to pair with Pro Bowl quarterback Donovan McNabb. T.O. would be playing in the same West Coast offense that had been used by the 49ers throughout his career and he'd be joining a team that had played in three straight NFC championship games. The Eagles were eager to prove their convictions as well. They gave Owens a seven-year, $49 million deal that included a $10 million signing bonus.

The impact was immediate. "We used to have about five thousand people come to watch training camp in the years before T.O. got to Philadelphia," said cornerback Sheldon Brown, who played for the

Eagles from 2002–09. "We had ten thousand people the first day he was there. He doubled the number of fans who wanted to see him before we ever played a game."

T.O. also was making all the right moves with his teammates. When McNabb's first daughter, Alexis, was born in 2004, T.O. arrived at McNabb's house carrying at least $1,200 worth of gifts. The two friends played cards and dominoes for nearly three hours while celebrating one of the biggest moments in the quarterback's life. McNabb had known T.O. from seeing each other at the Pro Bowl and he loved the wide receiver's noted tenacity. "He had that dog in him," McNabb said. "That's what every quarterback wants to see in a receiver."

As excited as people in Philadelphia had been, there were still many around the league who had their doubts. I was definitely in that group. When T.O. celebrated on the star in Texas Stadium a few years earlier, that had been a huge red flag as far as his potential. There was no question the guy could play and he was the league's best receiver when Philadelphia acquired him. But he was doing more controversial things with each passing year. Even when he pulled out a Sharpie marker and signed a football after scoring a touchdown in a game against Seattle in 2002—a move that drew laughter in some corners along with a stern lecture from then commissioner Paul Tagliabue—it seemed like he had his own agenda.

The scary part about his move to the Eagles was that it reinforced a growing belief about receivers. We weren't merely players running routes and catching balls anymore. Suddenly, receivers were hailed as saviors in some circles. If the Raiders needed a jump start, they acquired Randy. If the Eagles couldn't get to the Super Bowl with McNabb solely, then the addition of T.O. would put them over the top.

It wasn't just those two, either. Keyshawn was supposed to energize the Tampa Bay offense with his arrival in 2000, especially because the Bucs had been winning mainly with defense and in spite of mediocre quarterback play. In 2003, the San Diego Chargers (with David Boston) and the Atlanta Falcons (with Peerless Price) invested big money in receivers who were supposed to take their teams to the next level.

You'd be crazy to think other players didn't notice the symbolism in those moves. Top receivers were like pretty girls on a college campus. They never lacked for suitors.

In many ways, certain receivers were becoming comparable to NBA stars. In pro basketball, the players had immense control over their futures because they had massive guaranteed contracts and a league that built their marketing strategies around stars. NFL receivers didn't have guaranteed money, but the dollars were substantial enough to make them feel comfortable. Once that dynamic became part of the game, it was tougher to keep them under control.

"I don't know if personalities ever really change," Oben said. "Back in the seventies, they just didn't come out in public. You saw guys with big Afros in those days but they had to stay quiet. That's what the money and the fame did for the confidence at the position. We went from that to having players say, 'Fuck you—if you don't throw me the ball, I'm going to the media.' Suddenly the head coach and the general manager were no longer the strongest people in the organization. If receivers weren't happy, then somebody was going to hear about it."

"You had a lot of [receivers] who didn't understand that the game would go on without them," said former NFL cornerback Troy Vincent. "But nobody had really checked them on it. Once they got into the league and ran into coaches who tried to tame them, they were too far gone. They were taking it as a personal challenge if the coach said something to them. They felt like they were being handcuffed or muzzled and they fed off what people were saying about them."

We'd come a long way from the days when Harold Carmichael— the Eagles' all-time leader in receptions—claimed that owners would blackball players in the 1970s for being both gregarious and greedy. By 2004, it was apparent that receivers could say and do anything they wanted if they had Pro Bowl talent. The more teams salivated over stars like Randy and T.O., the more other receivers saw the benefits that came with the position.

Of the two, T.O. quickly proved to be the better deal. He enjoyed his fifth consecutive Pro Bowl year in 2004—with 77 receptions, 1,200 yards, and 14 touchdowns—but numbers couldn't solely define his impact. "He was so much better than everybody else that all the other receivers wanted to prove they could be that good," Brown said. "We had a young guy named Greg Lewis who improved because T.O. took him under his wing. Our defense was better because we had to go against him in practice every day. His work ethic and his mentality were the best thing about him. He felt like there was nobody on the field who could stop him."

It's impossible to think of a more courageous effort in a Super Bowl than what Owens gave Philadelphia during that season. Six weeks after sustaining a fractured fibula and severely sprained ankle, he caught 9 passes for 122 yards in a 24–21 loss to the Patriots. Many people thought T.O. was done for the season when he broke his leg. Instead, he would've walked away with Most Valuable Player honors if Philadelphia had pulled off the victory.

That should've been the first of many great seasons for T.O. in Philadelphia. I had played in that city long enough to know how Eagles fans reward their heroes. T.O. could've been as beloved in that town as Allen Iverson, Mike Schmidt, Reggie White, and, yes, Donovan. But there's something about T.O. that makes it impossible for him to enjoy anything. He reverted to old form before the buzz of his performance ever settled down.

First, T.O. started complaining about his contract a few months after the Super Bowl. He hired Drew Rosenhaus as his new agent and groused over his second-year compensation in that deal (after making $9 million in 2004, T.O.'s $4.5 million salary didn't rank among the ten highest-paid receivers in the league that year). T.O. also started taking shots at McNabb in the media. First he suggested that McNabb got tired toward the end of the Super Bowl, and then he claimed McNabb didn't do anything to help with his contract demands.

"T.O. never called me when he started all that talk about me throwing up in the Super Bowl, which wasn't true," McNabb said. "He never called me to help him with his contract situation. It would've been one thing if he called and said he needed help. I had told him earlier that he could get a new contract, but we also needed to take care of [Pro Bowl running back] Brian Westbrook. If we had done that, then all three of us could've stayed together."

T.O. wasn't hearing that. Once the 2005 season started, the rift between T.O., McNabb, and the Eagles front office worsened to the point that it was national news. T.O. intensified it even more by claiming Brett Favre would be a better quarterback for the Eagles. He also divided the team so much that former Philadelphia defensive end Hugh Douglas fought him one afternoon in the locker room.

The biggest problem, according to McNabb, was T.O.'s inability to exist in a world where he wasn't the biggest star. That meant T.O. was complaining more if the ball wasn't coming his way. It meant McNabb had to take more hard-line stances in the huddle to let T.O. know he wouldn't stand for his whining. "I've played with receivers who wanted the ball and thought they were open all the time," McNabb said. "And I'd tell them to straighten up, that this was my team and my huddle. With him, we'd butt heads and it would get sensitive. He would say things like, 'Nobody talks to me like that.' And I would tell him that nobody talks to me the way he would.

"I used to tell him all the time that I knew he could dominate games. But he could do his thing while other people got involved. He couldn't be happy with that or just being on the Philadelphia Eagles. It had to be Terrell Owens and the Philadelphia Eagles, just like David Ruffin wanted the Temptations to be David Ruffin and the Temptations."

McNabb added that T.O. created even more problems because "he had followers in the locker room. He would do certain things and then other guys would notice and wonder why they couldn't do them."

Said McNabb: "I know it wore [former Eagles head coach] Andy Reid out because he was meeting privately with T.O. at least once a week. So that was taking away from the team. You also had guys speaking up on T.O.'s behalf and talking about how the quarterback wasn't getting him the ball enough. We had [leadership] committee meetings all the time and you'd have guys saying we shouldn't suspend T.O. or we should talk about this more. There was one day when they tried to have a vote about whether to suspend him before I even got into the room. Somebody told me that after the meeting."

The drama that played out in Philadelphia wasn't surprising to the people who'd seen T.O. at his worst. "If T.O. got mad at you, he was mad at you forever," said Steve Mariucci. "That was a huge issue with him. Being verbal and animated on the sidelines is one thing. But you have to be able to let some things go and T.O. couldn't do that."

It was no shock that the Eagles eventually suspended Owens from training camp after he engaged in a shouting match with Reid in practice. What was more stunning was the press conference T.O. and Rosenhaus held in the driveway of Owens's suburban Philadelphia home. Wearing nothing but long, baggy shorts and a baseball cap turned backward, he performed sit-ups and lifted weights while reporters asked questions. It was a scene that made the Cowboys star celebration look like a simple two-step. In that moment, T.O. had everything he always wanted: The entire football-watching universe was focused on him.

Even if all those stunts were orchestrated—"It was a pretty smart business move on his part because something had to happen if the receiver and the guy throwing the football don't get along," Brown said—the sad part is that T.O. was a dominant player. There's never enough time to talk about that because of all his antics away from the game. He threw Jeff Garcia under the bus when those two became a Pro Bowl tandem in San Francisco. He trashed McNabb after the two had become fast friends in their Super Bowl run. It was bad enough that T.O. always felt disrespected. But he constantly seemed to be dragging others down with him.

McNabb was offended especially by T.O.'s willingness to attack another African American, saying, "He said things about me that he never would've said about a white quarterback." Added McNabb: "The crazy thing about it is that we started that year [3-2] and we had more attention on us than some undefeated teams. We thought we could've been like Peyton Manning and Marvin Harrison. We could've done in three years what those guys did in six. At the very least we should've gone to at least two or three more Super Bowls together. When T.O.

came to Philadelphia, he didn't just bring his talents. He brought so much energy that everybody thought they could do something different. We were so good at times that it felt like we were playing PlayStation out there. But then it got out of hand."

The Eagles eventually suspended T.O. after seven games in that 2005 season. A few weeks later, the team deactivated him for the rest of the season. By that point it didn't matter that T.O. had averaged more than 100 receiving yards a game and scored 6 touchdowns. He was tearing the Eagles' locker room apart with his constant drama. There was nothing left for the team to do as it stumbled toward a 6–10 record.

Randy, on the other hand, had different issues in Oakland. The more that team struggled on the field, the less Randy seemed to care about playing at a high level. By 2006, the receiver who'd been disinterested enough to walk into the locker room before the end of that Redskins game had become a full-fledged disappointment. I never thought I'd see the day when a player so gifted—and in his prime—would check out mentally.

I heard a story once about a play the Raiders called during a home game that season. Apparently, receivers coach Fred Biletnikoff had been waiting for the opposing defense to run a certain coverage that would leave the middle of the field vulnerable to Randy on a crossing pattern. But when the Raiders ran the play, the quarterback couldn't find Randy anywhere near the open area. The problem? Randy didn't like running across the infield dirt inside Oakland Coliseum, a structure the Raiders also shared with Major League Baseball's Oakland A's.

Of course, it would've been easy to attribute some of Randy's problems to a hamstring injury that plagued him all season. I didn't see it that way. He still played in thirteen games for a team that won only twice that year. That should've been more than enough time to produce more than 42 receptions, 553 yards, and 3 touchdowns.

"Losing didn't sit well with him," said Lance Johnstone, who played with Randy both in Minnesota and Oakland. "Not being able to contribute bothered him. It was a crazy year because we really didn't have a team in Oakland. We had three quarterbacks, the offensive line wasn't very good, and we went 2–14. We spent a lot of time talking about that season and all the frustrations that came with it. I know it was pretty hard on him."

To me, the most alarming sight that season came when ESPN analyst Merril Hoge broke down film of Randy. It was so bad that it hurt to watch. I'd never seen an elite player compete with so little intensity. Actually, I'd never seen any NFL player play like that because that kind of performance would end a career in a heartbeat. When you're as good as Randy was and you turn off the effort meter, it's like a flare in the midnight sky. Everybody notices.

"The thing about Randy is that he's a fierce competitor," said Matt Birk. "And when things don't go well, it really gets to him. He's probably always been the most dominant guy wherever he's been and he's used to dominating. But when he wasn't winning, that's when his frustrations would get the better of him."

I actually ran into Randy shortly after that 2006 season ended. He was driving around Boca Raton and he promised to stop by the house after seeing me. We spent a lot of time talking in my driveway after he arrived. We were mainly catching up on life stuff before I brought up his performance in Oakland.

"I have to tell you something before you go," I said. "I'm truly disappointed in how you stopped growing."

Randy didn't really say much as I spoke about issues such as his shoddy footwork and obvious laziness. He just nodded and listened in a way that let me know he wasn't happy with my candor. I imagine few people ever spoke to him as directly as I did. But I'd always told him that I wouldn't lie to him and deception wasn't an option then. Randy was too good to keep going down the road he'd chosen at that point.

I knew what a smart player Randy was. I knew he cared more than he ever let people see. Whatever went wrong in Oakland was destroying his career. He should've played six or seven more years there, then left the game as a sure-fire Hall-of-Famer without any additional con-troversy.

Instead, he had reached the point where opposing scouts thought he was done as a player. They didn't see the explosiveness or ferocity, and they damn sure didn't see any desire. At least you could say T.O. played hard when he wasn't causing drama. Randy wasn't even doing that.

On that afternoon, I had no idea where Randy was going to take his career. I just sensed that he wasn't going to immediately embrace my advice. When I was done talking, we said good-bye and he drove off. It was long a time before we ever spoke again.

CHAPTER 11

Underdogs and Underachievers

The toughest challenge in my first few years of retirement was mainly physical. I'd been competing in organized sports for nearly twenty-seven years when I left the NFL—or nearly three-quarters of my life by that point. I'd grown quite accustomed to preparing my body for football in the fall. Suddenly, I didn't have that outlet anymore. The days of winning one-on-one battles with defensive backs and diving for passes in heavy traffic had ended.

That's not an easy reality to embrace if you're a professional athlete. What's even more dangerous is thinking that you're going to stay in shape without off-season training, minicamps, and two-a-days. So I made one promise to myself before I ever got too deep into retirement: I wasn't going to let myself go physically. Whatever it took, regardless of the discomfort, I was going to keep my body from blowing up in a way that had become all too common with other former players.

As for the mental aspect of life after football, that was surprisingly easier. Every retired athlete goes through some form of mental withdrawal, but I had the benefit of knowing my career had ended on my own terms. It wasn't shortened by an injury or impacted by a contract too hefty to fit under the salary cap. I had left when I was ready. I had made my peace with the game.

My job with HBO's *Inside the NFL* also offered plenty of incentive because my future in television was far brighter than what football offered. I knew it would be a mistake to ignore that reality. So many players fall into the trap of thinking they need to find something to replace football after their careers. I looked at it differently. I had to accept that nothing could ever replace life in the NFL.

There's no way anyone is going to find another job that pays grown men millions in order to compete in front of huge audiences every weekend. You can't duplicate the emotion, the pressure, or the elation that comes with achieving something at the highest level of the sport. It's really easy to get addicted to those highs. Even the players who have a plan can struggle to move on after experiencing the joys of the NFL.

Fortunately for me, my television job kept me connected to the game. I was still in contact with the Minnesota Vikings on a regular basis. I was conducting interviews and gaining valuable information from people all over the league. I also had a built-in excuse to watch every game. Believe me, I had no problems staying busy.

That gig gave me a front-row seat to see receivers in ways I never really had as a player. When I was in the NFL, I was focused mainly on my job and helping my team win. Now I could study film of everybody while learning the intricate details that led to their success or demise. What I saw was a wide receiver position that wasn't just filled with players who were generating negative headlines as the twenty-first century began.

Marvin Harrison was torching defenders annually with the Indianapolis Colts, so much so that he set a league record with 143 receptions in 2002. Torry Holt blossomed into an explosive target in the aerial circus that was the St. Louis Rams. You also had two old-timers in Oakland still doing their thing before Randy arrived there. Forty-year-old Jerry Rice caught 92 passes for the Raiders in 2002 while thirty-six-year-old Tim Brown added 81 of his own. You had to be impressed with their staying power.

You want to know why Jerry lasted as long as he did? His former coach in San Francisco, Steve Mariucci, once told me a story about the 49ers' first training camp in Stockton, California, in 1998. Jerry was returning from major knee surgery and he wanted to practice with the rookies before the other veterans arrived a few days later. Mariucci balked at the idea. He didn't see any need for his star receiver to be running around with first-year players at that point in the preseason.

By the time Mariucci reached the team's offices that summer, he realized his words hadn't meant anything. Jerry hadn't even waited for the rookies to show in order to start his own work. Instead, Mariucci found him on the practice field running routes as team managers tossed passes in his direction. The last thing Jerry wanted to do was waste valuable time jump-starting his comeback.

That same desire could be found in various receivers around the league, especially those who had to fight for respect and opportunity. Jacksonville had a dangerous Pro Bowl duo in Keenan McCardell (who played for the Jaguars from 1996–2001) and Jimmy Smith (a Jaguar from 1995–2005). McCardell was so lightly regarded that he was the Washington Redskins' twelfth-round pick in 1991. Smith had been a 1992 second-round pick of the Dallas Cowboys but injuries—along with drug problems and a rift with Cowboys owner Jerry Jones— resulted in him barely playing during the first three years of his career. He didn't shine until then Jaguars head coach Tom Coughlin noticed his talents as a kick returner in Jacksonville.

Denver also had two terrific receivers in Ed McCaffrey and Rod Smith, both of whom caught at least 100 passes in 2000. McCaffrey had been a former third-round pick of the Giants before bouncing to San Francisco and then Denver. Smith hadn't even been drafted when he came into the league in 1994. He had to beat out two former first-round picks (Anthony Miller and Vance Johnson) just to keep a spot on the roster.

These receivers weren't interested in the attention that somebody like T.O. coveted. They only wanted to survive in a league where their talents were too often missed by decision-makers. That was the obvious downside of being a receiver around that time. If you didn't have the size of a T.O. or the speed of a Randy Moss, you had a harder time impressing NFL scouts.

Smith and McCaffrey, in particular, took great pride in their blocking. They were key figures in a Broncos attack that opened space for countless runners—including 2,000-yard rusher Terrell Davis in 1998—and they often didn't receive enough recognition for their work. "My son grew up watching me but he always idolized the flashy guys," Smith said. "I used to tell him that I put cleats on when I go to work, not makeup. I wanted people to respect me as a player, not a celebrity."

"The more high-maintenance guys brought more attention to the position but that helped and hurt," McCardell said. "If you played wide receiver, some people automatically thought you had some diva in you. They thought you might go off a cliff at any time. The position became a lot more like basketball, where it was about going one-on-one, talking trash, and being seen. But guys like me couldn't see ourselves being that way. We'd look at those other receivers and think they didn't need to be doing all that."

Those less heralded receivers did have one quality that always resonates with fans: They were underdogs. When a guy like Derrick Mason, a former return specialist, developed into the best receiver for the Tennessee Titans (and later the Baltimore Ravens), people respected his rise to stardom. The same was true of Pittsburgh's Hines Ward, a player who earned his success through hard-nosed blocking and fearless routes over the middle. The Steelers never foresaw him becoming their top pass-catching option when they used a third-round pick on him in 1998. He eventually played in four Pro Bowls and won MVP honors in Super Bowl XL.

It wasn't hard to see why those players blossomed. There were more opportunities than ever to catch passes for a living and less pressure placed on those unheralded wideouts who eventually thrived. Free agency also had become such a perilous path that teams were focusing more on cultivating their own talent through the draft. Instead of dumping big money into a Peerless Price or David Boston—both of whom bombed after being hailed as fortune-changing free agents—coaches and executives were eager to find a young talent clamoring for a shot.

The Carolina Panthers found such a guy in Steve Smith. A third-round pick in the 2001 draft, he went from being an elite kick returner to being a Pro Bowl receiver, one who teamed with Muhsin Muhammad in helping the Panthers reach the Super Bowl in 2003. Granted, he did have some anger management issues: Smith had two separate incidents during his career when he attacked teammates and was arrested for fighting and hospitalizing teammate Anthony Bright during a film session in 2002 (that case was ultimately dismissed when Smith entered a deferred-prosecution program). But you also couldn't deny his skills. He had speed, toughness, and the same nastiness that made Randy such a terror early in his career.

Another unheralded receiver who entered the NFL in the 2001 draft happened to have played junior college football with Smith in Los Angeles. His name was Chad Johnson and the Cincinnati Bengals made him their second-round pick that year. Despite playing for an organization that had been lousy for years, Chad thought he could be a star who helped Cincinnati rise out of the cellar. He even tracked Jerry Rice down after a game early in his career just to pick the future Hall-of-Famer's brain on how to thrive at the highest level of football.

When the Bengals hired Marvin Lewis as their head coach in 2003, it didn't take him long to understand Johnson's hunger. They first met at a community relations event in Cincinnati, a trip to a local school where tutors had been hired to help students improve their test scores. Lewis rode to the event with Chad and T. J. Houshmandzadeh, a third-year receiver who had played with Chad at Oregon State. Since Lewis didn't know much about either player, he asked them about their backgrounds.

Houshmandzadeh talked about how he stole cars as a thirteen-year-old kid in Los Angeles, dropped out of high school four years later, and needed a GED to get into junior college. Chad had grown up in Miami before going to Langston University and later Santa Monica College before finding a home at Oregon State. Lewis was stunned by their candor. He eventually said, "You guys probably shouldn't tell these kids your story because you're lucky to just be alive let alone be in the NFL. You should drop down on your hands and knees and thank God every day because you've definitely beaten the odds."

Both players certainly understood that. They drove each other in practice as if their lives depended on every rep. They'd work with the first-team offense against the scout team defense. When the first-team offense was taking a break, they'd run routes on the scout team offense against the first-string defense. Chad wouldn't stop there, either. He would call Lewis at night to see about training in the facility after hours and he wouldn't let up in the off-season.

Chad and Houshmandzadeh would work out relentlessly to refine their skills in the summer. They'd train in Los Angeles with star quarterbacks like Tom Brady, Drew Brees, and Bengals teammate Carson Palmer. Their sessions would generate so much buzz that other receivers and defensive backs would show up unannounced, just to get some serious work. As Houshmandzadeh remembered it: "Chad was football, football, football. That's the way he was all the time."

It also helped that Chad—who is a cousin of Keyshawn Johnson—had serious natural ability. He had tremendous quickness off the line of scrimmage, making him nearly impossible for defenders to jam. He was a little unorthodox in his route-running but he usually found ways to get open. At his best, he could create all types of nightmares for opposing defenses. "If he had man-to-man coverage on any pass play, I knew I could just jog through whatever route I was running," said Houshmandzadeh. "We all knew the ball was going to Chad in those situations."

The beauty of Chad Johnson back then was his combination of talent and desire. He'd never gained great recognition for his game before then and it didn't really seem to matter. When he found himself strolling through a Cincinnati mall in 2002 with Houshmandzadeh and fellow Bengals receivers Ron Dugans and Peter Warrick, not one person noticed Chad. The fans all swarmed around Warrick that day, worshiping the man who had been the team's first-round pick in 2000.

But that celebrity bug did bite Chad eventually. It came with every little bit of progress he made on the field. He made the first of his six Pro Bowls in 2003. That success gave him a platform to showcase his flair for entertaining, which he had no problem doing at any given moment. At first, Chad amused fans with a variety of touchdown-celebration dances, including an imitation of Michael Flatley's *Riverdance* in Chicago one season. Later on, he became more outlandish in his ideas to keep the spotlight focused squarely on his persona.

Chad would call out opposing defensive backs publicly before upcoming games. He openly talked about how wild his touchdown celebrations would become, even when he knew a large fine from the league might result from his actions. Before long, you didn't even have to wonder what Chad would do next. By the time he legally changed his last name to "Ochocinco" in 2008, he was the biggest showboat in all of pro sports.

It wouldn't be fair to put Chad in the same category as T.O. because their agendas were completely different. T.O. wanted everybody to pay attention to him, regardless of the damage it caused. Chad wanted everybody to have a good time, even it meant a hefty fine from the NFL every now and then. He thought he was merely making the show all the better with his ingenuity.

What Chad couldn't see was that with his huge grandstanding came huge risks to his career. The people who knew him best all emphasized he was a good guy with a big heart, and nobody could question his talent. But the more he behaved like the class clown on Sundays, the more it made people wonder what was really most important to him in the end. Chad was easily the biggest name in Cincinnati and he too often didn't realize the responsibility that came with that status.

There's little question Chad enjoyed being the most visible face of that franchise. He had the charisma and the nerve, and Carson wasn't nearly as assertive as most quarterbacks you'll meet. There was a need for leaders in Cincinnati and Chad felt equipped to fill that role with his unique style. And he wasn't the only wide receiver in the NFL who thought it was his job to raise his franchise's profile.

New Orleans had a Pro Bowl receiver who had similar beliefs about his own organization: Joe Horn. Like many of the wideouts previously mentioned, Horn didn't have anybody anointing him as a star upon his joining the Saints in 2000. He'd been the lowest member of that famed 1996 class—a fifth-round selection—and he didn't even play Division I football. Horn had attended Itawamba Community College in Fulton, Mississippi, because he couldn't qualify academically at a four-year school. When his grades there still weren't good enough after two years, he worked odd jobs and played in the Canadian Football League until the Kansas City Chiefs drafted him.

Talk about the swagger of a receiver. Horn had all that and then some. Even when he was playing for teams like the Shreveport Pirates and the Memphis Mad Dogs in the Canadian Football League, he didn't doubt his talents. "I felt like I'd arrived as a player when I was in the CFL," Horn said. "The NFL was just waiting for me to get there."

Horn wasn't all talk, though. Like Michael Irvin, he had a work ethic to go with his mouth. He learned strong fundamentals from his receivers coaches in Canada, and Pro Bowler Andre Rison mentored him in Kansas City as well. By the time Horn hit New Orleans, he was ready to prove his worth. He wound up making four Pro Bowls and bringing his own flair to the game.

When the Saints prepared to meet the New York Giants in a late-season Sunday night game in 2003, Horn was leaving his house when his five-year-old son asked to come with him. Horn told the boy he had to stay home because of school the next day, but he also promised the kid a phone call during the game. That call came in the second quarter of that contest, after Horn scored on a 13-yard touchdown. He jogged to the goal post and searched the padding for a few seconds. When he couldn't find what he was looking for, teammate Michael Lewis came over and pulled a cell phone out of the padding, and Horn started dialing his boy.

That stunt resulted in Horn receiving a $30,000 fine from the league, but you couldn't argue with the impact. Horn's play and personality were helping to make the Saints relevant. "When I got to New Orleans and saw how bad the franchise had been, I immediately wanted to bring notoriety to that town," Horn said. "And I was going to kill the myth about the Saints. I had that chip on my shoulder because everybody had disrespected us for so long. That's who I was as a man. I believe leaders are born, not made."

Now as brash as I was, I never considered myself the face of the Vikings. I had the biggest salary and the greatest influence, but we also had leaders like John Randle, Randall McDaniel, and Randy during my career. Being in New Orleans and trying to turn around a bottom-dwelling franchise had to be a different challenge. Somebody had to raise the expectations on the Saints and Horn thought he was the right man for the job.

But Horn wasn't just a leader on the field. He was also a leader in the community. He signed autographs when fans interrupted his meals in restaurants. He started conversations with people while standing in the checkout aisle at the grocery story. When Hurricane Katrina devastated New Orleans in 2005, he stepped his game up even more.

The Saints played that entire season in San Antonio. They also faced constant rumors about whether they would return to New Orleans, none of which owner Tom Benson completely dispelled. At one point, Horn was invited to talk with former NFL Players Association chief Gene Upshaw and then commissioner Paul Tagliabue about the ramifications of uprooting the Saints to San Antonio permanently. Horn didn't like the possibility from the start.

"A lot of people don't know that we were two minutes away from being the San Antonio Saints," Horn said. "When I talked to Tagliabue and Upshaw, they asked me what I thought about that. I said, 'How can you walk away knowing that these people have trusted and supported us? If you're talking about taking football away from them, we can't do that. I can't be a part of that.' The next morning the announcement came down that the Saints were staying in New Orleans. I'm not saying that happened because of me, but I felt like I helped the cause."

Unfortunately, Horn didn't have much more time to enjoy New Orleans. When the Saints hired Sean Payton as their head coach in 2006, he quickly clashed with Horn. In Horn's eyes, Payton wanted an offense that proved his play-calling was the key to his offensive success, not a need for high-profile receivers. "You look at the team now and you know Marques Colston could be a fifteen-hundred-yard receiver or Devery Henderson could be a star," Horn said. "But Payton wants the quarterback to get all the glory. You can't really argue against that, though. They won a Super Bowl with that approach."

That Super Bowl run during the 2009 season wasn't the hardest thing for Horn to stomach—and he actually watched the Saints' NFC divisional playoff win over Arizona from the stands to avoid any potential drama with Payton that day. It was the way others received credit for helping the city when they weren't around for the major devastation. "Sean Payton, Reggie Bush, Drew Brees—none of them were around when we came back from San Antonio," Horn said. "They gave those guys an ESPY award [for Team of the Year following the 2010 season] and that hurt me. My brother called me and he was upset."

Horn still calls the Saints' return to New Orleans after Katrina his Super Bowl moment. When the Saints released him in 2007, he signed with Atlanta and started mentoring a struggling receiver named Roddy White. The Falcons had used a first-round pick on White in the 2005 draft, only to watch him turn into an early disappointment. White was lucky to have such a blessing appear in his life. Some first-round picks weren't nearly that fortunate.

By the time White was drafted, it had become more popular than ever to invest big in rookie receivers. That didn't prove to be the greatest idea for some teams that made those calls.

I've long believed in an important premise about offense: A great receiver can make an average quarterback look a hell of a lot better. Ask Brian Billick. When he left Minnesota to become head coach of the Baltimore Ravens in 1999, the common belief was that his new team would become as explosive as the Vikings were when he was our offensive coordinator. But as he soon learned, you can't replace talent. Billick's offenses annually fizzled in Baltimore, where a defense led by Ray Lewis and Ed Reed dominated.

By the end of the 1990s, it was apparent that more teams were seeing just how much receivers could help an offense. A total of thirty wide receivers were selected in the first round of the NFL draft between 2000 and 2005, more than any other position. There were only nineteen quarterbacks drafted between those years, along with twenty-two running backs and eighteen offensive tackles. There also were twenty-four cornerbacks selected in the first round during that time but that clearly had to do with need: Somebody had to cover all those wideouts.

What I was seeing was the same philosophy Denny Green had preached back when he became my head coach in Minnesota: The more receivers you can put on the field, the easier it's going to be on your offense. We had all types of quarterbacks during my twelve seasons with the Vikings, ranging from Hall-of-Famers (Warren Moon) to retreads (Jim McMahon, Jeff George, Randall Cunningham) to young stars (Daunte Culpepper). Meanwhile, we had at least one Pro Bowl receiver every year I was there.

The only difference between our situation then and what was happening in the draft later was talent. We knew we had plenty of that with the Vikings. The same couldn't be said of all those players who went in the first round starting at the turn of the century. Most of those bright prospects never should've been selected that high.

Some were maddeningly inconsistent, like Cincinnati's Peter Warrick (fourth overall in 2000), Denver's Ashley Lelie (nineteenth overall in 2002), and Detroit's Roy Williams (seventh overall in 2004). Others were done in by injuries (Kansas City's Sylvester Morris) or problems with substance abuse and/or alcoholism (Jacksonville's R. Jay Soward, Seattle's Koren Robinson, and Detroit's Charles Rogers). There were some who just flat out couldn't play, most notably San Francisco's Rashaun Woods, the thirty-first pick in the 2004 draft.

All these players could thank one factor for their prominence: The need for receivers was so great that they simply became overvalued. "Football had become a chess match and you started to hear the term 'game-changer' enter the sport," said Roman Oben. "It wasn't just about having a guy who can make a catch on third down or move the chains. You had to have somebody who could demand double coverage."

Of all the first-rounders taken during that time, there were some who clearly thought talent alone would be enough to help them succeed in the NFL. Pittsburgh's Plaxico Burress, the eighth overall selection in 2000, fell into this category as a rookie. One afternoon after practice, when teammate Hines Ward asked Burress why his playbook wasn't in his locker, Burress said he only studied on certain days of the week. Ward diplomatically explained that professional football players studied their playbooks as much as possible.

Burress eventually grew into a reliable target for the Steelers (and later the New York Giants), but the same couldn't be said for Detroit's Mike Williams, the tenth overall pick in the 2005 draft. Lions general manager Matt Millen had made Williams the third consecutive receiver taken by Detroit in the first round—joining Charles Rogers and Roy Williams—and the belief was that Mike Williams was a can't-miss prospect. The red flags started revealing themselves when team nutritionists tried to put the 6'5", 235-pound receiver on a diet as a rookie. Williams balked, and weight issues plagued him for the rest of his days with the Lions. They released him after only two seasons.

The case of Mike Williams exemplified why it's so hard to evaluate wide receivers coming into the NFL. The ones who are truly dominant at the college level have a decided advantage over their competition. They can look better than they actually are because they're more athletic than the people covering them. When Williams became a star at USC, he probably faced many cornerbacks who didn't have the size to match up with him every down.

It's also hard to find many general managers with the courage to give a receiver time to develop. They can't go to the public and say that a first-round pick needs two years to find his way, even if that is the case. Most college players today have been exposed to sophisticated systems that require them to run a variety of routes and make adjustments based on coverage. That wasn't always the case at the end of the

1990s and the start of the new millennium. Some of these young guys were as raw as could be.

Jacksonville selected Arkansas quarterback Matt Jones with the twenty-first pick in the 2005 draft, all because he ran a 4.37 40-yard dash (while being listed at 6'6" and 237 pounds) at that year's NFL combine. They released him four years later after inconsistency and drug problems ruined his career as a pro receiver. The Philadelphia Eagles thought they had a future playmaker when they selected UCLA's Freddie Mitchell twenty-fifth overall in 2004. He became better known for running his mouth than running valuable routes, so much so that New England head coach Bill Belichick called him out before Super Bowl XXXIX. "All he does is talk," Belichick told reporters. "He's terrible, and you can print that."

"A lot of [receivers] came out for the money and then had to be taught fundamentals at the pro level," McCardell said. "They probably thought they'd be all right because they were big and fast. Once they got to the league, their teams thought they were supposed to know certain things and they didn't. A lot of busts happened because of that."

"I always tell young players that the difference between who you are and where you want to go is potential and production," said Troy Vincent. "When you come into the NFL, it's about what you can do today. But I'm not sure whether some young receivers really loved the game or just loved what things came along with [being in the league]. You look at the Jerry Rices, the Andre Reeds, and people like that, and they loved their craft. They didn't do it for the self-satisfaction of me."

The single biggest reason for the rising popularity of receivers was the rulebook. When the NFL decided to open up the game back in 1978, they declared it illegal for defenders to touch receivers more than 5 yards beyond the line of scrimmage. The idea was to keep aggressive cornerbacks like Pittsburgh's Mel Blount from manhandling wideouts on pass plays. The rule gave receivers more room to maneuver, but some felt like defensive backs still got away with violating the restrictions too often.

It wasn't until 2003, a few months after the Indianapolis Colts lost to New England in the AFC championship, that the league literally gave receivers free rein. Colts general manager Bill Polian had been outraged by the Patriots' attempts to hold Indianapolis receivers as they ran routes. New England got away with the tactic and went on to win their second Super Bowl. The Colts went home and let Polian make their case to the league's rule-makers.

The end result was that the illegal contact rule would be a top priority for officials from that point on. "They put the rule into effect in 1978, but having a rule and enforcing it are two different things," said Hall-of-Fame receiver James Lofton. "It really didn't get enforced until Bill Polian started getting on the competition committee about it."

The timing couldn't have been better for the first-round picks who actually did have bright futures. Future stars—like Roddy White, Reggie Wayne (Colts), and Santana Moss (Redskins/Jets)—all benefited from the stronger push for a pass-heavy league. So did another first-round pick taken in the 2004 draft. I'd known this player since he was a kid, and he was destined to bring a more palatable image to the position.

CHAPTER 12

A Different Model

One of my favorite experiences in football involved working with Randy Moss. I met him at a time when he was hungry to prove himself, and we enjoyed four years as teammates. As it turned out, I was fortunate enough to bond with another young, talented receiver as he set his own sights on NFL stardom. His name was Larry Fitzgerald, and we went back even further than Randy and myself.

My first memory of Larry was as a slender, earnest ball boy for the Minnesota Vikings in 1997. His father, Larry Fitzgerald Sr., was a local reporter who also happened to be really tight with both Denny Green and myself. Since Denny liked to provide jobs to children of close friends, the younger Larry found such an opportunity that year. He worked training camp in the summer and home games during the season.

It didn't take long before Larry and I became good friends. He was fourteen years old at the time, a kid looking for any advantage that might help him prosper as a football player. It was clear that he had the potential to grow and that toughness wasn't an issue. Larry loved playing outside linebacker in high school. He never backed away from being physical.

From what Larry Sr. said, his oldest son had always had a little mean streak in him once he started playing football. When Larry was ten years old, his mother, Carol, signed him up for a youth league. Larry Sr. showed up for his son's first practice in pads to find a boy racing around the field and launching himself at whoever stood in his path. There was no fear in Larry even then. Unlike most kids who face contact for the first time, he was wired to enjoy the tougher aspects of the game.

But Larry wasn't perfect. His father pulled him out of training camp one week after he started his first year as a ball boy. Apparently, some security guards had informed Larry Sr. that Larry had missed curfew one night. "I took him home and explained that he wasn't coming back if it happened again," Larry Sr. said. "I wasn't going to be embarrassed with the head coach. This was my livelihood."

Larry learned his lesson fast. He also impressed everybody with his hands once we moved deeper into camp. It wasn't uncommon for Larry to join us in pass-catching drills after practice, especially once Randy joined the team in 1998. Jake, Randy, and I would usually take at least fifty balls off the Jugs machine to finish a session, with the last twenty-five requiring one-handed grabs. Even at that tender age, Larry rarely let a ball slip through his fingers.

It wasn't long before Larry was a constant presence around the Vikings receivers. You'd see him at the hotel before games and in the locker room afterward. He spent plenty of time at my house as well, where he'd hang around with my children and enjoy my family life in the same way Randy later did. The players would also give him gloves and cleats, which made him even giddier.

You want to talk about a diehard fan? Since Larry worked the opposing team's sidelines during games, I'd glance over and see him proudly strutting around in our gear. If we were losing, then you'd really see the passion in him. He'd try to hide his emotions, but you could tell he wanted to scream out his frustrations in those moments.

Still, what I liked most about Larry was his curiosity. Most teenagers usually want to tell you what they can or will do with an opportunity. They think the most important thing is showcasing their skills, telling the world how talented they are. Larry cared more about the fundamentals of being a good player. He understood that sheer talent alone didn't mean anything if a receiver didn't take his craft seriously.

There were many days when he would walk up to me and say, "Uncle Cris, how do you do this or how do you do that?" He didn't want to just talk about route-running. He wanted to know what it took to set up a defensive back. He didn't want to only out-jump defensive backs. He wanted to learn how receivers position themselves for the best possible angle to go after the ball. The kid had a razor-sharp focus from the moment he started playing high school ball.

"It was a dream come true," Larry said. "Every kid who follows professional football would've loved that opportunity. I got to watch the best play the game. I saw how they studied and how they worked. Most people only know what they did on Sundays. I saw what they did to separate themselves from everybody else playing the game."

"I told Larry to soak up as much as he could," Larry Sr. added. "He was around two future Hall-of-Fame receivers, a head coach who won a hundred games, and an offensive coordinator who would win a Super Bowl. He was able to see who showed up early, who stayed late, and who was going home as soon as practice ended. I even tested him on the things he saw out there. I wanted him to see the good and the bad, because there definitely was bad."

One thing Larry didn't have a hard time understanding was humility. He had been a huge fan of Barry Sanders, Detroit's Hall-of-Fame running back, and that had been Barry's trademark. Barry embarrassed more defenders than any ball carrier in NFL history. But when he scored a touchdown, he never danced or dazzled fans with rehearsed celebrations. He just tossed the ball to the official and jogged back to his sideline.

I know Larry's parents loved to see the influence Barry had on their son. They constantly reminded him of the importance of carrying himself with a certain level of integrity whenever he stepped onto the field. Larry also gained plenty from watching the way Jake, Randy, and I attacked practice every day. He knew we weren't thinking about anything except maximizing every last bit of our abilities.

Before long, Randy and I—along with Daunte Culpepper, once he arrived in 1999—were attending Larry's games at the Academy of

Holy Angels high school in suburban Minneapolis. That was powerful motivation for him, because it wasn't like we went to only one game. We usually saw about three or four contests per year. We knew it meant a lot to him to see us in those stands. You could see his talent developing with every game he played.

Larry Sr. had moved Larry to that small school because the coach, Mark Pendino, stressed team values over individual gain. Larry played linebacker and safety and didn't even press his coach to try receiver until injuries to teammates presented an opportunity during his sophomore year. After Larry made a spectacular one-handed touchdown catch in a playoff game, his coaches knew where he belonged on offense. He received plenty of college scholarship offers as a linebacker, but his future was in catching passes.

In fact, I remember Larry Sr. approaching me one day and asking, "Do you think he could play in the NFL?" I told Larry Sr. that there was a possibility and I kept it at that. Larry was still at a point when just having a college scholarship opportunity was a blessing. The last thing I wanted was to inflate expectations for the boy.

It's not that I didn't understand why Larry's father would ask that question. It's just that I always told young players the same things when they wanted to know what it took to become a pro. The most important advice was this: It's a really hard thing to do. The people who play the game sometimes create the illusion that any talented athlete can reach the professional level with enough hard work, but it actually takes a lot of good fortune along with the ability to avoid injuries and distractions as well. If it were easy, then more kids would be able to look around their neighborhoods, cities, or counties and find NFL players.

Larry also had another issue affecting his chances of even playing in college: his grades. It wasn't that he was a dumb kid. He was just one who didn't put enough emphasis on academics when he started high school. He wasn't taking care of business at that point, and his school let him slide every year after that. By the time Larry was a senior, he didn't qualify for any four-year program. He wound up at Valley Forge Military Academy and College instead, a prep school that helped him improve his grades enough that he could accept a scholarship to the University of Pittsburgh.

Once Larry joined that program, I had a more reassuring answer for Larry's father about his son's pro potential. There was no question that he was going to be in the NFL very soon. Larry didn't only have great hands by then. He also had tremendous size (6'3" and 220 pounds), outstanding body control, and more speed than I ever imagined him gaining. When he was in high school, I worried that he might not run faster than 4.7 seconds in the 40-yard dash. By the end of his sophomore year, he was clocking below 4.5.

Larry was balling. He was in a sophisticated offense that built most of its attack around his talents. He was catching touchdowns like crazy (he would score 34 in twenty-six career games) and averaging 100 receiving yards a game. The only downside during that time was the tragedy brewing in Larry's home life.

Carol Fitzgerald died in 2003, following a seven-year fight with breast cancer. Larry was undoubtedly close to his father, but his mother was the soul of that family. When Carol fell ill, she didn't spend her days feeling sorry for herself. Instead, she became a huge activist in Minneapolis, one who encouraged other women to get regular mammograms and stay informed on the disease. The more I knew that family, the more I realized how much strength Larry took away from that woman.

When Carol died, it was a crushing blow for Larry. He had been arguing with Carol after his second year at Pittsburgh, apparently because she felt he was being disrespectful to a girlfriend. "[Carol] wasn't happy about how he was handling his stardom," Larry Sr. said. "Larry was the big man on campus and he responded by shutting her down."

Larry then made matters worse by staying away from home. "I'd tell him to call his mother and he wouldn't do it," Larry Sr. continued. "By the time he came home, it was too late. She had slipped into a coma. After that, Larry realized he'd made a terrible mistake because he was being hardheaded. He was hard on himself, but I told him he couldn't carry this with him the rest of his life. He had to move on."

Said Larry: "It was tough because it was a selfish thing on my part. I didn't know how sick she was but I still should've called. What I learned from that is the mistakes you make as a young person shape you as a man. After that point, I wasn't going to shut down if I was arguing with my father or my brother [Marcus]. I wish I had that same skill when I was younger, but it didn't work out that way."

Larry decided the best way to honor Carol at that point was through symbolism. He vowed to keep growing his trademark braids because that's exactly how his mother wore her hair in her final years. He also dedicated himself to terrorizing the world of college football. By the end of his sophomore season, Larry had won the Biletnikoff Award (given to the nation's top wide receiver) and finished second in the Heisman Trophy voting in 2003. He also earned a 3.5 GPA to prove he really was growing up in all the right ways.

As much as Carol's death crushed Larry, it also brought more purpose than ever into his life. He was always hungry. After that adversity, he'd never settle for being anything less than the best.

Larry was good enough for the Arizona Cardinals to select him with the third overall pick in the 2004 draft. Once again, Denny Green (then the Cardinals' head coach) had given Larry a job, and it wasn't hard to see the team's thinking. The Cardinals already had one talented, young receiver in Anquan Boldin, their second-round pick in 2003. With Boldin and Larry working together, Arizona had the potential to inflict some serious damage through the air.

It didn't take long for Larry to make his mark, either. He went from catching 58 passes as a rookie to grabbing 103 receptions (a franchise record) in his second year. He went to three Pro Bowls in his first five seasons. Larry also contributed to a trend that was counter to what we were seeing from other top receivers of his day: He practiced humility on a daily basis.

As with his college career, Larry didn't apply any extra sizzle to his game. He wasn't into touchdown dances, and his quotes were meant to inform instead of entertain. One day I asked Larry why he didn't want to be flashier in a league where individuality was more prominent. "Uncle Cris," he said, "I'm just trying to get the ball to the officials as soon as I can when I score. After that, all I'm thinking about is getting back to the end zone so I can do it all over again."

I suspect Larry's commitment might have been aided by what he saw in Randy's career. Larry had seen Randy at his best and at his worst. Larry wasn't naive. He knew that once the diva tag was established, it would be hard to shake.

More than anything, Larry was at peace with himself. He was quiet and respectful by nature, a player who never felt the need to win the approval of others. It also helped that he'd been a huge star at the college level. You don't earn the kind of attention he gained at Pitt without realizing the responsibilities that come with it.

If Larry ever forgot that reality, he had a father who could reiterate the importance of shaping a strong public image. "Larry has been around stars his entire life," Larry Sr. added. "Not just the Vikings but people like Michael Jordan, Magic Johnson, Kevin Garnett. He's been able to see what it was like to have those expectations on you all the time. What he learned is that to win, you don't just have to be a star. You have to be a big-time player in big games. And that meant he had to do more every year he stepped out there."

That mind-set had to play a serious role in Larry never crying out for attention. If you looked at somebody like T.O., he was a relative unknown when he arrived in the NFL. The same was true of Chad Johnson and Joe Horn. Those players craved the opportunities to show the world their talents. You'd be blind to not know what Larry was doing before he eventually entered the league.

In fact, Larry was no different from another rising star receiver at the time, Houston's Andre Johnson. The third overall pick in the 2003 draft, Johnson was another freakish combination of size (6'3", 229 pounds) and speed (4.41 in the 40-yard dash). His alma mater, Miami, had long been known for big personalities and even bigger trash-talkers at the height of its power. Johnson was a strange fit in that regard. I'd followed him for years and even in high school he didn't spend much time chattering at opponents.

Andre was so talented that I often tried to motivate Larry by pointing out Andre's considerable gifts. If somebody asked me to list the league's best young receivers, I usually started with Andre before mentioning Larry. Nobody could compete with Larry's hands. But running by people was a gift that I always envied in a receiver's skill set.

Because of certain circumstances, people didn't hear a whole lot about Larry and Andre in those days. Andre was stuck on a Texans team that didn't know how to improve quickly. They didn't stabilize their quarterback situation until Matt Schaub arrived in 2007 and disappointing seasons were commonplace for most of Andre's career. Larry faced the same challenges in Arizona.

The Cardinals had three straight losing seasons in Larry's first three years with the franchise. The team also thought Matt Leinart was going to be their quarterback of the future until Kurt Warner proved to be a better option. Larry never complained about those issues at the time. He was always a consummate professional, a receiver fully aware of what he actually could control on a football field.

Larry brought that same maturity to our friendship as well. He truly believed in the value of maintaining tight bonds with the people closest to him. It didn't matter where he was in the world or what was happening in his life. He'd usually find time to call, text, or simply send a photo explaining what he was doing. There may have been a few times when we lost contact briefly, but Larry was committed to not letting our relationship slip.

You could see that same devotion in Larry's craft. The more time he logged in the league, the more he focused on fine-tuning even the smallest details in his game. He actually made the biggest strides in his progress in 2007, when Todd Haley became Arizona's offensive coordinator. Though Haley didn't coach receivers for the Cardinals, he did challenge Larry to raise his game.

Haley's major concern with Larry was his yardage after the catch. Larry had been putting up huge numbers, but he was only averaging 1.5 yards after his receptions in the year before Haley arrived. "I talked about his run after the catch on one hundred receptions," Haley said. "I told him to stand there with the ball and fall forward. That's three yards right there, which would be three hundred yards more on a one-hundred-catch season. Then I told him to think about what could happen if he got five yards after the catch. At first he would just catch a ball in practice and toss it back to the defensive back. After a while, he was running all the way down the field after every catch."

Larry showcased that same intensity during the off-season. We would spend at least one week a year every summer working out together in Minneapolis. Every summer would end with him having spent ample time improving a flaw in his repertoire. As Haley said, "Larry's sole goal was to be the greatest receiver ever."

I wasn't the only person who admired that quality in him. He'd have Jerry Rice come to those workouts in Minneapolis. Andre Rison would show up, along with Michael Irvin. Anybody who had information that could help him grow was welcome at his sessions. Larry would pick all our brains, keep notes on the best suggestions, and then add them to his game.

That intense work ethic didn't happen as soon as he walked into the NFL. Larry built it over time, by studying and separating himself from his peers. "If you took the best young receivers in the game and had them work out with Jerry Rice in his prime, most of them couldn't keep up with him," said Atlanta Falcons receivers coach Terry Robiskie. "The only one who I think would survive would be Larry Fitzgerald."

"When I look at the way I'm wired, I call it a gift and a curse," Larry said. "It's a gift because it's made me a great football player but it definitely affects my personal life. I'm never satisfied. I always want to do more. If I go on vacation, I can't just sit on the beach and stare at the ocean. I see a mountain and I want to go climb it. That's just how I am."

Within four years, that attitude had turned Larry into one of the league's elite receivers. In his fifth season, he delivered a performance that would give him a strong claim to being the best.

It's an incredible feeling to hit your stride as a receiver. There comes a point when relentless training catches up with rare talent and the game slows down in ways that once seemed unimaginable. I remember the calm I felt in 1994, when I set the NFL record with 122 receptions. It was the first time I was playing at a level that satisfied my own personal expectations.

I'd have to think Larry sensed something similar in 2008. He'd been to the Pro Bowl and produced stellar numbers by that point in his career. What he hadn't done was separate himself from all the other elite wideouts in the league. The only way he could do that was by helping the Cardinals go places they'd never gone.

That year started well for Larry because Arizona finally had settled on Warner as the quarterback. The Cardinals had been hoping Leinart would win the job eventually, but Warner was too good to ignore. He had played in two Super Bowls in St. Louis—winning one during the 1999 season—and he'd regained the touch that had vanished from his game in the wake of recurring thumb injuries. For the first time in his career, Larry knew his job would be much easier heading into the regular season.

That's something people often don't realize with receivers. It's not only about when the player is ready to take his career to another level. It's also about whether he has the right guy throwing the football to him. Receivers know the best signal-callers can get the ball to them in the most critical of situations. In Warner, Larry had a quarterback who could hit him exactly in stride, creating opportunities for longer runs after the catch.

Larry's numbers that season weren't much different from what he'd produced throughout his career (he had 96 receptions, 1,431 yards, and 12 touchdowns). But what did change was the impact he had in the moments that counted most. The Cardinals had plenty of other weapons on offense, including Anquan Boldin and running back Edgerrin James. But when they needed a critical play, Larry was the player whose number was called most frequently.

There's a term in football called the "fifty-fifty" ball, which applies to a pass that is thrown to a receiver who isn't open. The term basically means that both the offensive and defensive player involved in the play have an equal shot at catching the ball. Larry was spectacular in those situations throughout that season. I'm talking about timing his leaps, catching the ball at the apex of his jump, and snatching it in traffic. There weren't many receivers who could make those plays as consistently as Larry did.

Larry also became more versatile within the Cardinals offense. "We were able to move him around and create more schemes for him," Haley said. "He wouldn't just line up at split end. We'd put him in the slot. We'd put him in motion. We'd line him up inside in a three-by-one set so we could get him isolated on a linebacker. Larry used to be comfortable just lining up and running the routes he knew. He grew a lot that season."

Once the Cardinals won the NFC West and qualified for Larry's first postseason opportunity, the expectations on him increased even more. Before the playoffs started, we had a long conversation about what that stage meant to his career. I was looking at my first shot at making the Hall of Fame—and hearing all sorts of criticism about how I never reached the Super Bowl—so I used that as a reference point. I wanted Larry to know exactly what success in these games could do for his own career.

"Don't be like me," I told him. "Don't let people look at your career when it's over and say that you had a lot of catches but you didn't do this or that."

Larry didn't need me to hammer that point home. He knew that Arizona had been an obscure franchise that rarely drew the kind of attention that was coming its way. He also understood that such a chance might never be within his grasp again. It had been ten years since the Cardinals had last appeared in a playoff game at that point. They could easily go another decade with a similar drought.

Larry didn't waste any time making an impact. He caught 6 passes for 101 yards and a touchdown in Arizona's wildcard victory over Atlanta. He was even better the next game, with 8 receptions for 166 yards and another score against Carolina. By the time the Cardinals hosted Philadelphia in the NFC championship, everybody expected the Eagles to slow Larry. He wound up with 9 receptions for 152 yards and 3 more touchdowns.

No receiver had ever looked that dominant in the postseason. Not Lynn Swann. Not Michael Irvin. Not even Jerry Rice. As much as Warner was thrilling people with his revival, Larry was redefining what a receiver could do in the most pressure-packed moments. It was like watching Michael Jordan score 50 every night. People couldn't believe how unstoppable Larry had become in those few games.

"Kurt was awesome that year but Larry really put us on his back," said Haley, who now works as the Pittsburgh Steelers offensive coordinator. "He was just in a zone and I would tell Kurt to trust that. Kurt was such a progression passer that if you weren't open, he would go to his next read. That [postseason] he went against every instinct he had. Even when Larry was covered, I told him to throw in his direction because Larry was going to make the play."

After all the bad press that had come down on the position in the preceding years, here was a star proving that props, temper tantrums, and blatant disrespect weren't the only ways for receivers to end up in the headlines. Larry was showing the world an old-school route to notoriety. He was simply doing his job as exceptionally as he could do it. In return, the football-watching world was mesmerized by the sheer brilliance of his talents.

When I spoke to Larry in the days leading up to that Super Bowl XLIII matchup with Pittsburgh, I reminded him to keep the same focus that had brought him and his team that far. "Be patient. You know [Pittsburgh Steelers defensive coordinator] Dick LeBeau is going to have something planned because he's not going to let you beat him. They'll get the ball to you eventually."

As it turned out, Larry had to wait a long, long time for his opportunities to arrive. He caught only 1 pass through the first three quarters of that contest and the Cardinals trailed by 13 going into the final period. That's when Arizona decided that their best chance at victory would be getting the football to Larry. He caught a 1-yard touchdown pass from Warner early in the fourth quarter and then electrified everybody as the game neared its conclusion.

The Steelers were leading 20–16 when Warner dropped back from his own 36-yard line with 2:48 remaining in the contest. Pittsburgh had been keeping safeties Ryan Clark and Troy Polamalu deep in coverage while having underneath defenders jam the Cardinals receivers off the line to disrupt their routes. It was a safe late-game defense to prevent a big play. But when Larry ran through the jam of Steelers cornerback Ike Taylor and darted toward the middle of the field, Pittsburgh's comfort level evaporated quickly.

Warner hit Larry perfectly in stride, as Taylor and outside linebacker James Harrison tried to keep up. Since Clark and Polamalu had drifted toward the sidelines to cover other receivers, nobody was there to stop Larry's path to the end zone. There were days when I often wondered if Larry would ever be fast enough to be an elite NFL wide receiver. But when he raced to that 64-yard touchdown and left countless defenders in his wake, he looked like he'd been shot out of a cannon.

I watched that play from my hotel room because I was supposed to be on ESPN after the game (I joined the network in April 2008). I had stayed at the stadium until halftime—to support Larry—before preparing for the show later. But the game became so suspenseful that I found myself waiting anxiously for Larry to do something huge. After he scored that touchdown, I sprinted five blocks to the set to catch the end of the game.

That touchdown had put Larry in position for so many bigger things in his career. There's no question he would've been the game's Most Valuable Player, which would've made him the third receiver to win that award in the previous five Super Bowls (joining New England's Deion Branch and Pittsburgh's Hines Ward). He also would've elevated himself above all the other receivers in that generation. All the Cardinals had to do was hold on for two minutes and thirty-nine seconds. Once the game clock expired, Larry's place in history would've been set.

By the time I walked into the ESPN offices for makeup, Steelers quarterback Ben Roethlisberger was dropping back from Arizona's 7-yard line and pump-faking in the midst of a collapsing pocket. When he finally fired the pass, it sailed over three Arizona defenders before wide receiver Santonio Holmes snatched it in the corner of the end zone. I couldn't believe my eyes. Larry had gone from the highest of highs to the lowest of lows in the time it took me to get to my job.

My heart sank as I thought about what he was feeling as the game ended. The losing team in a Super Bowl always seems to be forgotten once the postgame celebration begins. Hordes of reporters and photographers rush the field. Game crews set up the victory stage and rope off the field under clouds of confetti and streamers. The winners hug and cry and laugh. The losers vanish amid the chaos, as if their mere presence might interfere with the party about to jump off.

I never did find Larry on the television screen as the network cameras focused on Roethlisberger, Holmes (the game's MVP), and their teammates. It wasn't until our broadcast was about to start that I received a phone call from him. Given how devastated I was after losing the NFC championship to Atlanta during the 1998 season, I was waiting to hear the same pain in Larry's voice. Instead, just as Randy had done ten years earlier, Larry said something that totally changed my feelings about the moment.

"I want you to analyze the season," Larry said. "And tell me what it's going to take for me to get better."

We had enjoyed some great moments in Larry's career but that was the best in my book. I was sitting there on an ESPN set, wiping tears from my eyes because of what he'd lost. He was halfway across town in a locker room filled with crushed teammates and coaches. He easily could've felt sorry for himself after producing 7 receptions, 127 yards, and 2 touchdowns that night. But his refusal to do so convinced me that he had plenty of great moments left in the NFL.

That postseason ended with Larry having enjoyed the most prolific playoff run by a wide receiver ever. He set NFL records for receptions (30), yards (546), touchdowns (7), and—if they actually kept track of this stuff—memories. It was later revealed that Larry had played all those games with a broken left thumb and torn cartilage, making his performance all the more amazing. Still, what I'll always remember most about Larry during that year was the phone call.

People say he's a different kind of receiver. They have no idea how correct they actually are.

A few months after Larry tore up the postseason, the debate raged even more about who was the NFL's top receiver. Larry had plenty of supporters, because no other wideout had accomplished as much as he had during a playoff run. Andre Johnson had his people as well. He was a matchup nightmare for a Houston team that was desperately searching for more weapons to put around him. There also was a talented receiver coming off his second year in Detroit—a player named Calvin Johnson—who had a chance to eventually enter that conversation.

As much as I loved Larry and Andre, Calvin had even more upside than the both of them. He was bigger (at 6'5" and 235 pounds), faster (having run a 4.35 40-yard dash), and a dominant performer in a run-first offense at Georgia Tech. I thought Randy was a freak when he entered the league. Calvin could hurt defenses in the same way, especially by making plays anyplace on the field.

What was interesting about Calvin was that he brought the same personality to the league that Andre and Larry already had. He was an introvert. He rarely did things to draw attention to himself. He also had to deal with the same quarterback issues that they had, as the Lions' quarterback of the future, Matthew Stafford, battled shoulder problems during the first two years of his career after being the top pick in the 2009 draft.

The collective presence of all three of these players didn't seem so critical at the time, but it was a welcome change. The talk about receivers didn't mainly focus on the high-maintenance characters anymore. Now we had young rising stars who had a seasoned maturity to their games. They didn't need to go the extra mile to draw attention to themselves.

The more you looked around the NFL, the more you saw receivers with a similar desire to remain more low-key. Reggie Wayne wasn't making crazy headlines in Indianapolis nor was Wes Welker in New England. Greg Jennings had a similar approach in Green Bay, as did Derrick Mason in Baltimore. That isn't to say all the characters had vanished from the game. They just weren't dominating the spotlight in ways they once had.

Larry wasn't totally responsible for that new approach, but he did play a huge role in it. As Troy Vincent said, "Larry Fitzgerald is a throwback player when you think about how he handles his business. He's not doing all that commercial stuff but he's still very marketable." Larry grew so large that President Bill Clinton invited him to Uganda to help open a school for impoverished kids there. If we didn't already know it, this was confirmation that this was one player who was widely held in high regard.

"When it comes down to it, I catch footballs for a living," Larry said. "That's not some great feat. It's not like I'm saving lives. Now, do I love my opportunity? Yes. But I don't take myself that seriously. I try to know my place and I understand I'm the last part of the play. The line has to block and the quarterback has to make the throw in order for me to succeed."

"It's been great to watch him handle his success," said Larry Sr. "He's shown that you don't have to be a diva or show your unhappiness when the ball isn't coming your way. I'm proudest of that more than anything. He's still a great football player and he realizes the ball isn't going to come his way twenty times a game. The only thing that matters is what he does with his opportunities."

I doubt Larry spent much time celebrating his success. Just as he had done as a child and after the Super Bowl, his sole focus was on maximizing his potential. That desire eventually became visible in other receivers who needed to find their own sense of purpose. While Larry ushered in a new youth movement with his rise to stardom, there were other receivers surprising people in different ways, and Randy was still among them.

The last time I had seen Randy, he was driving away from my home after a tense conversation about his future in the spring of 2007. He was traded from Oakland to New England a few weeks after that talk. The compensation—a fourth-round pick—revealed how much his value had shriveled during those two disappointing years with the Raiders. Oakland was so tired of him that they basically gave him away to the Patriots.

I would've had a hard time believing Randy would reinvent himself after I watched him play in Oakland. As it turned out, he became a perfect example of what a talented wideout could do when given a shot at redemption in a model franchise. It wasn't just more focused, younger stars like Larry who were changing the image of receivers as we moved toward the end of the first decade of the twenty-first century. That transformation was also aided by something far less predictable: an assortment of troubled veterans who decided it was finally time to grow up.

CHAPTER 13

The Art of Reinvention

It's difficult for a player to get a face-lift once he's earned a bad reputation in the NFL. The average professional career lasts just over three years and that doesn't allow much time for resurrection. Regardless of the player's commitment, he can't fathom how much effort goes into such a change. Even the most talented receivers can struggle to undo the damage they've done to their respective livelihoods.

All I had to do was look at my own career to understand that. I was considered damaged goods from the moment I left Philadelphia to the time I proved myself in Minnesota. It didn't matter that the Vikings didn't know everything about why the Eagles had dumped me in 1990. All they knew was that there had to be some reason behind my departure.

I still question if Minnesota would've taken me if they had known about my addiction problems at the time. I might have been too big a gamble, a player unworthy of that kind of support. They also had no idea how much I wanted to push my life toward a better place at that time. Every day counted when I stepped onto a football field. It was a grind unlike anything I had ever known.

When I heard that Randy Moss was going to New England in 2007, I suspected he would understand the challenge of those circumstances. Everybody knew he had worn out his welcome in Minnesota and checked out mentally in Oakland. The question on many minds was: Which Randy Moss was going to show up in New England—the all-world talent who had blown people away in his younger days or the disinterested diva who vanished when times got tough?

I had an inside track on Randy's whereabouts, so I suspected the old Randy was making a comeback. We used the same stretching therapist near my home in Florida, so I usually heard about Randy's business through those folks. The word in the spring of 2007 was that the Patriots were coming at Randy the right way. The New England front office talked to a ton of people before making that trade. Despite everything that had happened, most of what they heard about Randy was complimentary.

I liked the idea of Randy being in New England because all the right factors were in place there. He had a strong head coach in Bill Belichick, a man who commanded respect because of his three Super Bowl victories between 2001 and 2005. Long gone were the days when a disgruntled receiver like Terry Glenn felt comfortable waging open war with Belichick. He had become a coach with enough clout that no player dared cross him. If that happened, the player would be run out of town—and miss a chance at a championship—before he ever had time to call a moving van.

Randy may have had issues with authority figures, but he also loved winning. He saw that Patriots quarterback Tom Brady was the best signal-caller whom he'd ever have a chance to play with in his career. New England also had an excellent offensive system that would combine Randy's deep speed with the quickness of slot receiver Wes Welker operating on underneath routes. Throw in other reliable targets like Jabar Gaffney and Donté Stallworth, and the Patriots had weapons all over the field. All Randy had to do was take the top off every defense he faced.

It might sound ironic to some people—especially given Randy's rebellious image—but he thrives off structure. He likes having strong leadership around him because it means fewer distractions. Randy could've cared less about being a star. When he was in the right environment, he only cared about playing at the highest possible level. If

Randy had his way, he wouldn't talk to the media at all. He'd simply do his job and go home to hang out.

Coming to New England offered him that benefit. Belichick was notorious for shielding his players from the press, so Randy didn't have to worry about reporters misconstruing his words (not that he cared about that stuff). In fact, the most noteworthy comments Randy made after joining the Patriots were mainly pointed at Brady. He said that Peyton Manning had plenty of dangerous receivers over the years. It was time Brady had some of his own weapons.

That statement revealed plenty about where Randy's head was coming into that 2007 season. I knew he was physically healthy because he always worked hard in the off-season. I also knew his head was in the right place as that season drew closer. The Patriots didn't use him much in the off-season, claiming that his hamstring was acting up, but he looked perfectly fine once the games started counting.

Randy had 9 receptions for 183 yards in a season-opening win over the Jets. The most impressive part of that performance was a 51-yard touchdown pass he caught in the third quarter. The Jets shadowed Randy with a cornerback, a safety, and a linebacker as he raced to the post. He was still 3 yards ahead of everybody when Brady's pass hit him on the way to the end zone.

Belichick was the only person who seemed to be running as hard as Randy on that play. While the ball soared through the air, he raced down the sideline, waiting for it to land in Randy's hands. When Randy jogged back toward his teammates, Belichick yelled, "That's the Randy Moss I know." I think the entire football-watching world agreed with Belichick's words that day.

The Patriots weren't just better with a revitalized Randy on their roster. The NFL was a better league with him locked in. He spent that regular season—one that saw New England go 16-0—reminding everybody of what made him so special in the first place. And it was beautiful to watch.

The Patriots did things with Randy that nobody else had ever tried. They threw the deep post pattern more instead of only asking Randy to run go routes that kept him outside. They hit him on slants, seams, and crossing patterns in the red zone. In one game against Miami, Brady twice threw to Randy in the middle of double coverage. Both times Randy leaped over the defenders for touchdowns.

The most historic moment of that season for Randy came in the week-sixteen win over the New York Giants. Brady had tried to hit him on a deep pass in the fourth quarter that sailed over Randy's head. The Patriots were so confident that year that they called the same exact route on the next play. This time Brady found Randy for a 66-yard score that put them both in the NFL single-season record books. It was Brady's 50th touchdown pass (breaking Peyton Manning's mark) and Randy's 23rd touchdown catch (surpassing Jerry Rice).

Nobody could understate the impact Randy had made. Along with producing 98 receptions for 1,493 yards, he also helped New England set a single-season scoring record with 589 points. "The 2007 Patriots and the 1998 Vikings are the two highest-scoring teams in NFL history," said former Vikings offensive coordinator and Baltimore Ravens head coach Brian Billick. "I don't think it's a coincidence that Randy Moss played on both of them."

The only downside for Randy that season was a loss few people could've seen coming. The New York Giants upset the Patriots in Super Bowl XLII, with Randy catching only 5 passes in that defeat. The most memorable highlights on that day actually belonged to two Giants receivers. David Tyree made a near impossible one-handed grab with Patriots safety Rodney Harrison draped all over him to keep New York's game-winning drive alive. Then Plaxico Burress—the same man who had guaranteed a Giants victory earlier in the week—caught a 13-yard touchdown pass from Eli Manning to give New York the lead for good.

The history books will say the Patriots finished 18-1. What can't be underestimated was the way Randy dominated the league that season. He once again proved that he was at his best when he had something to prove. He also spent the next two years reminding people that there were plenty of reasons for defensive backs to fear him. I'd never seen a player go from looking so abysmal to so awesome in the span of twelve months.

Randy had pulled off a feat in New England that had been far more difficult than what he'd done as a rookie in Minnesota. He had to look within himself and acknowledge that he wasn't being the player he was capable of being. It takes courage and self-awareness to address that flaw after enjoying his level of success. As we learned with some other receivers, it isn't so easy for certain stars to change their own colors.

When I looked at receivers at the end of the 2000s, I saw plenty who were trying to accomplish a feat similar to Randy's with their own careers. Take Terrell Owens and Chad Johnson. They both had become so well known for what they did off the field that their on-field performances didn't have the same impact any longer. They were personalities instead of players; stars who seemed to be driven more by their need for attention than their desire to win.

T.O. had forced his way out of Philadelphia—after a relentless battle with the Eagles—and landed in Dallas in 2006. He was so coveted by the Cowboys that owner Jerry Jones signed him four days after his release and gave him a three-year, $25 million contract. As much as Jerry liked T.O.'s playmaking ability, he also surely coveted his entertainment value. T.O. was a traveling road show by then. He could keep people riveted anywhere he went simply by opening his mouth.

Even his former teammates sensed that Owens was more manipulator than madman. "T.O.'s issues in Philadelphia were never as big as the media made them out to be," said former Philadelphia cornerback Sheldon Brown, a teammate of T.O.'s with the Eagles. "There were supposed to be all these problems between him and Donovan McNabb but they'd always dap each other up and laugh when he was in Dallas. It was always about business with T.O."

That may have been true, but after a certain point business went bad for T.O. After famously encouraging Dallas fans to "get your popcorn ready" upon his arrival, he fell victim to the same reputation that he spent years building. You could argue that T.O. was still a dangerous weapon, given his 166 receptions and 28 touchdowns in his first two seasons. What he couldn't do was convince people that the problems he created in San Francisco and Philadelphia weren't going to happen in "Big D."

By 2008, news reports claimed that T.O. once again had become a divisive presence inside another locker room. Anonymous reports surfaced that he was jealous of how heavily quarterback Tony Romo relied on tight end Jason Witten in the Dallas offense. The underlying sentiment was that T.O. was up to his old tricks. And if he wasn't getting the ball enough, then he was a ticking time bomb waiting to explode.

In fairness to T.O., there were never any issues within Dallas that rivaled the problems he inflicted on the 49ers or Eagles. He never suggested that Romo was a homosexual, nor did he publicly denigrate then offensive coordinator Jason Garrett. Aside from a 2006 incident that was first reported as a suicide and later ruled an accidental overdose, he only made news on the field. It was as if he'd either gotten tired of his prior antics or had simply found enough attention to satisfy him.

"I had him his first year in Dallas and I didn't have a problem with the guy," said former Cowboys receivers coach Todd Haley. "He had some things happen off the field—and there were some drops—but I was fine with him."

Still, such impressions were lost on most people who followed T.O. He had become so controversial that Fox sideline reporter Pam Oliver did four separate stories on him in his first season with Dallas. "The Cowboys were a ratings bonanza anyway," Oliver said, "but when you added the most dysfunctional receiver in football to America's Team, it was too good to be true. I did a story on T.O. coming to Dallas. I did a story on T.O.'s relationship with Tony Romo. I did another story on whether T.O. was bringing the Cowboys down. Sometimes I was surprised that he talked to us at all because the guys on the [Sunday morning] studio show were always killing him."

The consensus was that T.O. would never stop being a potential headache and that meant teams had to be wary at all times. There's a reason why he bounced from Buffalo to Cincinnati after Dallas decided against re-signing him following the 2008 season. The more he aged, the less teams wanted to take a chance on the notion that he was a changed man. His reputation preceded him.

Chad was finding it just as difficult to maintain the success he enjoyed early in his career. Bengals head coach Marvin Lewis first sensed trouble with his star receiver in December 2005, when Cincinnati rewarded quarterback Carson Palmer with a six-year extension on a contract that still had three years remaining on it (and increased the total potential value on Palmer's deal to $118.75 million). When Bengals executive vice president Katie Blackburn called to give Lewis the good news, Lewis told her to wait before notifying the media. Lewis wanted to talk with Chad first.

"I told Chad to come in because I didn't want to tell him that over the phone," Lewis said. "And not too long after I told him that, he fired Jerome Stanley as his agent and hired Drew Rosenhaus. Chad wound up getting an extension in 2006 that was basically guaranteeing him the same money he would've made anyway. But things were different after that. It got to be money driven."

Lewis wasn't the only person seeing a difference in Chad by then. "Chad and I trained every off-season until around 2006 or 2007," said former Bengals receiver T. J. Houshmandzadeh. "That's when he stopped coming to L.A. to work out. And when he did come, he wasn't there every day. I eventually made a comment to him like, 'Damn, Chad. What are you doing?' He looked at me like I was hating on him—or calling him out—and then he'd tell me he was working out in Miami. I eventually left it alone after a while because I felt like I'd said my piece."

Chad didn't help himself much after that. In June 2007, he participated in a publicity stunt that involved him racing a horse in a 100-meter dash in Cincinnati. About eight thousand people showed up for the event. I was also in town but for a different reason. Lewis had invited me there to speak to his team—and specifically Chad—about how to be professionals and leaders in the NFL.

I was supposed to talk to the entire team, and then with a few key veterans and Chad individually. The only person I didn't get to see was Chad, because he never showed up for the meeting. Here I was preaching accountability, and the team's biggest star was nowhere to be found one day after his big race. The kicker was that he called Lewis and asked if I could stick around for an extra day to accommodate him.

That situation gave me a clear sense of where Chad was heading in Cincinnati. I realized even more when the Bengals opened that year with a game against the Baltimore Ravens on Monday night. After catching a 39-yard touchdown pass from Carson Palmer in the first quarter, Chad sprinted back to the bench and donned an oversized yellow sports jacket that Houshmandzadeh handed to him. In huge letters on the back of the jacket was a question that proved Chad had lost all perspective: FUTURE H.O.F. 20??

Chad would've been fine if he had stuck with the touchdown celebrations and the random funny anecdote. Instead, he kept pushing the envelope until he crossed the line with that stunt. It wasn't just an immature move. It was a downright foolish one. It also wasn't funny and outsiders started to see exactly what the Bengals were dealing with on a daily basis.

Moments like that became more annoying for Lewis because Chad was pulling more people into his acts—"We were always trying to figure out who was getting this stuff to him on the field," Lewis said—and it was undermining the team. "The people inside the building knew it was just Chad being Chad most times," Lewis continued. "But I think his teammates also got tired of answering questions about him. He saw it as being his way of competing but the Hall-of-Fame jacket went too far. That was sacred."

It was clear by then that Chad was becoming more focused on his celebrity than developing his game. He probably listened to too many enablers or thought it was helping his image off the field. What he didn't understand is that you entertain people in football with your ability. When you're trying to think of ways to keep the game fun for fans, you tend to lose focus and credibility.

That 2007 season was the beginning of the end for Chad. He enjoyed just one more 1,000-yard season (which earned him Pro Bowl alternate status in 2009). He also found more people complaining about his lack of explosiveness, productivity, and desire. It seemed that all people associated Chad with were his stunts. Once he wasn't finding the end zone on a routine basis, his entertainment value spiraled in the same downward direction as his statistics.

One Bengals coach said the team had issues with Chad's inability to play anything other than split end and his toughness declined as his celebrity grew. "He was never really courageous from the start, but the amount of routes he was willing to run with vigor declined around 2007 and 2008," said the coach. "He wasn't as interested in running inside and his attention to detail—which was never great—became a problem. He got to a point where he would just get into a route and say he was open. But the issue was that the play called for an eighteen-yard pattern and he was at thirteen. It's hard for a quarterback to throw the ball when guys are constantly in different places."

What I never understood about Chad—who changed his name from Ochocinco back to Johnson in 2012—was why he couldn't reel himself in once his career slide began. He was an extremely talented receiver in his prime, one who could do just about anything a team needed. He eventually became a one-man reality show, a celebrity hell-bent on amassing Twitter followers and finding his way onto *Dancing with the Stars*. Even when his actions were leading to fines, he didn't care about the consequences. Good or bad, it was all publicity in the end.

At the very least, one would think that he'd be concerned about the cash. When the NFL fines a player, it's not like getting a parking ticket, where you just go down to the police department and pay it. They take the money away from players before they ever see it. All you get is a letter from the commissioner's office explaining the punishment and a much lighter check than the one you received a week earlier. And trust me—it's hard to make money, even at that level.

The sad part about Chad was that he could've been far better than what he became. As I learned through my own experience, you need good people around once you start becoming successful in the NFL. Without that, it's too easy to get lost or distracted. In Chad's case, he started caring more about what the NFL could do for him than what he could do to capitalize on a tremendous opportunity. Instead of becoming a transcendent player, he became just another talented receiver who entertained fans for a few years.

"Chad is a pretty good guy but he's just like a twelve-year-old kid," said one Bengals assistant. "Other things started to get his attention as his career went on and he lost the focus he used to have. He'd always tell the coaches things like, 'I have to be me and do my thing.' But when you start becoming a distraction, it becomes selfish because you're taking away from the team. He never saw it that way because deep down he cared more about feeding his ego. When he was taking fans to dinner on the Saturday before games or doing late-night chats in training camp, it was taking away from his game."

"He got so big so fast that he didn't know how to deal with it," added Houshmandzadeh. "The bigger you get and the more money you make, the more you have people tugging on you. Aside from Peyton Manning, Chad was probably the most popular player in the league [during his Pro Bowl years]."

The disappointing part of Chad's career was that he could've done so much more with it. The difference between good receivers and great ones is how long they can stay in their prime. Chad was at his best for about five years when he could've stretched that number to eight or nine. He's not a future Hall-of-Famer because he couldn't maintain that level long enough.

Like T.O., I don't think Chad ever envisioned the day when he might be expendable. It's like they both thought they'd never have to pay a heavy price for their behavior, that people would eventually cut them some slack once they asked for it. They had plenty of opportunities to change. It wasn't like they were Denzel Washington and Will Smith playing roles in a movie. They were being themselves when they craved all that attention and eventually—as it does for everybody—the fun ran out.

In the case of T.O., at least he can say he was consistent on the field for a long period of time. Between 1998 and 2008, he had at least 1,000 receiving yards in nine seasons. Obvious issues affected his production during the other two seasons in that time period (the 49ers lost starting quarterback Steve Young in 1999, while the Eagles suspended him after seven games in 2005). But when it was time to play, he usually got it done on the field.

T.O. and Chad took the NFL for granted in the same way I had in my early years. When you're a professional athlete, it's easy to forget how rare that opportunity really is, especially at the start of a career. But once you blow it, you realize how lousy it feels to have somebody else in control of your own destiny. It's a purgatory that always lasts much longer than one would expect.

The deeper they went into their careers, the more publicly frustrated they became over what they perceived as constant slights. T.O. felt like reporters were baiting him into controversial remarks while he played in Buffalo, as he told the *2 Live Stews* radio program after one game in 2009, citing that "[the media] took some more than initiative to try to get me to kind of go down the wrong path." Chad complained that critics saw him as a selfish, undisciplined player when he was only trying to enjoy himself. They were trapped in the personalities they'd created for themselves. They couldn't see that it was too late to alter the perceptions most people had of them.

If a player truly wants to change, then he needs somebody to be brutally honest with him about what's involved in that process. Sugarcoating the facts won't help, nor will dancing around the issues (or with the stars!). When T.O. was in his driveway pumping weights in front of reporters—shortly after the Eagles suspended him in 2005—somebody should've said to him, "You're really killing your career right now." Instead, the show went on, along with the belief that he'd always be capable of pulling such stunts.

There's a Bible verse that says "The truth will set you free." I believe that understanding the truth is what ultimately gives one supreme liberty. For me, that kind of honesty came from Buddy Ryan and later Betty Trilegi. I tried to give the same candor to Randy, especially when his career was spiraling in the wrong direction.

Some receivers never encounter that kind of help when they're destroying their own livelihoods. Like T.O. and Chad, those are the guys who have to learn their lessons the hard way.

All players need a catalyst when straightening out their careers. For me, it was family. My wife, Melanie, was pregnant with our first child, Duron, when the Eagles cut me. We had a newly purchased home, plans for another child someday, and hopes that the NFL would set us up for life. All that was jeopardized by my immaturity and ignorance to my own weaknesses. I thought I could control everything around me because I was a talented player. I learned how quickly that attitude could lead to trouble.

I've seen plenty of athletes fall into that same trap, both during my playing days and during my career. They reach the league and they start feeling entitled, as if the game has always owed them something. When I talk to young players, I point that out to them as candidly as I can. Football has given them countless benefits their entire lives, whether it's scholarships, money, notoriety, or access to a pretty girl who might not look at them otherwise. They've gotten used to taking from the game because of that. It's easy for some to forget their stature always has been a privilege.

It's very dangerous for players to feel too comfortable in the NFL. There should always be a healthy fear of losing one's job. It can happen in so many different ways—and for so many different factors—that players are sometimes stunned when they find themselves cut, waived, released, or looking for work in the Arena Football League. They've been coddled for so long that it's devastating when a team eventually says they're not good enough to earn a paycheck anymore.

For some reason, receivers—more than players at any other position—have a hard time grasping this concept. We haven't been responsible for all the major feuds with coaches and management over the last ten to fifteen years, but it certainly feels like we've been involved in the biggest. We're not the only players in the game who have acted immaturely or irresponsibly, but it certainly feels like everybody noticed when we were. In some cases, we behaved as if football wouldn't go on without us. We forgot that it could humble us as easily as it could the next guy on the roster.

Take former Giants wide receiver Plaxico Burress. When he left Pittsburgh and signed a free-agent deal with New York in 2005, he immediately gave quarterback Eli Manning a valuable weapon. His 6'5" frame included a massive wingspan that meant Eli could feel comfortable throwing the football anywhere in Plaxico's vicinity. With that kind of height and athleticism, Plaxico was the only person catching Eli's passes if they were thrown with the proper trajectory.

Plaxico became Eli's favorite target and then showed up big in the 2007 postseason. Despite playing on a bum ankle that plagued him all season, he caught 11 passes for 151 yards in an NFC championship win over Green Bay in frigid Lambeau Field. Two weeks later, Plaxico scored the game-winning touchdown against New England in Super Bowl XLII. He was at the highest point of his career. That success should've elevated him to an entirely different level.

Instead, Plaxico openly complained about not being happy with his contract the next year. He also feuded so much with head coach Tom Coughlin, a noted stickler, that Plaxico was suspended and benched at different points early in the 2008 season. Plaxico had never been a big fan of Coughlin's rules. In that year alone, the *New York Daily News* reported that he lost more than $200,000 to the Giants and the NFL for assorted fines and suspensions.

Of course, that was before Plaxico walked into a New York nightclub on November 28, 2008, and accidentally shot himself in the leg with an unregistered gun he'd been carrying. That mistake led to a weapons charge that ultimately landed him in jail for nearly two years. Just like that, a series of bad decisions demolished all the good faith that Plaxico had created during his career in New York. He'd gone from baller to bonehead in the blink of an eye, leaving what was left of a promising career in tatters the minute they locked him up.

Plaxico did get another shot in the league—signing with the Jets after his release in 2011—and he did mature plenty in prison. It also didn't have to come to that. Even before he landed in jail, Plaxico was becoming a huge headache for his team. He'd let his unhappiness with his contract mushroom into justification to act out at any moment. Once his legal problems started, he'd just solidified himself as another spoiled receiver who didn't get it.

The truth was that Plaxico's teammates loved having him on that roster. He was also smart enough to avoid his eventual legal troubles. But he had to cry in a jail cell—where he missed the birth of his daughter and watched two years of his career evaporate—before he realized how bad things could get. The man lost far too much to learn the lessons he eventually gained.

Most people have a hard time understanding how a pro athlete could wind up in that situation. What they fail to grasp is that NFL players are human beings, too. Fat paychecks, packed stadiums, and all the other fringe benefits associated with the game don't change that. We're still prone to the same errors as the middle-class middle manager making ends meet at his nine-to-five. It's actually easier for us to slip up because we're conditioned to think we can overcome anything. As Bengals head coach Marvin Lewis said, "Some guys think they're invincible."

People also don't realize the emotional and psychological stress that comes with life in the league. If a guy making $60,000 loses his job and has to move his family, there aren't any reporters around to compound that unsettling feeling. The player who is released faces the same fears as that working man, all the while knowing there are only about sixteen hundred jobs total in the NFL. That's not an easy plight to handle. It would eat most people up.

That's why I laugh when I occasionally hear fans say they'd handle things well if they were ever in the NFL. I always think, *No, you wouldn't.* They have a hard enough time managing their own personal lives. The pressures and the traps of this job would destroy them in a heartbeat. They might never recover from the career-threatening mistakes that I've seen some young players make in the game.

Mike Williams, the Detroit Lions' first-round pick in the 2005 draft, literally ate himself out of the league in three years. It wasn't until his former coach at USC, Pete Carroll, took a job in Seattle that Williams actually became a productive player. Williams caught all of 44 passes in his first three NFL seasons. He had 65 receptions with the Seahawks in 2010. Though Seattle released Williams after the 2011 season—to make room for younger receivers—he'd resuscitated his career by understanding that conditioning and discipline were key aspects of being a professional.

Williams wasn't the only young receiver who learned what it took to be successful in the league. Brandon Lloyd was accused of having a poor attitude early in his career until he put himself on a better path. He eventually made the 2010 Pro Bowl after leading the NFL in receiving yards as a member of the Denver Broncos (he's now with New England). Kansas City's Dwayne Bowe, a 2007 first-round pick, didn't blossom into a Pro Bowl player until former Chiefs head coach Todd Haley rode him about paying better attention to detail. Before that point, he was known for his ego and inconsistency.

Haley actually demoted Bowe after taking over the Chiefs job in 2009. His main beef was that Bowe reported to camp weighing 234 pounds that season, nearly 15 pounds over his listed playing weight. Haley wound up pushing Bowe all the way down to 209 before the start of 2010, Bowe's Pro Bowl season. In the process, Bowe learned something that Parcells also had preached about receivers: that even a little bit of weight gain can impact their performance.

Bowe had to learn that everything mattered, not just nice stats he earned during losing seasons. "So many of these guys don't have ideal lives growing up that they dangle carrots in front of themselves to escape their circumstances," Haley said. "Larry Fitzgerald didn't have a horrible upbringing, but his carrot was to be the best receiver ever. In the case of somebody like Dwayne, his carrot was to be a celebrity, to make money and be in the NFL. I had to always tell him to not be content with just that."

Those players had to reevaluate their careers in the same way I had to look at mine in 1990. I suspect they probably had to do the very things that helped me thrive. They couldn't worry about what people thought or said about them. They had to focus on helping their families, honing their skills, and improving every time they stepped onto a practice field. People talk about the pro game being 90 percent mental and 10 percent physical ability. Players truly learn that when they are reinventing themselves.

Atlanta Falcons wide receiver Roddy White is another example. He was that team's first-round pick in the 2005 draft, a big-time talent out of an unheralded school, the University of Alabama, Birmingham. The Falcons envisioned White becoming the dangerous target that then quarterback Michael Vick always needed in their offense. Instead, White let the allure of NFL life immediately derail his career.

It was bad enough that White had inconsistent hands and a lousy work ethic. He compounded his problems by partying so relentlessly that there were nights when he slept at the team facility to make morning meetings. The pull of the NFL nightlife was too much for White to handle, especially in a city with as many distractions as Atlanta. His hectic lifestyle eventually reached a point where he'd nearly wasted all the money in his $7 million rookie contract in just under a year.

That news forced White's mother, Joenethia, to go to Atlanta and swipe all of her son's credit cards as he slept one night. She also told his financial advisers that she needed to be informed of all his future business dealings. What White later admitted was that all the partying was a means of escape. He said, "I tried to find other ways to deal with things, because football wasn't going good. I came in with so much promise but I also felt like I wasn't getting a fair opportunity. I'd drop one pass and the fans would start booing, but that would be the only pass I'd see all day. I felt like I needed the ball more and [the coaches] felt like I wasn't working hard enough."

Now I'm a big believer that sometimes players can make a lot of excuses for themselves. In White's case, there was a reason why he wound up at Alabama-Birmingham in the first place, and he needed to realize that he had to work harder to succeed in the NFL. However, I'll concede that unlike Larry Fitzgerald and Randy Moss, who were some of the most highly recruited players in the country when they entered college and became accustomed to dealing with scrutiny, White didn't face that pressure until he was an NFL player. When you're lightly recruited and you play at a smaller program, it's much easier to perform at a high level, because there are no heavy expectations from fans and the media. The fear of being a bust isn't even part of the equation.

If it weren't for Joe Horn's one season in Atlanta in 2007—when Horn begged the Falcons to keep White on the roster—White might have seen his career flame out early. Horn explained that White "was taking food out of his family's mouth" every time the young receiver didn't make a play in the league. Over time, White followed Horn's lead because he could see the dedication in the veteran's game.

White had the same problem as many young receivers: confidence. He wanted to do all these great things and his athletic ability had always been his saving grace. He was bigger, stronger, and faster than most of the people who covered him in college. As a pro, he had to learn the same lessons that Mike Quick taught me as a rookie: No receiver is going to thrive in the NFL unless he has the discipline and the smarts to understand the game on a higher level.

Even when White made his first Pro Bowl in 2008, he gave a hint of how much self-doubt had shackled him in his early days. While strolling through Hawaii, he admitted to Joenethia that he never saw himself being an elite player. When his mother asked why he felt that way, White said, "I never thought I was this good." White made three more Pro Bowls after that year, likely because he recognized that the best receivers work their way to the top.

That's actually something every wideout in the NFL has to learn eventually. There isn't much difference in the skill level between the least talented players and the average ones. The same is true of the difference between the good players and the great ones. It all comes down to how much the receiver really wants to thrive. Once he succeeds, it's about how badly he wants to stay at an elite level.

What's even harder to figure out these days is how you separate the elite from the transcendent. That's a reality I've been living with since my career ended in 2002. It used to be easy to know what a Hall-of-Famer looked like, especially when it came to receivers. The deeper I went into retirement, the more I realized that it's a much tougher distinction for some people to make.

CHAPTER 14

Blowback

My first year of eligibility for the Pro Football Hall of Fame was 2007. I'd been retired for five years—the minimum amount of time required before induction eligibility—and I was feeling pretty good about my chances of election. Normally, I try to not let others influence my opinions. But the more I ran into people that year, the more I sensed a good reason to start preparing for terrific news.

That was my first mistake in that process. I hadn't really paid much attention to the Hall before that point. I didn't understand that a lot of great players didn't become first-ballot inductees. Basically, I figured it would be fairly simple to determine who belonged in the Hall when it came time to vote. The problem, as I eventually learned, is that every finalist can make a strong case for why he should be elected.

My class alone included some of the biggest names of my generation: Darrell Green, Richard Dent, Derrick Thomas, and my longtime Vikings teammate Randall McDaniel. There were also old-timers with plenty of their own strong credentials, including five-time Pro Bowl cornerback Emmitt Thomas and Oakland Raiders punter Ray Guy. If that wasn't enough competition, the ballot was also cluttered with receivers. Both Art Monk and Andre Reed had been passed over for enshrinement before I ever joined the list of finalists.

The sheer volume of talent in that group should've deflated my optimism from the start. I certainly was proud of my own accomplishments, especially since only Jerry Rice had more catches and touchdown receptions in NFL history when I retired. It's just that you can never predict the thoughts of other people and the voting process isn't determined by statistics alone. I also knew enough about the politics of voting to sense there were some other factors against me. I hadn't played in a Super Bowl, which is usually the first knock they applied to differentiate great players. The position I played also had seen a glut in recent years. Even Michael Irvin had to wait three years for induction despite the fact that two of his longtime teammates—quarterback Troy Aikman and running back Emmitt Smith—went in the first year they were eligible.

Despite being the heart and soul of those great Dallas championship teams, Michael's enshrinement clearly was affected by his problems off the field. Instead of judging him on his play, people likely viewed him as a flawed hero who was a cut below his other star teammates. That didn't mean Michael savored his selection any less when it finally came in February 2007 (he learned the news while Super Bowl XLI was held in his hometown of Miami). It only meant that every other receiver not named Jerry Rice should've been paying close attention to how he was treated by the process.

I was thinking about that reality around the time that the Hall-of-Fame committee actually invited me to attend the announcement ceremony in February 2008, during the week of Super Bowl XLII. They wanted me to fly to Phoenix—where the Giants were facing the Patriots—and be immediately available for a press conference following the vote. The Hall-of-Fame selection members always meet on the Saturday before the Super Bowl to decide on that year's class. By midafternoon, we'd all know who was next to have a bust mounted in Canton, Ohio.

My initial reaction was to not go to Phoenix. I didn't want to arrange all the transportation and lodging, drag my family across the country, and get all dressed up without feeling certain the day would end well. I remembered talking to Dan Marino once and having him tell me about his own experience with the Hall of Fame. "After all the years I played," said Marino, "I've never been more nervous than I was when I was waiting for [the voters] to elect me."

If an automatic, first-ballot Hall-of-Famer felt that way, you could imagine what was going through my mind. My anxiety was equally strong when I arrived for the announcement. Even though all the finalists who were there had great chances of getting in—they only invited you if they sensed your odds of enshrinement were high—we all knew somebody was going home disappointed. The Hall only takes four to seven members each year, and you need 80 percent of the votes to make the cut.

The waiting process is even less reassuring once you're actually at the Super Bowl. The staff shuttled me into a room at the convention center, where I was supposed to remain until the announcements were made. I bumped into Darrell Green, another finalist, while he strolled toward his own assigned location, and I could tell he was nervous as well. It's wild to think of all these accomplished stars just sitting in sterile rooms, waiting for somebody to pass judgment on their careers. It's almost like you're part of some crazy game show.

It was even less fun once they started announcing the names of the inductees. They did it alphabetically, so I didn't have to wait long to know where I stood. Fred Dean, the great pass rusher for the 49ers and Chargers, was the first name called. After that, I heard Darrell Green, Art Monk, Emmitt Thomas, Andre Tippett, and Gary Zimmerman. There wasn't even enough time for me to raise my hopes.

It's difficult to summarize the range of emotions I felt in that moment. The only thing I did understand was that I wasn't the first receiver to be surprised in that situation. I later did my research and learned more about the Hall's history. Aside from Jerry Rice and Steve Largent, most receivers were as stunned as I was when they first were denied admission.

The hardest aspect of that day was knowing I'd gone against my natural instincts. I'd let public sentiment convince me that I had a better shot than I did. That was the last time I made that mistake. I was a finalist every year and I always spent that time in my hotel room with my family. Even though my job with ESPN took me to the Super Bowl annually, I didn't want to be around other people when that news broke. I was too raw in that moment.

It was always the same scene. We waited for the call to see if I'd made it. We rented a movie to kill time and coped with the anxiety. We all checked our phones for e-mails and texts to keep busy. And once the deadline for announcing new members passed without any word coming my way, we all understood what that meant: Everyone in that room would be shedding tears within seconds.

It's not that I couldn't handle the rejection, but after a while, it began to feel like everybody was bringing the subject up. Anytime somebody referred to me as a future Hall-of-Famer or a player with a Hall-of-Fame career, it put me in an awkward situation. I didn't want the voters thinking I had anything against them, because they had my respect. The election system is a process. We all have to accept and live with that.

I'm sure other receivers feel the same way, which is why it was hard to talk to other finalists about the Hall. Once you've been passed over on that first ballot, you have instant empathy for anyone else who's ever been in that same position. I talked to Michael Irvin many times when he missed on his first two opportunities. It pained him to not be a first-ballot inductee, especially because he had all the requisite credentials. Super Bowls, Pro Bowls, All-Pro, team leader.

Andre Reed was in a similar predicament. He was a huge part of those prolific Buffalo Bills offenses in the 1990s, a team that sent quarterback Jim Kelly, running back Thurman Thomas, and wide receiver James Lofton (who did most of his damage in Green Bay) to the Hall. When compared to Lofton, Andre had more career receptions (951 to 764) and touchdowns (87 to 75) and was nearly comparable in yardage (13,198 to 14,004). That apparently didn't sway the voters, because he'd been waiting for induction since 2006.

The obvious problem all eligible receivers face is the numbers game. Receivers became so prominent in the 1980s and 1990s that the production at the position spiked. Just look at Steve Largent. When he retired in 1989, his 819 career receptions were a league record. By the end of the 2011 season, that total ranked him twenty-first of all time. Eight other players—including yours truly—had surpassed the

1,000-catch mark by that point. As Keenan McCardell said, "Lynn Swann made some great plays but his numbers [336 receptions, 5,462 yards, and 51 touchdowns] are what a good third-down receiver can produce today."

"Jerry Rice changed the game so much that he changed how people looked at the position," said Atlanta Falcons receivers coach Terry Robiskie. "If a Cris Carter retires in 1986, he goes into the Hall of Fame in his first year of eligibility. But Jerry set the bar so high. People don't look at receivers and judge them just off catches, yards, and touchdowns. It's about rings and what you did off the field and in the community. When Jerry did what he did—and did it with his mouth closed—he made it hard for every receiver who came after him."

The evaluation process becomes even harder when there are only so many prolific receivers who won championships. I thought my accomplishments were impressive when my career ended, but I'm sure Andre felt the same way about his. We actually bumped into each other after the 2012 voting, and it was awkward to discuss our situations. You don't want to start comparing yourself to somebody you respect, even though it's easy to fall into that trap.

I also saw longtime Oakland Raiders wide receiver Tim Brown before the vote that same year. Like me, he had more than 1,000 career receptions and he'd hit the 100-touchdown mark. He hadn't been on the ballot as long as I had (he became eligible in 2010). Still, that was long enough for him to encounter all the ups and downs that come with the eternal waiting game.

As we talked briefly about what had been happening in our lives, Tim finally asked a predictable question.

"So what are you thinking?" he said.

I was honest with him. "Our numbers are pretty similar," I said. "So all I can say is to not get your hopes up. If I was asking for advice, that's what I'd want to hear."

What I learned is that statistics weren't the only thing impacting the voting process. The amount of high-profile players was becoming an issue as well. There was no way Andre, Tim, or I was going in ahead of Jerry Rice, who was eligible in 2010. Every year more candidates become eligible and crowd the pool even more.

"When you think about what defines a Hall-of-Famer, it used to just be on-the-field performance," said Troy Vincent. "Now there are so many worthy people that with each passing year, more relevant names emerge. That's when emotion comes in and the pool starts to widen. You look at the Cris Carters, the Andre Reeds, and the Tim Browns. Those guys didn't have to compete with people like Deion Sanders or Marshall Faulk when they first got on the ballot, but they eventually did. And every year there are more people like that coming up [for election]."

Still, it is worth noting that only twenty-one wide receivers are in the Hall of Fame. Only punters (none), kickers (three), and tight ends (eight) are less represented in Canton. Now I don't expect us to be like quarterbacks, who usually go in on the first ballot if they have any kind of serious credentials. But I do often wonder why wide receivers' numbers are not taken into account in quite the same way. You can only put so much of that on politics, personality conflicts, and professional failings. At some point, it also comes down to the perception of the position. I've long believed that receivers don't get enough credit for how we go about doing what we do. My experience with the Hall of Fame makes me even more certain that few people actually understand exactly how wide receivers operate.

I've long believed that the job description of a wide receiver is one of the most mysterious topics in pro football. Yes, we catch passes for a living and block when our team calls a run. After that, you'd struggle to find many informed fans who could break down what makes us successful. Most people only see what we do at the end of a play. Seldom do they appreciate what put us in that position in the first place.

Part of that is because we've benefited from watching so many receivers make the job look easier than it actually is. Also, it's more fun to marvel at a great one-handed catch or a diving grab in traffic. It takes more work to evaluate a receiver's release, depth, break, and understanding of how a defense is trying to cover him.

I guarantee you some cynics look at a guy like Andre Reed and dismiss him as a product of an explosive offensive system. They won't say Jim Kelly was any less amazing because they watched him throw all those passes. They won't question the brilliance of Thurman Thomas because they could see every move he made once the ball touched his hands. But Andre's greatness is easier to pick apart. The uninformed see all those numbers and assume he needed a little help to be considered elite.

It's convenient to think that way when you don't know what to look for in receivers. There's a lot of information out there, but too many people don't know what makes a wideout good. I hear talking heads throw around words like "separation," but nobody ever goes into detail about how receivers create that. It comes down to more than mere speed. It's more than sheer athletic ability that makes a wideout dangerous.

Brian Billick said, "As much as any position in football, there's been a huge change in the type of athlete that plays wide receiver. You look at what people like Michael Irvin and Jerry Rice did in their day and then you look at the sheer opportunity to catch passes in today's game. A lot of what we're talking about is just the maturation of the position. You've got so many types of receivers today—slot guys, move guys, outside guys, deep guys. It's just the evolution of the game."

When it comes to judging the greatness of a receiver, there are only five aspects that should really matter. First, the player has to be capable of dominating single coverage. Second, he has to be consistent when it comes to catching the football. Third, he has to be a game-changer, a weapon who tilts the field in favor of his team and continually produces big plays. After that, durability and reliability are the only qualities that come into the equation.

As simple as that sounds, it's still far too common for fans and pundits to throw around the word "great." For example, former Pittsburgh Steelers receiver and current NBC analyst Hines Ward was a great football player. He wasn't a great receiver. He got it done during a fourteen-year career that saw him catch 1,000 passes, but he couldn't do a lot of things other players at the position could do.

The biggest flaw in Hines's game was speed. He couldn't threaten the field when he was flanked outside because defensive backs could just sit on his routes (meaning they'd always anticipate him running shorter patterns because he couldn't beat them deep). What made Hines successful was his understanding of the game and his limitations. Even though a top-flight cornerback could create problems for him, he made the most of the skills he did have.

Now, would you want Hines on your team? No question. He was one of the best blocking receivers ever and his infectious spirit made him a natural leader. But a lot of his success came down to Pittsburgh's offensive system. He made countless plays out of the slot, capitalized on how defenses played him, and consistently displayed tremendous grit.

Even the Steelers took a long time to eventually see the upside in making Hines their number one receiver. After taking him in the third round of the 1998 draft, Pittsburgh spent first-round picks on both Troy Edwards (1999) and Plaxico Burress (2000) in consecutive years. Hines was always candid about how much those acquisitions irritated him. Instead of giving him an opportunity to prosper, the Steelers kept searching for others to tackle the role. After a few years, Hines literally willed his way into the lineup with his toughness and dependability.

A player like Detroit's Calvin Johnson creates a different dilemma for people who watch him consistently. His physical skills are so impressive—it's hard to imagine another 6'5", 235-pound man who runs the 40-yard dash in 4.35 seconds—that people underestimate the way he's refined his game. His release off the line has improved every year, as well as his conditioning, route-running, and ability to run after the catch. He hasn't just been a super freak. He's actually invested time and energy into distinguishing himself from everybody else at the position.

It would be enlightening if we heard more about those qualities of the player known as "Megatron." Instead, we get countless highlights of him racing by defensive backs and leaping over hapless defenders. He's bigger and faster than nearly everybody on the field, so it seems like the game comes easily to him. What most people don't see is his footwork, the way he uses his hands to ward off cornerbacks, the discipline he maintains at the top of his routes. You don't become that dominant merely by being more athletic than the competition.

Lions coach Jim Schwartz sums up Johnson best by saying, "If players were show horses, there wouldn't be a better one in the league than Calvin. But what makes him special is that he works like he's a plow horse. He doesn't think he's better than anybody. And he's always working to improve his game."

That effort comes back to another point about receivers: We always have to be preparing for those moments that take your breath away. There may be days when such plays result from mere improvisation, but there are plenty of others where we've trained ourselves to be dynamic. It could be practicing one-handed catches on a Jugs machine. It could be rehearsing our toe-tapping to stay inbounds on a pass near the sidelines. All that stuff matters when the games become real. We understand that it's easier to contort our bodies once we've given ample thought to how best to do it.

When the New York Giants beat New England in Super Bowl XLVI, the biggest play of the game occurred when Eli Manning hit Mario Manningham with a 38-yard pass late in the fourth quarter. That completion moved the Giants from deep in their own territory to midfield, with Eli earning ample praise for that throw. People admired how accurately he dropped the ball into Manningham despite tight coverage. It was one more example of what a talented quarterback can do for his team in a clutch situation.

Now think about what Manningham had to do on that play. He had to beat a jam off the line of scrimmage, which he did with a nice release. He had to get good depth as he raced upfield so Eli had enough space to fit the pass into once the secondary reacted. Once the ball reached Manningham, he also had to cradle it, keep his feet inbounds, and maintain control as he fell to the turf. Just another example of what a talented receiver can do when his quarterback needs somebody to make a play.

Mario isn't alone when it comes to such efforts. David Tyree did something just as spectacular for the Giants four years earlier, when he pinned a Manning pass to his helmet with his right hand as Patriots safety Rodney Harrison tried to violently strip it from him during New York's final scoring drive in Super Bowl XLII. The game-winning catch that Santonio Holmes made in Pittsburgh's win over Arizona in Super Bowl XLIII was similarly amazing. Steelers quarterback Ben Roethlisberger was practically throwing that ball away until Holmes snared it while falling out of the back corner of the end zone.

These plays have gotten considerable attention because they happened on the biggest stage in football. But they happen every week all over the league. We spend so much time talking about how quarterbacks drop back, read coverage, feel the pressure, and release the football. We don't spend nearly enough time discussing the little nuances receivers do to be exceptional.

I'm clearly biased about this because of my connection to the position. But I also understand how this issue impacts players long term. You'd think that the more the NFL becomes a predominantly passing league, the more the discussion would turn to how receivers do their thing. Instead, it's starting to feel more like what Joe Horn said earlier in this book: The quarterbacks are still getting most of the glory, while receivers are hardly getting enough.

"I know they call it the diva position," said Keyshawn Johnson. "But teams can't play or win without us. That's just a fact."

The blowback on receivers is going to be huge in the coming years. The more I think about it, the more I wonder how people are going to evaluate us. There are so many different types of wideouts today—and such huge numbers—that fans and the media are becoming numb to the productivity. Catching 100 balls doesn't generate nearly the buzz that it once did. The same thing is true for a 1,500-yard season or double-digit touchdowns. We live in a fantasy football world these days. People forget what it takes to generate those kinds of numbers.

I can predict some major frustration among the soon-to-be-eligible receivers with credentials that will earn them consideration for the Hall of Fame. Marvin Harrison is a first-ballot lock because he has every qualification a player needs. He has a Super Bowl ring, eight Pro Bowls, and plenty of statistics (1,102 career receptions, 14,580 yards, and 128 touchdowns). The only questions about him involve post-career issues, specifically his alleged involvement in a homicide in his hometown of Philadelphia in 2009. That case, which has been investigated by the Philadelphia police and the FBI, remains unsolved.

After Harrison, the choices become much harder. Take his longtime teammate in Indianapolis, Reggie Wayne. He's one of only twenty-four players in NFL history with more than 800 receptions, but he's going to be hurt by playing alongside Marvin. It's too easy for skeptics to say his success had more to do with having a better player on the other side of the offense. That's what they do to you when it comes time to assess your overall greatness.

Now think about this: Only four players with more than 800 receptions were in the Hall of Fame by the end of 2012 (Rice, Monk, Largent, and tight end Shannon Sharpe). Some receivers will be no-brainers once they become eligible, like Randy and T.O. (both of whom have more than 1,000 receptions and 150 touchdowns). I also imagine that three younger players—Larry Fitzgerald, Andre Johnson, and Calvin Johnson—will join them if they stay healthy and maintain their current levels of productivity. They have the benefit of being the defining playmakers of their generation. Other players may not be so lucky.

Hines Ward had more receptions than both John Stallworth and Lynn Swann combined, but he's likely to face some pushback. Isaac Bruce (1,024 career catches) and Torry Holt (920) were the key elements in the St. Louis Rams' prolific attack, but they won't be getting first-ballot love in the way running back Marshall Faulk did upon his induction in 2011. The same holds true for other members of that

800-plus-catch club, a list that includes Keyshawn Johnson, Muhsin Muhammad, Jimmy Smith, Keenan McCardell, and Derrick Mason. That spike in productivity has cheapened their numbers. "It used to be rare for a receiver to catch eighty balls when I played," Largent said. "Now eighty receptions is an average year for most guys."

"A friend actually asked me if I'd be considered for the Hall of Fame," said McCardell, who had 883 career receptions. "When you look at the great receivers who waited a long time to get in, you feel like you're not getting considered until they're actually in. The other thing I see—especially with players like Tim Brown or Andre Reed—is that these weren't receivers who promoted themselves. You look at T.O. and some people will say he's a first-ballot Hall-of-Famer. So does it pay to be a diva? I don't think so. But does it help your chances of getting into the Hall? It just might."

"Part of the problem for guys like Andre Reed and Tim Brown is they never drew attention themselves," said Bill Polian. "There's a bias in everything and there's a bias in the Hall of Fame. Why is Michael Irvin in the Hall of Fame when Andre isn't? Some people would say it's because Michael has three Super Bowl rings and Andre played on four teams that lost in the Super Bowl. But the guy in Dallas also brought attention to himself. He gave himself a nickname. You'd like to think that it doesn't matter but it probably does."

It will be interesting to see how the Hall treats T.O. and Randy when they become eligible. They've both had so many issues off the field that there will be considerable debate about them going in on a first ballot. We all know what Michael Irvin's off-field problems did to his candidacy. I've also read stories that my own wait was the result of people not caring for my personality.

If those factors were valid in the voting process, then Randy and T.O. should probably prepare for disappointment. I can't imagine another big-time receiver who has created worse public relations than Owens. As Polian said, "How can you put a guy like that in the Hall of Fame? He tore teams apart."

"Most of the time T.O. played, he played well," said Steve Mariucci.

"What hurts him is the stuff with coaches and teammates. The media knows about that stuff and they vote for the Hall of Fame. His numbers make him a Hall-of-Famer, but when you need 80 percent of the vote—and people remember what you did—I worry that some people will hold a grudge against him."

T.O. was already feeling the fallout from his reputation when the 2011 season began. Not one team wanted to sign him following a lockout-shortened off-season. Part of that had to do with a torn ACL he sustained earlier that year. But when T.O. held a private workout in October 2011 to prove he was healthy, there wasn't a single scout in attendance. He had reached a point where people weren't even intrigued by the possibility of what he could still do. He was so unwanted that he ultimately took a job with the Allen Wranglers of the Indoor Football League to make money.

That icy reception by the league carried over into 2012, when T.O. still couldn't attract much interest. That was even more telling. There are thirty-two teams in the NFL, which equates to sixty-four starting wide receivers. You couldn't tell me there were sixty receivers in the league who were better than T.O. at the start of the 2012 regular season. Even as he closed in on his thirty-ninth birthday, he likely had the skills to catch at least 60 to 70 balls.

A lot of teams wouldn't touch him because they didn't have a head coach strong enough to handle him if things went sideways. The franchises that were lousy or rebuilding surely didn't want the hassle of him being unhappy on their sidelines. Finally, the Seattle Seahawks took a flyer on T.O., signing him to a one-year deal when their training camp started in 2012. He wound up dropping enough balls that the team released him after its third preseason game.

If T.O. had a better reputation, he would've found more opportunities later in his career. But too many people thought he couldn't change. They didn't see a player who really hadn't caused any major issues in Buffalo or Cincinnati. They saw the guy who nearly blew up the first two franchises that employed him.

Cincinnati Bengals head coach Marvin Lewis would be the first to say that T.O. was far from being the headache he'd been in San Francisco and Philadelphia. When Lewis asked T.O. to show the team's younger receivers how to study, he would sit in front of meetings—highlighter in hand—taking copious notes. If T.O. couldn't practice because of an injury, he'd be on the sidelines with his playbook in hand, keeping tabs on what the offense was doing. One week he broke his hand in practice on a Thursday. He played in a game three days later.

T.O. still was prickly around coaches and vocal about his touches—"T.O. thinks he can get open and catch a pass on every play even though we can't always get it to him based on the defense," Lewis said—but the coach didn't have any major complaints. "The thing about T.O. was that he knew what the right way of doing things was," Lewis said. "He'd been taught that by Jerry. But I always say there is Terrell and there is T.O. If you get to know Terrell, that guy is a hell of a person."

Still, Terrell wasn't a good enough person to make the Bengals bring him back for a second year or for Seattle to keep him on their roster for the 2012 regular season. Those teams both likely thought the same thing—he wasn't worth the risk any longer. If T.O. had been a more model citizen, he could've been like Reggie Wayne in Indianapolis or Donald Driver in Green Bay. They lasted a long time with their respective teams because they were positive influences on younger players.

What T.O. eventually learned is that receivers become liabilities as they age. The best ones don't play on special teams, cover kicks, or return punts, so teams see them as one-dimensional players on the roster. That's not a good thing in the age of the salary cap. If an older receiver makes the team and then gets hurt, the team is on the hook for his entire salary that year (if he's vested in the league's pension program). Aside from financial reasons, it also doesn't make much sense to take on an aging receiver because of the potential for personality issues.

In T.O.'s case, he tried to be a celebrity throughout his career. Once he moved past his prime, he should've been thinking about ways to fit in with the teams who employed him. Instead, everybody kept wondering if he'd blow up another locker room if given the opportunity. He was a nightmare waiting to happen.

"T.O. went about things the wrong way," said Keyshawn Johnson. "Some guys won't openly say it, but they try to copy what they think is a blueprint [for dealing with management]. And it gets them caught in a pickle when things don't go the way they want. He thought I shot my way out of New York so he figured he'd shoot his way out of San Francisco. But that's not how it went down with me. When he was in Philadelphia, he thought he could cuss out the coach and force his way out of that franchise. But that wasn't how I left Tampa. I know I can meet with Bill Belichick, eat lunch with Bill Parcells, and get a job with ESPN. Some guys can't even get people to call them back."

Randy was fortunate that his career included enough stretches away from the headlines that controversy alone didn't define him. When he was in New England, money was a major factor in his undoing there. The Patriots weren't showing enough interest in giving him a new deal heading into the 2010 season, so Randy started to check out. One person with knowledge of the situation said Randy's attitude became so alarming to quarterback Tom Brady that he actually told Belichick there might be an issue with Randy's focus. Belichick must not have been seriously concerned at the time, but that changed once the regular season started.

When Randy dogged it on a couple routes in an early-season win over Miami, Brady expressed his frustration much louder. He told Belichick that the Patriots could keep Randy, but the quarterback was never throwing his way again. The Patriots traded Randy back to Minnesota two days later, where he lasted less than a month before the Vikings waived him. He finished that season as a bench warmer in Tennessee, with two different opinions emerging about Randy's inability to get on the field.

Randy's belief, as he later admitted, was that some Titans coaches wanted to blackball him. As he said, "Why they claimed me, I really don't know. There were some things where I could really tell I really wasn't liked, and that was coming from the coaching staff. To be able to still make plays . . . there were some things going on in-house that I probably won't speak upon until I write my book."

Randy added that he didn't know if those unnamed coaches were blackballing him because they didn't like him or because they thought he couldn't play. One coach Randy did appreciate was head coach Jeff Fisher, who was pleasantly surprised by what he saw in his new receiver. Fisher has contended that Tennessee never found a way to make Randy a productive player in their system because offensive coordinator Mike Heimerdinger wanted to use younger receivers who knew his system better. But Randy also didn't disappear as he had in Oakland.

Instead, Randy worked hard to help his teammates learn their craft. During one off morning, Fisher walked by a meeting room at seven A.M. and found Randy teaching the other receivers some tips on playing the position.

"That was a tough year all the way around," said Fisher, who now coaches the St. Louis Rams. "But one of the positives for me was being around Randy Moss."

Fisher said the Titans might have kept Randy for another year if Fisher wasn't fired after that season. As it turned out, nobody else was willing to give Randy the same benefit of the doubt. When the 2011 off-season lockout ended, there wasn't a single team that wanted to give Randy the long-term deal he coveted. He wound up retiring before the start of the season, believing it was better for him to focus on something other than football.

Randy did return to the league—signing with San Francisco in 2012—but he wasn't the only big-name receiver whose career path went through New England. The Patriots also traded for Chad Johnson before the 2011 season, after he'd finally worn out his welcome in Cincinnati. The deal was hailed as another steal for the Patriots, who had been searching for another elite receiver to team with Wes Welker since dropping Randy. That acquisition eventually became one of the most disappointing moves of the year, with Chad catching only 15 passes all season. If that wasn't painful enough, the Patriots also deactivated him for their AFC championship game against Baltimore.

I give Chad credit for being a team player and not complaining about his struggles. He also curtailed his obsession with Twitter while trying to blend in with Bill Belichick's squad. When the Patriots dumped him after that season, he signed with the Miami Dolphins—who badly needed help at receiver—to take another shot at resuscitating what was left of his playing days.

In a press conference with local Miami reporters before the start of the 2012 season, Johnson admitted that he'd gained plenty from his disappointing year in New England. "I learned so many things," he said. "That's one of the greatest coaches ever in the game. Learned a lot of things: Discipline, learned to shut the f— up for a year. I never thought I could do it, but I did it."

"I think Chad would tell you one hundred percent that he had everything under control before he got to New England," said T. J. Houshmandzadeh. "And that was a problem. He wasn't training with the same intensity. He was playing well enough in Cincinnati and that blinded him. When he got to New England, he realized it. I didn't see him in Los Angeles for years before that. After he left New England, he came back."

It seemed like Chad was primed for a fresh start in Miami until his reputation caught up with him there. New Dolphins head coach Joe Philbin was unwilling to let Chad's personality become an issue in their first year together. When Chad gave a profanity-laced press conference to local reporters on his first day of training camp, Philbin immediately chastised him. The coach was even less forgiving when Chad was arrested for allegedly assaulting his wife two weeks into training camp. The Dolphins released Chad as soon as he was released from an overnight stay in jail. (He eventually pleaded no contest to the charge and was ordered to serve twelve months probation and enroll in a batterers' intervention program.)

The message that Philbin sent with that decision was obvious: Chad didn't have enough talent anymore to be a distraction. I also felt bad for Chad, because the entire world could watch his dismissal on HBO's *Hard Knocks*, which was televising Miami's training camp that summer. When the Eagles cut me, I was so humiliated that I told Buddy Ryan that I'd be in two hours before my teammates to receive the news. I could only imagine how Chad felt with all those cameras taping his last hour with the Dolphins.

Still, that was the fate he had created for himself. The world was wonderful when people were celebrating his play and his creative antics. It was a little different when he was perceived as a detriment. "It got to the point where people didn't want to deal with that drama anymore," said Donovan McNabb. "They'd seen it for the last ten years and they were tired of those players. I feel bad for Chad because he was the last of the Mohicans."

"Chad isn't a bad kid," Keyshawn said. "He gets a bad rap because of the position. He's never done anything illegal off the field [before his 2012 arrest] or torn up a locker room. He likes to have his fun but he just gets caught up in the perception. We all get lumped together, and I shake my head when I get linked with certain guys. I see my name mentioned with T.O. and Chad and I wonder why people think they did things the same way I did. I never put on a fucking Hall-of-Fame jacket while standing on the sidelines."

Chad's experience in New England felt like an aberration because of another fact: If a big-time receiver plays long enough, he's going to have a hard time accepting a lesser role. We all still think we can do it, regardless of the proof on film. There's simply something in our genes that keeps our egos substantially inflated. We're like boxers in that sense. We need to be knocked out to understand we're truly finished.

When Jerry Rice went to Seattle after Oakland—in 2004—he openly acknowledged that he was unhappy with being underutilized. It didn't matter to Jerry that the Seahawks had plenty of younger receivers who needed playing time. He wanted to still compete like he always had. When he moved on to Denver the following season, he finally accepted that it was time to retire. Apparently, Jerry didn't like the idea of only being a fourth receiver in that offense.

I can relate to that feeling. Even though I left Minnesota on my own terms, I also played in Miami for a few games in 2002 before returning to TV. It's hard to let go when you've done one thing for so long. It's even harder when you're accustomed to being a difference-maker with that one thing.

Still, the curtain comes down on us all. That's what all receivers have to understand. It's going to be painful regardless of how it happens. It's really a question of mental preparation.

What also helps is the support you receive from other people along the way. When I didn't make the Hall of Fame in 2010, I spent a lot of time trying to make sense of what kept going wrong. Then I received a phone call from John Randle, my former teammate and a defensive tackle who was voted in that same year. He told me that I was going to make it eventually and then he added something that raised my spirits. "We all know you were the heart of the team for all those years," he said.

Words like that made a huge difference when I was waiting for validation of my own career, as did the encouragement I received from others. After I didn't make the Hall in 2012, Minnesota Vikings public relations director Bob Hagan offered to create a new plan for improving my chances with the voters. With the help of his assistant director, Tom West, they broke down my best eight seasons (1993–2000) and compared them to other receivers in my generation. Even I was amazed by what they found.

No wide receiver during that time caught more passes than me (779). I also had more touchdown receptions (90), more catches of 25 or more yards (77), and more third-down receptions that turned into first-downs (235). Not even Jerry Rice outdid me when looking at the numbers from that perspective. In other words, I'd been the most productive receiver in the league during my prime years.

As satisfying as that evidence was, I knew there was more work to be done before the Hall voted in 2013. Part of that process included altering my presentation to the voters. Every candidate for the Hall has a voter who covered them speak on their behalf, and Mark Craig, a reporter for the Minneapolis *Star-Tribune*, had always been my advocate in those meetings. I'd encouraged him to talk about my overall numbers in those sessions but this time I asked him to focus on impact. I felt that could be my edge, especially with the evidence from the Vikings and some powerful quotes I'd gotten from Deion Sanders, Dan Marino, Tony Dungy, and former Vikings head coach Bud Grant.

The final advantage I had was my own research. I had been among the final five candidates who had been voted on in each of the previous two years. From what people told me, players who fall into that category generally get inducted the third time their candidacy is discussed. I guess it makes sense. The longer you stay in the conversation, the more people start believing in your right for inclusion.

That last bit of information kept me in an optimistic mood throughout the entire week of Super Bowl XLVII. I knew the percentages were in my favor. I also figured that one of the first-ballot nominees probably would be passed over despite the class being especially strong. What I didn't count on was Tim Brown publicly accusing former Raiders coach Bill Callahan of sabotaging his team when Oakland lost to Tampa Bay in Super Bowl XXXVII. I knew Tim seriously hurt his image by being so negative so close to the selection process.

But I won't lie: The day of the vote became much harder as the announcement neared. I spent most of that afternoon talking to sponsors at a corporate event that lasted until 3:30. Since the vote was going to be announced around 5:00, I knew those last couple hours would be hell. I actually felt a sickening feeling in my stomach during the last twenty minutes of the event. The more fans approached me—with comments like "We'll hear soon" or "We know you'll get in this time"—the more I wanted to run back to my hotel room and wait quietly for the news with my family.

I eventually returned to my hotel thirty minutes before the announcement and there was at least some good news by then: I was among the final five candidates for the third straight year. Now it was a matter of earning 80 percent of the votes. I wanted to be more excited, but I couldn't do that to myself. I just curled up in my bed with Melanie and stared at the flat-screen television a few feet in front of us.

I tensed when the announcer prepared to break the news to the world. Since I knew he was going in alphabetical order, I exhaled briefly upon hearing that former Cowboys Pro Bowl guard Larry Allen was the first on the list. The broadcaster then paused briefly before uttering the second name and that's when I noticed how he was curling his lips to enunciate. Before he ever finished saying "Cris," my wife and I were screaming manically. I never even heard the man say "Carter" because I blacked out a split-second later.

The next thing I remembered was hearing a knock on my door from my brother John. Then I jumped into the shower, threw my suit back on, and raced to the lobby to catch a cab to the press conference. When I couldn't find a taxi—we were staying at the Baltimore Ravens team hotel that week—I accepted a ride from a friend of Keyshawn Johnson. To be honest, I probably could've floated to the Super Bowl convention center for that event. That's what six years of waiting for a lifelong dream can do to a man.

Aside from Allen, I really didn't know who else had made the Hall once I arrived at the press conference. It wasn't until that point that I saw former Ravens offensive tackle Jonathan Ogden, former Tampa Bay defensive tackle Warren Sapp, and longtime head coach Bill Parcells. The emotions surging inside me were especially raw as we all congratulated one another. I knew I'd be crying once the questions started but I also had a strategy for dealing with that.

I wasn't going to talk about numbers or the voting process. I was going to talk about my journey. I was going to focus on the people who stood by me, who saw me at my weakest moments and still gave me opportunities to succeed. I was going to talk about how my faith in God helped me stay on the right path even when it was rockier than ever.

More than anything, I was grateful. As I told the press, there wasn't one undeserving player who was voted in during all those years that I sat in my hotel room heartbroken. I also was thankful for the effort Mark Craig put into presenting my case to the voters. I was later told that he did a tremendous job of selling my merits, which told me plenty. It takes a lot to get Mark excited so his passion had to really move that room.

The amazing thing for me was how much my world changed after that vote. I started to receive standing ovations when I walked into restaurants. Augusta National Golf Club invited me to spend three days playing on the same course where the Masters tournament is held. It was just as exciting to be standing there with my fellow Hall inductees before the coin toss at the start of Super Bowl XLVII. It's hard to describe how thrilling it is to hear yourself announced as a Hall-of-Famer to the entire world.

What I've always believed is that players with a story like mine rarely get to be considered among the greatest of anything. That's why it means so much today. Knowing how far I've come—and that my son, Duron, had the opportunity to introduce me during the induction ceremony—reinforced everything I'd learned throughout my life. Good things could happen as long as I kept my faith and kept fighting.

The best feeling that came from my selection was the undeniable sense of freedom. It no longer seemed that I was being punished for not winning a championship or playing most of my career in a smaller-market city. I didn't have any regrets about how things had played out because I'd done my best. Thankfully, that was eventually enough to get my name off that list of potential Hall-of-Famers.

This is why I don't spend much time entertaining people who say I should've gotten in earlier. There's simply no need to ruin this moment by thinking about what it could've been like five years sooner. The truth is that it felt pretty damn sweet exactly when it happened. And that tells me that regardless of the pain that went with it, I made the Hall of Fame at precisely the right time.

CHAPTER 15

The Next Wave

I was the guest on another episode of ESPN's *Mike and Mike in the Morning* in August 2011 when I made a mistake that turned me into an instant enemy of Motown. Mike Greenberg asked me to name my top receivers in the NFL and a list instantly popped into my head. I had to have Larry Fitzgerald on there because he was my boy. Andre Johnson came next, followed by Minnesota's Greg Jennings and Atlanta's Roddy White. I thought I was rolling by that point, since I had plenty of options for my final selection.

Remember, this was an impromptu question thrown at me on a morning radio show where at least a hundred topics are discussed every day. Since I wanted to move the conversation forward quickly, I pondered the receivers who had most impressed me recently. For some reason Philadelphia's DeSean Jackson came to mind first. Even though he'd let his unhappiness with his contract distract him at the time, his two Pro Bowls and big-play ability made him a safe choice in the end.

As soon as I said DeSean's name, Greenie jumped on my glaring omission. "What about Calvin Johnson?" he asked. I didn't even think about the Detroit Lions Pro Bowl receiver when I began making that list. I also wasn't going to make the mistake of downgrading him beyond that. I basically said Calvin would've been next on the list and even higher if he was more consistent.

Talk about your uproar. I spent the next three days hearing all kinds of comments about how I'd disrespected Megatron and I must have been crazy to put five receivers ahead of him. The anger died down after I later admitted my mistake on *Mike and Mike*.

Truth be told, if you wanted to know what the near future of the wide receiver position looked like, it could be found in a Detroit Lions uniform every weekend in the fall of 2011. Calvin scored 8 touchdowns in his first four games, prompting Lions quarterback Matthew Stafford to tweet:

Does anyone think 8 tds in 4 weeks will change chris carters mind about an "elite" receiver? #megatron

By season's end, he had set career highs in receptions (96), yards (1,681), and touchdowns (16). Calvin then capped his season with 12 receptions, 211 yards, and 2 scores in an NFC wildcard playoff loss to New Orleans. Even in defeat, Megatron took your breath away.

As much as people didn't like my omitting Calvin from that list, there was no question that he was the league's best receiver when that season ended. Even Larry was willing to concede that. If a player is averaging a touchdown a game in the regular season, that's a pretty good indication of consistency. If he's dominating in clutch situations—as Calvin did often that season—that's the epitome of a game-changer. Calvin had become so dangerous that the New Orleans Saints once covered him near their goal line with two defensive backs, as if he were about to run downfield to cover a punt.

When I think about how far the game has come for receivers, I look at what Calvin has meant to the Lions. Nearly two months after they enjoyed their first winning season in eleven years, Detroit rewarded him with an eight-year, $132 million contract extension. It is one of the largest deals ever given to an NFL player (and Calvin backed it up with 1,964 receiving yards in 2012, which broke Jerry Rice's single-season league record). That contract also put Calvin in the same company as Larry, who had signed an eight-year, $120 million extension with Arizona in 2011.

There was no denying the value of receivers after that. It was a big deal when Keyshawn Johnson was demanding to be paid more money than the Jets' starting quarterback as a rookie in New York in 1996. Five years later, Randy Moss made even more noise when Minnesota gave him an eight-year deal worth $75 million. But to see teams compensating receivers at a higher rate than almost anybody else in the league? It made me wish I had better timing.

The most rewarding part about that change was that Calvin and Larry deserved that money. They had produced at the highest level. They had carried themselves with class. They had proven they could be everything their franchises had hoped they'd become. In other words, they had raised the bar once again for what a receiver could do in the NFL.

"The money definitely changed things," said Jerry Rice. "When I was playing, we probably had three or four receivers who could've been stars on other teams. But teams need that marquee guy who can go out and make plays for them today. Look at the money Detroit gave Calvin Johnson. There are no Super Bowl rings on his fingers. That's just how the game has evolved."

Andre Johnson is another receiver who was on the same level as Calvin and Larry, even though he struggled through a difficult season with the Houston Texans in 2011. A hamstring injury limited him to seven regular-season games that year. He played well in two postseason games, but his impact could've been greater had Houston not lost quarterback Matt Schaub to a season-ending injury before they reached the postseason. The 2012 postseason didn't help Andre's legacy, either. Though healthy, he didn't produce a 100-yard performance or score a touchdown in two playoff games.

Still, you couldn't talk about NFL receivers without mentioning all three of those players. Their play didn't just alter the league. It also affected many of the receivers who followed them into pro football. A potential star receiver with a penchant for professionalism was someone a smart team couldn't pass up. In the 2011 draft alone, the Cincinnati Bengals took one such talent with the fourth selection (Georgia's

A. J. Green) to be Chad Johnson's replacement. The Atlanta Falcons were even more aggressive, as they traded five picks in order to move up and select Alabama's Julio Jones sixth overall.

Both players made immediate impacts on their teams. Jones was so impressive when he first started training with the Falcons that quarterback Matt Ryan told some people that he had to start raising his game to accommodate such talent. Jones went on to lead all rookies with 8 touchdown receptions and produced 959 receiving yards. Green was even better. He made the Pro Bowl with 65 catches and 1,057 yards.

Most important, they only drew attention to themselves because of their production. They're more stable personalities and it's not hard to see why. "The difference between A.J. and Chad is that when A.J. walks into a stadium, he hears people cheering his name and he just keeps on walking," said Bengals head coach Marvin Lewis. "It doesn't faze him one bit. When that would happen with Chad, his head would be on a swivel. He'd be looking all over to see who was calling his name. But A.J. is used to being a star. I vacation in South Carolina [Green's home state] so I know how big a deal he's been since he was in high school. He's a legend in that state and at Georgia. That makes a difference in how you handle things."

"You have less controversial guys coming into the league all the time now," Keyshawn said. "I call it the Larry Fitzgerald–Andre Johnson–Calvin Johnson model. You look at younger guys like A. J. Green or Julio Jones and they are nice kids. It wasn't like the class of '96. That draft basically launched the era of the loudmouth receiver, which ran for about fifteen years. There really aren't many of those guys left."

I suspect the massive increases in top-end salaries had something to do with that. When receivers are making at least $8 to $9 million annually, they usually have much less reason to complain about disrespect or lack of notoriety. Younger players also understand now how bad it can look if they go overboard with their antics. The ones who do get out of control can see what happens if they don't reel themselves in soon. Some players just don't want the headaches that come with too much controversy.

"My approach comes from my upbringing," Green said. "I have a big family, so they keep me grounded and humble. I know football is my job and I'm blessed to do it. I think it's just better to let my play speak for myself."

The players who actually do attract negative headlines these days generally aren't trying to do so for the attention. DeSean Jackson didn't really have any major issues in Philadelphia until his contract negotiations hurt his production in 2011. Chicago's Brandon Marshall has been involved in a variety of legal issues—and also publicly feuded with former Denver Broncos head coach Josh McDaniels while playing for that franchise in 2009—but he's not pulling Sharpies out of his socks after touchdowns.

Even a character like Buffalo's Stevie Johnson isn't somebody you'd classify as a loudmouth. He's lost money with some ill-conceived touchdown celebrations, like when he scored against the Jets in 2011 and pretended to shoot his leg in a mocking tribute of then Jets receiver Plaxico Burress. Such moments come across as juvenile. But I also suspect Stevie wanted to be as entertaining as Chad Johnson was in his early days.

Aside from those guys, I agree with Keyshawn: The oversized personalities aren't nearly as abundant as in the past. When I think about the receivers who are going to stand out in years to come, I see Green and Jones going to multiple Pro Bowls. A speedster like Miami's Mike Wallace jumps out as well, while the Giants have to like their options at the position. As long as Hakeem Nicks and Victor Cruz are together, Eli Manning's life will be much easier.

In fact, there are so many talented quarterbacks in the NFL these days that there should be an even greater need for productive wideouts in the future. You'd have to go back to the 1990s to find so many players who can throw the rock at the elite level, which includes Super Bowl winners like Drew Brees, Tom Brady, Aaron Rodgers, Ben Roethlisberger, and the Manning brothers. The next group features Pro Bowlers like Matt Ryan, Tony Romo, Philip Rivers, and Michael Vick. There might be twenty quarterbacks who can get it done for their respective franchises.

The more players at that position continue to blossom—especially in an era when the league has cracked down so much on player safety that hard-hitting defensive backs can't tee off on defenseless receivers any longer—the more coaches are going to ask of their passing games. Atlanta was a perfect example of that in 2011. They went after Jones in that draft because they knew Ryan needed more help around him. The Falcons already had a Pro Bowl veteran in Roddy White and a future Hall-of-Fame tight end in Tony Gonzalez. Surrendering a handful of draft picks for Jones, in their eyes, meant defenses would eventually struggle to contain them.

It's easier for teams to take such gambles because of how receivers are groomed for the NFL. When I came into the league, I had a veteran like Mike Quick telling me to forget some of the tricks that led to my college success. Today's young players don't have nearly the learning curve if they come from the right programs. Some know more about playing receiver than I ever knew when I walked into the league.

I never saw myself coaching football until the day my wife and I signed up our son, Duron, to play. He was ten years old at the time, about two years older than me when I took up the sport, and I was looking forward to watching his experience. Melanie also wanted to make sure I wasn't too excited about the opportunity. As we drove to see what the program was all about, she explained that I needed to follow some explicit ground rules.

Melanie said I basically had two options. The first was to look at the volunteer sign-up sheet she had noticed when she checked out the team. They needed coaches to help with the kids, which—as Melanie wisely noted—meant I could say as much as I wanted about what was happening on the field. My other choice was to keep my butt—and my opinions—in the stands and let Duron do his thing. "I better volunteer," I told Melanie. "Because there's no way I'm going to stay quiet all year."

I tell that story because coaching kids gave me an entirely different perspective from the one I had as a lifelong receiver. I later moved over to Duron's eventual high school—St. Thomas Aquinas in Fort Lauder-dale (the alma mater of Michael Irvin)—and saw the thrills that came from kids winning national and state championships while also earn-ing full college scholarships. I was able to pay more attention to the game from the ground up. It gave me a better feel for what was hap-pening to the future of the wide receiver position.

I quickly realized there is a simple reason why so many young re-ceivers are better prepared to enter the NFL when they reach that level: They're getting more exposure to sophisticated passing games. They're learning more about coverages, route-running, and all the fundamentals that help wideouts thrive as they grow older. The talent level isn't that much different from when I played. However, the overall football intelligence is far greater in some of the kids you see today.

That isn't only the case at schools as prominent as St. Thomas Aquinas, which had six alums in the NFL at the time this book was written. I've seen the changes at football camps all over the country in the off-season. Everything is more specialized and advanced. Younger players are getting far more reps in the passing game at an early age and it's helping them mature faster.

You'd have a hard time finding more than a handful of teams that ran some form of a spread offense twenty years ago. Now high schools all over the country are operating it. I watch college games as much as possible and there's a huge difference in the efficiency of receivers at that level. Several are more polished and savvy. I see plenty who under-stand the importance of techniques and fundamentals.

Going into the 2012 season, USC had two receivers—Robert Woods and Marqise Lee—who looked like they had bright futures in the NFL. They weren't thriving off bubble screens and fades, the kind of simplified plays that college coaches use to get the ball to raw talents. These guys were running serious routes that professional wideouts have to master: the post-corner, the comeback, the deep-in. They couldn't do those things if their coaches didn't put high expectations on their techniques.

Keep in mind that these kids weren't impressing people because they were experienced upperclassmen. Woods had 111 receptions as a sophomore and Lee had 73 catches as a freshman during the 2011 season. They combined for a 194 receptions a year later, with Lee winning the Biletnikoff Award as the nation's top receiver. Woods and Lee weren't producing those numbers in a spread system designed to create and capitalize on mismatches. They were running out of a conventional pro offense used by head coach Lane Kiffin, who spent twenty games coaching the Oakland Raiders from 2007–08. He clearly wants his receivers living up to pro standards.

I saw the same kind of potential in a receiver I coached at St. Thomas Aquinas, Rashad Greene. I wasn't surprised when he went to Florida State in 2011 and became a freshman All-American. He looked like a good fit for the NFL when he was killing people in high school. He had quickness, deep speed, and a real hunger to learn as much about the game as possible.

These are the types of receivers who will come into the NFL looking to make an immediate impact. They won't be as overwhelmed by the complexity of a league that has changed drastically in what it expects from wideouts. As James Lofton said, "When I came into the league in 1978, the Green Bay Packers used nine routes. When I stopped coaching with the San Diego Chargers in 2008, we were using fifty-five different route combinations. That's a big change in the game. It's like going from a typewriter to doing things with an iPhone."

That isn't to say every receiver who enters the league is going to be ready for the professional life. Just consider Dez Bryant. The Dallas Cowboys made him the twenty-fourth overall selection of the 2010 draft, fully believing they'd found their next Michael Irvin. Bryant had size, speed, and so many accolades coming out of Oklahoma State that his talent was tantalizing. But he struggled with consistency, injuries, and off-the-field controversy during his first two seasons.

In July 2012, Bryant was arrested on a misdemeanor domestic violence charge for allegedly hitting his mother. (The charge was moved to conditional dismissal in November 2012, granted that Bryant complete general counseling and avoid any legal run-ins.) That incident—combined with everything else that had happened with Bryant before that point—was enough to drive Cowboys owner Jerry Jones to action. Jerry made it clear that Bryant needed to shape up if he wanted to stick with that franchise (and even made Bryant agree to avoid strip clubs and alcohol while also adhering to a midnight curfew). That's a heck of an ultimatum to receive after only two years in the NFL, but Bryant also responded with his best season. He had 92 receptions, 1,382 yards, and 12 touchdowns in 2012.

Still, receivers have so many opportunities today that teams don't have to fret so much about slowly developing draft picks. The New York Giants certainly didn't expect Victor Cruz to be their best wideout when he showed up as an undrafted free agent out of UMass in 2010. A year later, that's exactly what he became. Taking advantage of an injury to Mario Manningham, Cruz led the Giants in receptions (82), yards (1,536), and touchdowns (9) that season, while also helping them beat New England in Super Bowl XLVI.

Cruz was no different from most receivers who go overlooked coming out of school. Whether you're talking about undrafted guys (like Denver's Wes Welker or Dallas's Miles Austin) or late-round picks (New Orleans's Marques Colston or Buffalo's Stevie Johnson), coaches are always searching for a difference-maker. They understand that it's not always pedigree that turns a player into a success. A lot of times it just comes down to how badly the receiver wants to be remembered.

"Those lower-tier guys are hungry," said Rod Smith. "When I was in Denver, Coach [Mike] Shanahan cut two first-round picks to make room for me, but I also earned my way onto the roster by playing special teams. You have guys today who won't even cover a kick if they're drafted in the fourth round or earlier. Those [unheralded] receivers want to prove what they can do. They know the draft too often comes down to forty times and how many people you played in front of in college. Too many times people don't consider something far more important: a player's heart."

———————

I've been invited to speak at the NFL's annual rookie symposium several times, where I've often given the final address to those first-year players. I've always viewed that opportunity as an honor because it's one more way to give back to the game. Coaching is great because you're really in the trenches. The symposium is a different vibe. It's a chance to be real with players about what they can expect at the highest level of play.

I tell them that being drafted only means that they've got a job in the league. Now they can tell all their friends and loved ones that they're actually working as professional football players. After that, I ask them something else: Do they think they have sixteen NFL seasons in them? Can they deal with all the heartaches, headaches, distractions, attractions, and everything else that can shorten a player's career?

Some kids in those sessions will be out of the league within three months. A good amount will be gone in about three years, the average career span for players in the league. I emphasize that nobody gets far in this game if they don't respect it. They need to look around that room and be grateful for all the legendary players in those photos lining the walls—the Walter Paytons, Joe Montanas, and Ray Nitschkes. When they leave the NFL, they have to make sure it's a better place than when they arrived.

I had to learn that same respect for the game through my own journey, and I see current receivers learning important lessons on their own paths. When Terrell Owens first met with local reporters prior to Seattle's 2012 training camp, he looked much different from the man who once did shirtless sit-ups before media members in his suburban Philadelphia driveway. He also talked about being grateful for the opportunity and humbled, an obvious reference to his bankruptcy case and his brief tenure with the Indoor Football League's Allen Wranglers.

"It's all about, for me, now being part of something rather than being the center of something," Owens told reporters. "I understand a lot of the media is here because of me and again, I have changed in a lot of ways. A lot of things have occurred in the last two years, and I've had a lot of time to think about things and put things in perspective, and I just want to move forward and leave all the things that happened five to ten years ago behind me."

Keyshawn Johnson, of all people, preached a similar message of humility when he talked with Santonio Holmes during the New York Jets training camp in 2012. Holmes spent most of that summer doing damage control after his meltdown at the end of 2011. He mended his relationship with Jets quarterback Mark Sanchez during players-only workouts and he vowed to be more diplomatic when publicly commenting on teammates.

Keyshawn also encouraged Santonio to think about his long-term image. "I told Santonio that you have to take your jersey off at the end of your career," Keyshawn said. "I said, '[The media] will dig up everything you do in New York City but they can help you if you handle things properly.' He can't tell them to go fuck themselves but he can do it with his play. If he comes out of every game with seven catches for 110 yards and a touchdown, they can't say shit. But if he stinks up the joint, they'll kill him. And the perception they'll have won't help him when he's done."

It's hard to know how long Holmes will follow that advice, especially on a team with a slowly developing young quarterback and a penchant for relying heavily on the running game in hard times. What is clear is that Holmes needed to listen to somebody. His career in Pittsburgh ended when that franchise tired of his off-the-field issues. He didn't need to get sideways with his second team before ever making one Pro Bowl.

Many receivers can benefit from such guidance at certain points of their careers. The key is how it's offered and taken. When Joe Horn helped Roddy White in Atlanta, it wasn't merely his wisdom that made White follow his lead. It was Horn's actions that caught White's attention. "If you're telling these young guys one thing and they see you're acting differently, they aren't going to listen to you," Horn said. "They have to know that you're real."

Authenticity was a major factor in the relationship that Randy Moss and I built at the start of his career. As his playing days were winding down, I was happy to see him find another shot in the league with San Francisco. When Randy Moss called me in early 2012—while I was in the midst of my vacation—I was thrilled by the hunger in his voice. He talked about working out that summer, having me stop by to see his progress. Randy wanted to regain his stature in the league. He knew it wasn't right to leave the game with tainted memories.

That conversation was enough to let me know Randy would be in the right frame of mind once he returned to the field with the 49ers. He'd been focused as a rookie in Minnesota and he thrived as a result. The same thing had happened when the Oakland Raiders traded him to New England in 2007. The 49ers also gave Randy the same important factors that always helped his productivity: a strong head coach (Jim Harbaugh), a talented team (they'd played in the NFC championship in 2011), and a chance at a championship.

That move paid off for Randy, even though he only caught 28 passes in 2012. The 49ers reached Super Bowl XLVII and he proved his value as a mentor to some of San Francisco's younger wideouts. Randy did make headlines during the week of the Super Bowl—when he proclaimed himself "the greatest receiver ever" during Media Day—but I was happy to see him have another shot at a ring. The only negative was that the game didn't go his way. The Baltimore Ravens won that contest, 34–31, marking the first time in 49ers history that San Francisco actually lost a Super Bowl.

There was something poetic about Randy returning to the league when the passing game was stronger than it's ever been. "A great wide receiver with an average quarterback is always better than a great quarterback with an average receiver," said Merton Hanks. "[Cincinnati's] Andy Dalton is an average quarterback but A. J. Green makes him look better. Randall Cunningham had some great years but he was on a different level with Cris and that rookie from West Virginia in 1998 [Moss]. In today's NFL, you can't win if you don't have a legitimate receiver. It's become a space game and a size game, and that's why guys like Randy Moss are still viable. If you're big and can run, you can play forever."

Every wideout who's ever played this game understands that reality. It helps explain why our egos can grow so large. It's a by-product of the job. We all want to impact the game. We all believe we have that potential inside us.

I'm old enough now to also see the rewards that come from being selfless. People can talk about the way I screwed up my final college season, but now I can offer that experience and its ramifications to the high school kids I coach at St. Aquinas. They can talk about the addiction problems that cost me my career in Philadelphia, but now I can tell my story to those rookies every year I'm invited to speak at the symposium. It would've been great to have a Super Bowl ring or a speedy induction into the Hall of Fame. But I also had the satisfaction of watching Randy become a star and hearing Larry call me "Uncle Cris."

I've always considered myself fortunate to have sixteen years in the NFL. I've been just as lucky to be a receiver for almost half my life. Quarterbacks may get all the glory, but I'll be damned if we don't have more fun. You could see that much in Hines Ward's constant smile, Victor Cruz's salsa, Chad Johnson's crazy antics, and all the other spectacular highlights on the reel that we've created over the last forty years. We've all helped raise the game's overall entertainment value.

What other position—in any sport—draws so much attention to it? Pitchers don't have that appeal in baseball. Basketball has given us superstars like Dwyane Wade, Michael Jordan, and Kobe Bryant, but guards haven't been the only magnetic personalities in that game. Hockey plays to a much smaller fan base, while individual sports—like boxing, tennis, and golf—don't have enough true characters.

People still can't get enough of receivers, even if the wildest personalities aren't as abundant as they once were. As Keyshawn said, "The next ten years are going to be really interesting for receivers. You're always going to have a Dez Bryant or a DeSean Jackson—somebody who needs a little time to get his act together—but you're not seeing too many guys who want to be lightning rods. They all saw the last group of receivers who acted that way and a lot of those players had their careers come to screeching halts. Those guys got a lot of splash during their playing days but nobody wanted to hire them at the end."

That is true but I also see things differently. The game evolves. It's always changing. When I started playing football in the 1970s, I couldn't name five receivers who really caught my eye. When I started writing this book, NFL running backs were becoming increasingly less relevant, while the fullback position had nearly disappeared altogether. Pro football had become a game played predominantly through the air.

Many receivers played a role in the offensive explosion that hit the league over the last thirty years. Most did it through awesome productivity. Others brought productivity in addition to a sheer force of personality to the game. In the end, we all were part of a bigger movement—a cultural shift in a league that never really saw us coming.

So let the world talk about the NFL as a quarterback league. The signal-callers can have most of the credit because God knows their jobs are far more difficult than ours. But when it comes to keeping fans captivated, entertained, and consistently wondering what's going to happen next, that's an entirely different story. That domain, without any question, now solely belongs to the wide receivers.

Epilogue

As much as I've enjoyed speaking at the rookie symposium, there is one reason why I haven't done it since 2009: The NFL moved the event to the Pro Football Hall of Fame instead of holding it in previous places like Southern California and Washington, D.C. My absence had nothing to do with my feelings on spending four or five days in Canton, Ohio. It had everything to do with the Hall itself. It would've been too difficult for me to be at a place where I felt I belonged. My conscience wouldn't let me be comfortable with going there until I was finally part of that exclusive membership.

The people who run the symposium understood that as well. They didn't press the issue nor did they try selling me on what my speeches mean to all those rookies. They know how important those opportunities are to me. They realized that I've taken tremendous pride in connecting with all those first-year players.

Most of the receivers we've talked about in this book have heard me at that event: Randy, Chad, T.O., Keyshawn, Megatron. I can remember the year Larry Fitzgerald was drafted, and he was sitting right there in the front row, taking in everything I was saying. I've even had several former players from St. Thomas Aquinas in the crowd. It's just as gratifying to see how far they've come from the days when I was touting them as future NFL players.

The more I've attended the symposium, the more I've thought

about what that kind of orientation could've done for my career. There wasn't anything like that when I came into the league in 1987. For better or worse, players were pretty much on their own. If you weren't fortunate enough to land in a locker room filled with selfless, caring veterans, you had to learn to be a professional through trial and error.

It would've helped me to hear firsthand stories about the perils of drugs and alcohol in the NFL. I had great veteran teammates in Philadelphia, but it would've been nice to have had more forewarning about all the traps that come with a big paycheck and free time. Then again, I wouldn't be who I am today if I'd had that kind of good fortune. I certainly wouldn't have the perspective that made me comfortable writing a book this ambitious.

My career put me in the ideal position to see exactly where receivers came from and where they are headed. It helped me understand what it takes to be great as well as why some wideouts come off as being so crazy. When I think about it, there are very few things that have happened to the game's most prominent receivers that I didn't experience myself. I could relate to almost anybody who played the position in my era.

I had my addiction problems. I had my run-ins with coaches. I knew what it was like to have players dislike you and strangers question your overall impact on the game. I also understood the rewards of resilience and the power of perseverance. I could talk about consistency because I could take pride in being a fourth-round supplemental pick who lasted sixteen years in the NFL.

I didn't simply get an education in football during my playing career. I gained a deeper appreciation for the job I had. No position in the NFL went through a more thorough transformation than wide receiver over the last four decades. I was lucky enough to be around for most of it.

What I've found interesting while writing this book is how much other people have been fascinated by the position. Everyone I talked to embraced the concept of this project. That trend was an affirmation of all the beliefs I had going into this process. I didn't have to embellish anything to make the story more attractive. There was so much information to work with that the hard part was deciding what to eventually cut.

You always hear people throwing around the term "swagger." Well, no position in sports has more of that than the NFL wide receiver. Maybe it's always been that way. Maybe we just needed the right time and opportunity to let people see what was really going on with us, especially during all those years when relentlessly running the football was considered genius.

The game we see today almost demands that swagger be a part of it. This is still big business, and as Merton Hanks said, "You don't want too many quiet guys out there." I agree that it's huge to have both talent and juice in the game. That combination means the entertainment value of pro football is never really in jeopardy.

Strategies also help receivers more than ever these days. Offenses can't just produce twelve- and fifteen-play scoring drives like they used to in the 1970s and 1980s. Defenses are too strong and the potential for a costly mistake is too great. Teams need the capability of gaining yardage in huge chunks. They need receivers who can make big plays when the ball is in their hands.

If you want to know how much the game is changing, look at what's happened to the running back position. Forty years ago, this was the glamour position, right after quarterback. Today running backs are practically expendable in the eyes of most teams. The 25-carry workhorse has given way to the running-back-by-committee approach, all because teams don't expect ball carriers to last like they once did.

You can forget about fullbacks, too. They're about as relevant today as the Gap Band. The ones who haven't been transitioned into H-back roles are hoping enough throwback coaches stick around to utilize them. With so many teams favoring one-back offenses, it's hard to find fullbacks who play even 30 percent of their team's snaps.

Consider how the Baltimore Ravens—a team that once relied on a conservative offense to complement a strong defense during their Super Bowl run in 2000—stormed their way through the 2012 postseason. As much as people celebrated the brilliant play of quarterback Joe

Flacco, his wide receivers supplied clutch performances in helping the Ravens reach and win Super Bowl XLVII. Anquan Boldin had two 100-yard receiving efforts during the Ravens' four postseason games and scored just as many touchdowns as he had in the regular season (4). Torrey Smith also was invaluable in a divisional playoff win over Denver. He caught 2 touchdown passes in that game, with both scores coming against future Hall-of-Fame cornerback Champ Bailey.

The 2011 New York Giants also offered a great example of what receivers mean in these times. They won the Super Bowl during that season for many reasons, but their wideouts were at the top of that list. Hakeem Nicks had 165 yards and 2 touchdowns in an NFC divisional playoff win over Green Bay—a heavily favored, defending Super Bowl champion that went 15–1 that year—in Lambeau Field. Victor Cruz had 10 receptions and 142 yards in another road upset, this time a win over the 49ers in the NFC championship. Finally, it was Mario Manningham who delivered that highlight-reel catch to set up New York's game-winning score in Super Bowl XLVI.

Yes, the Giants had Eli Manning and a rejuvenated pass rush in all those games. They also had the perfect weapons on the outside: receivers who understood the enormity of the moment and the importance of changing a game anytime a pass floated in their direction. This is a crucial aspect of the position that every receiver has to grasp today. They don't pay us to be insurance anymore. They expect us to alter outcomes.

That's a big responsibility and it takes a sizable ego to handle it. Sometimes that means taking on a receiver who can drive a coach crazy and keep reporters constantly hanging on his every word. What I've learned throughout my career—and in writing this book—is that there really isn't much difference between the receivers who do a lot of talking and the ones who rarely say a word. We all want the ball in our hands. We all want to do the very things that blow people away on Sundays.

If you catch some highlights from Super Bowl XLVI, you'll understand exactly what I mean. For all the attention given to the Giants' receivers in that contest, there was a pregame moment captured by NFL Films that encapsulates all the central themes of this book. It's a shot of former New England Patriots wide receiver Wes Welker—one of the least vocal players in the game despite having four 100-catch seasons at that stage of his career—talking with quarterback Tom Brady as they warm up. They're both focusing on the task that lies ahead of them, the opportunity to give New England its fourth championship in eleven seasons.

After firing a few passes to a receiver 20 yards away, Brady looks down at the diminutive Welker and gushes about returning to football's biggest stage. He tells Welker how hard it is to contain his excitement. Welker nods, clearly feeling equally charged. He also tells Brady something that every receiver has uttered at one point or another, a line that sums up the mentality that has helped the position become so prominent.

"I'm open," Welker says, as if to educate Brady on something the quarterback didn't already know. "Remember, I'm always open."

Acknowledgments

I am deeply grateful to Jeffri Chadiha for all the work he provided to make this project a success. My marketing agent, Maury Gostfrand, and my literary agent, Peter Steinberg, both deserve credit for encouraging me to pursue this book and showing me the possibilities in what it could become.

We also wouldn't be able to make *Going Deep* a reality without the confidence and guidance of Hyperion—specifically, executive editor Kerri Kolen. She saw the potential in this book from day one and never wavered in her commitment to it.

Along with Hyperion's support, *Going Deep* benefited from the contributions of numerous NFL players, coaches, executives, and media members. I'm touched by their willingness to give so much to a project that has meant so much to me.

Finally, I want to thank my family. I grew up with great support, and I've been fortunate to be blessed with two terrific children, Duron and Monterae. More than anything, I've been lucky enough to marry my best friend, Melanie. God has been great to me. I see that every day in her love.

Index